BECOME A WRITER TODAY: THE COMPLETE SERIES

BOOK 1: YES, YOU CAN WRITE! | BOOK 2: THE SAVVY WRITER'S GUIDE TO PRODUCTIVITY | BOOK 3: THE ART OF WRITING A NON-FICTION BOOK

BRYAN COLLINS

BECOME A *Writer* TODAY

PREFACE

This book uses British English.
Thank you for supporting this work.

GET YOUR EXCLUSIVE BONUS

Before you start reading, I've created a **FREE video masterclass**. You'll cut months off how long it takes you to write your book by using my best tactics and strategies.

DID YOU CLAIM YOUR FREE BONUS?

VISIT
becomeawritertoday.com/author

If you want to get this free video masterclass today, please visit and sign up here: http://becomeawritertoday.com/author

CONTENTS

THE ART OF WRITING A NON-FICTION BOOK

YES, YOU CAN WRITE!

101 PROVEN WRITING PROMPTS THAT WILL
HELP YOU FIND CREATIVE IDEAS FASTER
FOR YOUR JOURNAL, BLOGGING, WRITING
YOUR BOOK AND MORE

YES, YOU CAN Write!

Proven Writing Prompts that Will Help You Find Creative Ideas Faster for Your Journal, Blogging, Writing Your Book and More

BOOK 1
IN THE BECOME A WRITER TODAY SERIES

BRYAN COLLINS

INTRODUCTION

I felt delighted with my prize until I climbed to the top of the crane and looked down.

The grey, jagged rocks lurched upwards towards me, and my head began to spin. I stepped back from the edge of the crane seat, and I held onto the thick, yellow bungee jump cord as if it were life itself.

"I'm not doing it," I said. "I won't jump."

The bungee jump instructor smiled and raised the palms of his tanned, oversized hands.

"You can't climb back down." He shook his head. "You must jump."

"No, no, no," I said.

The day before, I had won a swimming competition in the Greek resort where friends and I were spending our summer holidays. My prize was a bungee jump from the crane overlooking the rocks on the beach. At the time, I felt delighted. Now, my pale legs were rattling against each other like twigs in the wind.

Our stand-off lasted for twenty long minutes, all the while me holding onto the crane rails and my friends calling from down below:

"Jump! Jump! Jump!"

"That guy is a coward," someone shouted. "He'll never do it."

That was enough.

I sat down on the edge of the metal crane seat, closed my eyes, and using two hands, I eased myself off the seat and into the air...

Down I went.

Writing can feel a little like bungee jumping. I've perched myself over the blank page for hours at a time, unable and unwilling to get started.

When I tried to write my first book, I brewed a cup of coffee and pulled a chair up to my desk in my bedroom and arranged a notebook and pen before me.

My hand hovered over the blank page, but sitting in a chair in front of the blank page was an alien experience. Eventually, I put my pen down, stopped to refill my coffee, played some music and filled a bowl with crackers and cheese.

It went on like this for an hour... I'd sit down, try to write and then get back up to open the window, walk around the room, call the dog and do anything but write.

I just didn't know what my book was about or how to begin – or even where to begin. Finally, I threw away my notebook and pen, feeling like a failure and that I didn't know what I was doing.

The painful truth is *I didn't know what I was doing.*

Like the reluctant bungee jumper who worries about being embarrassed in front of his friends, I needed a prompt.

If you haven't written much before or you're unsure what to write about, writing prompts can help you improve your craft and get into the habit of spending more time in the chair, in front of the blank page.

A writing prompt should encourage you to write. It could be a single word, sentence, phrase, question or even a picture that you focus on. It should encourage you to jump.

In this book, you'll find 101 examples of writing prompts that you can use for various types of non-fiction writing. These prompts should help you to overcome common problems like writer's block, to find ideas for your books and to become an author.

I've broken the book into seven sections to cover seven different types of non-fiction writing, and each section contains around 10 to 15 writing prompts. It's best to use the writing prompts in this book without fear or expectation, as a warm-up for the main event.

Now, let's strap in.

PRACTISING YOUR CRAFT

"One of the main aims in writing practice is to learn to trust your own mind and body; to grow patient and non-aggressive." – Natalie Goldberg

Some days, I like to close the door, open up a blank document on the computer, set a timer for 30 minutes and write about whatever comes to mind.

I start by writing about an idea I'm wresting with or something that's bothering me, but I never know where I'll end up.

I don't expect to publish what I wrote, although occasionally I pin a creative problem to the page.

Ultimately, freewriting is a form of writing practice.

In 1986, author and artist Natalie Goldberg introduced the concept of writing practice in her book *Writing Down the Bones: Freeing the Writer Within.*

It involves turning up and writing about a particular topic, theme or idea for a pre-determined period. If you want to freewrite, avoid editing yourself, overthinking your work, or worrying about spelling punctuation or grammar.

It's an expressive, exploratory type of writing that almost every type of writer can use to improve their craft. It's also a useful way of finding ideas, stories and interesting arguments for your books.

Natalie says, "Don't try to control it. Stay present with whatever comes up, and keep your hand moving."

So set a timer for 15 or 30 minutes, open up your favourite writing application and use the writing prompts below to practice your craft:

1. Look out the window. What's happening outside, and how have things changed since you last sat here?
2. Write about an everyday or intimate object and what it means to you. It could be something on your desk, in your bedroom or in your fridge. It could even be an item of clothing. What does it look, taste, sound and smell like? What does it mean to you?
3. What do you do when you're alone? What keeps you up at 3 a.m. and how do you handle these worries?
4. Draw upon a memory. "I remember the first time I...", "I remember the last time I..." and "Can I trust this memory?" The more visual the memory, the better.
5. Consider a painful moment from your past. A job you didn't get. A relationship that broke down. Use this as the starting point for what you write next.
6. Think of your childhood hero. What impact did they have on your life and how? What would you say if you could meet them now?
7. When was the first time someone disappointed you? What did they do? And how did you react?
8. When you were in school, you were probably asked to write about what you did on your summer holidays. Now that you're all grown up, write your epitaph.
9. What was it like to revisit a place from your childhood as an adult? Did the visit match your memory of this place?
10. Take a photo with your phone of an occasion or a

YES, YOU CAN WRITE!

memorable event (yes your memory will fade, so photos are important), or find an old picture from your library. Now, write about it.

11. Put on a pair of headphones, and listen to a piece of music outside of your comfort zone. Now write 300 to 500 words about how it makes you feel.

12. Describe a physical injury. How did it happen, what did it feel like and what was the result?

13. Consider a small private victory or, better yet, a small, private defeat. Now write an honest account of what happened.

14. Describe an experience, event or conversation that you feel angry about today. What would you like to do about it and say to those involved?

15. Do you have a secret that you haven't told anyone? Or do you know a secret about somebody else? It should be something you don't want your mother to read. Now, start writing.

CONQUERING WRITER'S BLOCK

"Writing about a writer's block is better than not writing at all." – Charles Bukowski

Many successful authors go through unusual rituals before they start writing. Roald Dahl, for example, wrote in a shed behind his greenhouse. Before starting on books like *Matilda* or *The BFG*, he got into a sleeping bag and pulled it up to his waist. His biographer, Chris Powling, said:

> He steps into a sleeping bag, pulls it up to his waist and settles himself in a faded wing-backed armchair. His feet he rests on a battered travelling case full of logs. This is roped to the legs of the armchair so it's always at a perfect distance.

So by all means, develop a personal creative ritual, such as going to a set place or turning up at a set time, if they help you start writing faster.

If you're still struggling with writer's block, you could also read a great book, watch an inspiring film or visit an art exhibition.

Surrounding yourself with other people's great ideas often inspires fresh thinking.

Then, there are these writing prompts:

1. Like Charles Bukowski says, write about what you're blocked about...and why.
2. Skip the introduction. Start your conclusion instead. Or start in the middle.
3. Take a great first line from a book you admire. Write at the top of the page. Now, keep going. When you're done, delete the first line.
4. Write down the facts and everything else you know about the topic you're having trouble with. Consider what it would mean if one of these facts were untrue. What if the world wasn't flat or we weren't the centre of the universe?
5. This prompt works better if you do it alongside the previous one. Write down the weaknesses of what you've written. Is it too long or too short? Figure out what's wrong with your work, and fix it.
6. When you think about the topic you're struggling with, what do you feel in your gut? What does your intuition tell you? Now, go.
7. Get into the habit of annotating important sections in the books you read. Now, before you start writing, review some of your annotations for ideas, material and inspiration. If you're reading on a Kindle, use your device's flashcards.
8. Make a list of 10 things you want to include in your current project. If that's too hard, try 20. Or 100. The harder you make your brain work to dump ideas onto the blank page, the more outlandish ideas it will give you.
9. Instead of trying to write, just work on an outline. Use single words and lists to identify key themes or topics. If you're a visual thinker, try a mind map.
10. Lower the bar. Instead of aiming for a word count or a

milestone, write whatever you want and without any standards.

11. Keep a notepad next to where you sleep. If you wake in the middle of the night, write down what you were just dreaming about so you don't forget. Now the following morning, write about this note.

12. Write a letter to a friend and help them with something they're struggling with. You don't have to send the letter. Instead your goal is to get your fingers moving over the keyboard and to relight your creative spark.

13. Describe a favourite walk. Better yet, bring your notebook and pen with you, and halfway through your walk, sit down and write about what you can see. You can try this with your commute too (presuming you're not driving).

JOURNALING AND INTROSPECTIVE WRITING

"It's not my job to entertain anyone in my diary." – David Sedaris

I've kept paper and digital journals for 20 years, and it's an honest and expressive form of writing. It takes about 10 or 15 minutes to write an entry, and I do this three or four mornings a week.

Journaling will help you document day-to-day life. It'll also help you identify negative thought patterns, set goals and track your progress. Plus, it's entertaining to read back on old entries from several years ago, and it's cheaper than therapy.

Here's an extract from a 2016 entry:

"Sometimes, I feel like I'm writing this journal with [my wife] or one of my friends in mind, but there are times when the entries are just for me. After all, they may never read these entries. Or they might. I'm not sure which is worse. Although if they do read it they either hacked the journal – it's password protected – or I'm dead.

[My wife] went to Birmingham with work last night and is not back until later tonight.

When I finished cleaning the house, I slept on the couch for an hour. I

woke up with a headache and took two paracetamol. It is still lurking in my left temple. When I die, it will involve a massive headache of some sort!

Sometimes what I write in here is just therapy and not an accurate reflection of how I feel.

I've been reading more about stoicism lately. There are some fantastic mental strategies in the writings of Seneca et al. for dealing with the demands of this modern materialistic life. He put forward the idea of picturing the worst happening and... using the realisation that this hasn't happened to be more grateful for and present with what's in front of you.

So I should be grateful for my headache... passing."

Famous authors like Vladimir Nabokov, Virginia Woolf and John Cheever all kept journals. At the very least, you can journal your progress while writing a book and document your ideas as they unfold.

That said, there's no wrong way to journal. Your entries are for you and you alone. If you need help journaling, ask yourself:

1. What did I do today, and what would I like to do tomorrow?
2. How am I feeling right now? Is this emotion affecting me physically in some way?
3. What one thing must I focus on this week, and how can I go about doing it?
4. What should I stop doing and why? What should I start doing more of and why?
5. What could I have done better this week, this month or this year?
6. When I think of a private or embarrassing mistake from my past, did I tell anyone about it, and what did I learn from it?
7. What did I learn from the last book/article I read? Now, how can I put these lessons into practice?
8. How did or could I help my friends and family?

9. In a month, a year or five years, where would I like to be, and what would I like to have accomplished?
10. What would I like to say to somebody who angered or wronged me in some way from my past?
11. What three things am I grateful for right now and why?
12. What would I like to say to the person who wrote an entry in my journal 12 months ago?
13. If I had more courage, what would I do?
14. What unpleasant or difficult conversations am I postponing?
15. What scares me most about death and why?

WRITING ABOUT THE SAME TOPIC IN DIFFERENT WAYS

"Writing non-fiction is more like sculpture, a matter of shaping the research into the finished thing." – Joan Didion

Trent Hamm has been writing about personal finance almost every day since starting the *Simple Dollar* in 2006. His focus on a single topic helped him discover what he was good at. He explains,

> What I ended up realizing I had a knack for...a particular flavor of half-memoir half-advice articles that I could write quickly and relatively well. Is the writing great, the kind you'd find in *The New Yorker*? Nope, and I don't claim that it is. Is it earnest and clear and helpful and always there with new topics and thoughts? That's what I'm striving for.

Today, the *Simple Dollar* is one of the biggest personal finance blogs in the world.

Many non-fiction writers, like bloggers, specialise in a niche. Like Trent notes, there's pleasure in going deep rather than wide, but some days you may feel like you've said all you have to say... and yet your publication deadline looms like a guillotine.

What's a committed blogger or non-fiction writer supposed to do? Try these prompts:

1. What's the one thing you know now about your topic that you wish you'd known before you got started? Alternatively, what don't you know about your topic or niche, and what would you like to learn? Document your experiences.
2. List posts are the staple of the blogosphere, and readers love them because they're quick and easy to read and digest. Use proven formats like "99 Reasons Why X is Better Than Y", "The Top 100 Tools of Savvy [Insert Your Audience]" or "The X Things Every [Insert Your Audience Type] Should Do Before..."
3. Blog readers love learning how to achieve specific outcomes. So share your expertise by writing articles like "How to Accomplish More By...", "The Ultimate Guide to..." or "A Step-by-Step Guide to..."
4. Instead of reinventing the wheel, why not trawl through your archives and give some old articles, opinions and ideas new life in the form of "My 5 Most Popular Posts of the Past Year," "An Always Up-To-Date Guide to...", "An Introduction to [Insert Topic]... Revisited" and so on.
5. Take a complicated topic you understand and break it down into simple steps your readers can follow. You could cover "How to Accomplish [Insert Outcome] Faster Checklist", "A Weekly Checklist for...", "Your Post [Insert Topic] Checklist" and more.
6. Ask one of your readers, "What are you struggling with?" Then, answer their question in your next post or article.
7. Feature a reader in one of your articles as a case study. Reveal how they put something you taught or recommended into practice and what happened next.

8. Type your topic or idea into Google News or a tool like BuzzSumo. Study what's trending or in the news. Then write a reaction.

9. Go to a Q&A site like Quora and search for your subject matter. Pick the question with the most replies and views. Write your answer.

10. Go onto Goodreads and search for a book you enjoy. Look at the most popular quotes. Pick one, and use it as your prompt.

11. Repeat the same exercise as in #10, this time searching BrainyQuote for a quote from an influencer or expert that you admire. Use it as your prompt.

12. Describe a recent personal accomplishment or failure for your readers. Write about what you set out to achieve, what challenges you overcame or what went wrong?

13. Find a scientific study or research, pull out a compelling statistic or quote and write your reaction or opinion. I use sites like *Harvard Business Review* and *Psychology Today* to do this.

14. Write about your creative process or your routine. How do you find ideas, write about them and/or create? How has your process or routine evolved?

TELLING PERSONAL STORIES

"Some writers squirm through the process, shifting uncomfortably in their seats. That's a good sign." – Sol Stein

I drank a large glass of green absinthe and smoked a badly rolled joint of hashish. Then, I took the bus into Dublin city centre, sipping on a plastic bottle filled with vodka and coke.

I was warm and buzzing when I arrived at Sarah's 21st birthday party. I ordered a pint of Budweiser and dropped a shot of vodka into it.

"She looks hot," I told Michael and his girlfriend. "I feel like it's Christmas."

"Who does?" says Michael.

I pointed my thumb at Sarah.

Michael and his girlfriend look at each other and laughed.

At midnight, we gathered to wish Sarah happy birthday. So I got in line behind the groomed, perfumed and more sober college party-goers. I put both hands around Sarah's waist, pulled her close, kissed her ear.

"Haaappy birthday, Niamh. It's Niamh isn't it?"

She pushed me back and drew her hand back to slap me across the face.

"It's Sarah. How could you forget my name?"

"Absinthe," I slurred.

Afterwards, I staggered to the bathroom cubicle, sat down on the toilet and rested my head against the tiles.

I woke up when a barman banged on the toilet door.

"Get out! You must leave now. We're closed," he shouted.

The bar was empty, and the lights were on. I looked at my phone. It was after 3 a.m.

No missed calls.

Sarah didn't say much to me in college after that. For years afterwards, I panicked about getting people's name wrong after even a single drink.

I still squirm today even thinking of that night, when people couldn't wait to get away from me.

I almost left my embarrassing moment out of this book, but there's nothing more disappointing than the non-fiction writer who looks away from their readers and doesn't reveal any personal details.

Even if you're writing a non-fiction book, you must tell personal stories if you want to connect with your readers. So try writing about:

1. A surprising event or change of fortune. Was this change for the best or the worst, and how did you respond?
2. When you first met your mentor, teacher or guide. How did you respond to them, and what did they have to show you?
3. When you first met an enemy or antagonist. It doesn't have to be a person... it could be an inner demon.
4. A rite of passage. How did the experience change you?
5. When you went too far or didn't go far enough. What were the consequences?
6. When you dealt with a problem in your external world or faced your inner demon. What did you do, and what happened next?

7. An occasion when you felt like all was lost. How did you pick yourself up off the dirt?

8. Something you did that makes you squirm even today. The more personal the better.

9. When you faced a conflict with your surroundings, friends or family. What was at stake, and how did you respond?

10. When you were last provoked into action. What did you do, and what happened next?

11. A difficult choice you faced. What were the stakes, and how did you decide what to do?

12. A time you got completely lost or didn't know what you were doing. How did you find your way back?

13. The aftermath of an unsettling, difficult or life-altering event. What did you and those close to you experience, feel or say?

14. Closure. What does it look like, and how did you get there?

BRINGING AUTHENTICITY INTO YOUR WORK

"Write the truth" – Robert McKee

They say you should never meet your heroes; I disagree.

The author and creative writing instructor Robert McKee is one of mine. In 2014, I attended his non-fiction writing workshop in Kerry, Ireland.

For an entire day, I listened to him explain the art of storytelling, but at the end of the workshop, I still wanted to know: "How can a writer tell better stories?"

At 5 p.m, I asked Robert to sign my copy of his book and pushed him for answers. He penned this advice, "Write the truth."

That night, on the train back to Dublin, I wondered about his advice. So, I re-read his book *Story*, where he explains:

> One of the sad truths of life is that there's only one person in this vale of tears that we ever really know, and that's ourselves. We're essentially and forever alone. Yet...the truth is we are all far more alike than we are different. We are all human.

Whether you agree or disagree with Robert, he writes about the truth as he sees it. And that's authentic. As a writer, it's your job to find the truth as you see it and bring this into your work.

So:

1. Give yourself or your subject a dilemma. It could be a moral, professional, personal, financial or something else altogether. But the bigger the better. Now, open with that.

2. Go to a coffee shop, bar or restaurant. Listen carefully and record a snippet of conversation you overhear. Now, use this snippet in what you write next.

3. Pick a piece of writing where you explain a topic or idea. Now, inject dialogue or a real conversation into what you just wrote or described. "I've got no time for this," he said. "Well, don't come around here complaining nobody reads your work," she replied.

4. Consider a great film you watched or book you read. What's the core idea behind this film or book? Now, write about that.

5. Distil the core of what you're currently writing into a single sentence. Now, use this sentence as a tool to decide what to write more of and what to cut.

6. Insert a sensory detail into your work. Did the coffee taste bitter? Was his skin cold to touch? Did her voice sound like a cat being castrated? Were his eyes bloodshot? Did he reek of gone-off tuna? And so on.

7. Write about a single image that will give your work more resonance. It could be an everyday object, a place, a colour or a decorative design.

8. Interview a would-be reader, and ask them about their biggest challenge related to what you're writing about. Now, use what they tell you next as your introduction.

9. Go back and review your work. Now, rewrite a section

from a different perspective i.e., from the point of view of an interviewee or a bystander.

10. Challenge your internal editor to... shut the hell up so you can get some work done. It doesn't matter if you succeed or fail (at least for the purposes of what you're writing). It's more important to write honestly about what happened and without holding back.

11. Every great hero possesses a flaw. Superman is vulnerable to kryptonite. Han Solo is brave to the point of recklessness. What's yours?

12. Ask why. Now, answer. Ask why again. Keep answering. Ask why again. Once more with feeling.

13. What values do you (or the people you're writing about) believe in, and what risks would you/they take to hold true to these values? Typical values and their antithesis include justice/injustice, freedom/imprisonment, honesty/deception, love/indifference and so on.

14. Write about a time when you or your subject compromised on what they believe in.

15. Rather than telling readers how an event unfolded, show them. Use dialogue and action. Dramatise it. Instead of "I felt angry", it's "I threw the cup against the wall."

INJECTING COLOUR INTO YOUR WRITING

"Chaos in the midst of chaos isn't funny, but chaos in the midst of order is." – Steve Martin

Great writing often lies in rewriting. When you get to this point, it's time to spice up your work so that it becomes more memorable.

Inject some colour and flavour by elaborating on your stories, playing around with your prose and clarifying your train of thought. These colourful writing prompts should help you do just that:

1. Abandon logic. See below.
2. Insert a historical figure or celebrity into your work. "Ernest Hemingway and I, we go way back."
3. Count up the numbers from an everyday activity you've described and have fun with them. "Today, I dealt with 147 emails, 37 WhatsApp messages, five text messages, three missed calls and one angry boss. Today, was a good day."
4. Write an inappropriate response. "I gave my boyfriend my

first draft to read. He told me he hated it. So I burnt down his house."

5. Poke fun at some prevailing wisdom from your area of expertise. Oscar Wilde said, "When I was young, I thought that money was the most important thing in life. Now that I'm old – I know it is."

6. Use the rule of three, remembering to save the most colourful word or idea for last. Homer Simpson said, "Bart, a woman is like a beer. They look good, smell good, and you'd step over your own mother just to get one!"

7. Put one of your characters in an unusual context. In his poem, *A Supermarket in California*, Allen Ginsberg wrote, "I saw you, Walt Whitman, childless, lonely old grubber, poking among the meats in the refrigerator and eyeing the grocery boys."

8. Inject some self-deprecation into your work. "I think writers should get paid what they're worth. So I wrote myself a cheque for a dollar."

9. Take two opposite, disconnected or competing ideas and mush them together. "After spending a day writing, I love nothing more than unwinding at a good book burning."

10. If you've written a longer piece, pick an idea from the start of your work, and write a throwback to this idea at the end. Do you remember when I compared writer's block to bungee jumping in the Introduction? Well, go read the Conclusion of this book.

11. Scott Adams, the creator of Dilbert, says, "Humour writing is a lot like business writing. It needs to be simple. The main difference is in the choice of words. For humour, don't say 'drink' when you can say 'swill'". So peruse through your masterpiece, pluck out an everyday word and in its place, leave an alternative delight from your thesaurus.

12. Overstate your solution to a problem. "I didn't feel like I was getting much done, so I started getting up early. After my alarm goes off, I meditate for an hour, lift weights, brew

coffee, write 2,000 words, catch up on my email, make breakfast and read the newspaper. Around then the sun is rising, so I really need to get going."

13. Increase the prize for success. "If you write your book, you'll be able to quit the job you hate, earn a full-time living from writing and maybe even buy your own island just like Richard Branson."

14. Raise the penalty for failure. "If you don't write your book, you'll have to hand back that fat advance you spent on a trip to Necker Island, your wife will leave you for the tanned pool cleaner with a six-pack and J.K. Rowling will stop taking your calls."

YOUR 101ST WRITING PROMPT

"I need a beer to calm my nerves," I said.

I crouched down on the ground, and while the bungee instructor undid the cord, I pressed my shaking hands onto the wet concrete.

"God, it's good to be back down here with all of you," I said to a friend.

He slapped me on the back.

"I didn't think you'd jump," he said.

"Neither did I."

To say 'jump' was a bit of stretch. I knew I'd just fallen through the air like a white egg on a string, and although my plunge lasted just a few seconds, I hated every moment.

Still, I felt good about proving my hecklers wrong. But that night I told a friend, "I'll never climb up a crane or jump off one like that again. We're not meant to fall through the air at speed. And besides, I just realised I hate heights."

"Who knew?" said my friend.

"I did," I said. "Or at least, I do now."

Trying to write a book for the first time or overcoming a creative problem like writer's block can feel terrifying in a different way.

But you can use a writing prompt to overcome your fears, and unlike bungee jumping, it'll help you figure out what type of writing you enjoy and what type of writing you dislike. You'll improve your craft too.

These days when I try to write a book chapter, an article or blog post, I usually have a good idea of what it's about in advance.

I look down at the blank page, and I hesitate.

But sometimes the blinking cursor asks me, "What have you got?" and I don't have an answer.

But sometimes I wonder if I even know what I'm doing.

So I turn to my list of prompts, write one at the top of the page, and I step out.

No fears. No expectations. No opening the window to call the dog.

Just me, my prompt and the rapidly filling blank page.

Now, my list of writing prompts works for me... because I wrote them. No, that's not the sound of my over-sized ego banging off the ceiling.

For your 101st writing prompt, I'd like you to *create your own list of writing prompts and add to it over time.*

Whether you're writing a journal entry, a blog post or a book chapter, keeping a personal library of writing prompts will save you hours of wasted time.

Use a notepad.

Use a digital app like Evernote. Use the back of your hand if you have to... but build your personal library of writing prompts.

Start by taking a great first line from your favourite book, writer or story. You could go on to record snippets of conversations, headlines you like and even ideas you come across in great books. Use what works and discard the rest.

If you do this, you won't have to perch yourself over the blank page and wonder if you've got what it takes to become a successful writer.

Instead, you'll be able to say, "Yes, I can write!"

FURTHER RESOURCES FOR FINDING WRITING PROMPTS

Bryan Cohen has written a series of books with writing prompts based around events, occasions and characters, the most comprehensive book being his boxset *1,000 Creative Writing Prompts Box Set*.

If you like using great first lines as prompts, *The First Line Generator* will spew one up at random from a great book.

Musicians Peter Schmidt and Brian Eno created *The Oblique Strategies* in 1975. These are a set of cards or prompts for musicians, but they can be used for all types of creative work.

Reddit has a comprehensive forum packed full of writing prompts, with a heavy emphasis on fiction writing.

Ryan Andrew Kinder has gathered more writing prompts than you shake a blank page at in his book *1,000 Awesome Writing Prompts*.

The Story Shack offers a useful writing prompt generator for fiction writers.

The New York Times has a specific list of writing prompts for narrative and personal fiction.

If you want to inject more colour into your writing, check out *The Comic Tool Box: How to Be Funny Even If You're Not* by John Vorhaus.

If you want to write more jokes, read *Comedy Writing Secrets* by Mel Helitzer.

Natalie Goldberg's book *Writing Down the Bones: Freeing the Writer Within* doesn't cover writing prompts specifically, but she goes into great detail about how to find ideas and tackle problems like writer's block. The audio version, narrated by Natalie, is a particular pleasure.

Robert McKee's book *Story: Style, Structure, Substance, and the Principles of Screenwriting* is essential reading if you want to tell better stories.

Evernote is a great place to build your library of personal writing prompts. Alternatives include Simplenote and Google Keep.

If you want to practice journaling, the app Day One is purpose-built for just that. You can even include photos alongside your time and location-stamped entries.

THE SAVVY WRITER'S GUIDE
TO PRODUCTIVITY

HOW TO WORK LESS, FINISH WRITING
YOUR STORY OR BOOK, AND FIND THE
SUCCESS YOU DESERVE

THE SAVVY, Writers GUIDE TO PRODUCTIVITY

How to Work Less, Finish Writing Your Story or Book, and Find the Success You Deserve

BOOK 2
IN THE BECOME A WRITER TODAY SERIES

BRYAN COLLINS

INTRODUCTION

Writing is hard work.

You've got to think of an idea. Shape it into something usable. Write it. Rewrite it. Edit it. And then rewrite it again. It's mentally and physically demanding, and many writers give up before they finish.

Perhaps you find it difficult to take an idea from concept to completion.

Maybe you struggle to produce anything meaningful from a few hours of writing each week.

Possibly do you just want to create a habit of writing every day?

Take a deep breath.

It's OK.

You're not alone.

If you opened up this book, you're ready to become a different kind of writer.

Any aspiring writer can learn how to finish their work. You don't need to be a genius, possess divine gift, or have the discipline of a Zen monk to finish a writing an article or a book.

So, don't feel intimidated by the blank page.

You can cultivate your ability to become more productive by

showing up in front of that blank page and cultivating your craft every day.

I've spent years working as a journalist, copywriter and blogger. I've made a lot of mistakes–some public, some private–and learnt many hard lessons about what productive, successful writers do.

I've studied and written about popular productivity methods on my blog *Become a Writer Today*. I've also read hundreds of articles and books about writing.

I'm going to share 33 simple but effective productivity strategies for any writer who wants to finish what they started and become more successful.

WHAT YOU'LL DISCOVER IN THIS BOOK

Why 33 productivity strategies?

I started this book by writing 101 writing strategies through studying how literary heavyweights and renowned non-fiction writers approach their craft.

I also spent time studying the methodology behind popular productivity techniques that business people use to accomplish more in their personal and professional lives.

I wanted to find that point where business and the arts intersect, and in this book, I regularly reference authors we can learn from.

But I'm not going to lie to you.

I almost gave up writing this book–twice, but starting with a goal of writing 101 strategies made the job of writing 33 strategies feel achievable.

Think of the marathon runner who has to run 26 miles—the first 13 are easy; it's the second 13 that present the real problems.

So once I had 101 strategies, I took Ernest Hemingway's advice.

He said, "The first draft of everything is shit."

Authors like Hemingway can teach the rest of us how to achieve anything with words, ideas and a blank page.

I worked through each of the 101 strategies and discarded what wasn't working. This kind of brutal editing is a process every productive writer becomes intimately familiar with.

Then I refined my research and ideas into 33 strategies that will help you get to the end of whatever you're writing.

What I've just described–the strategy of generating more ideas by setting the bar higher–forms part of one of the 33 strategies you'll learn about in this book.

HOW TO USE THIS BOOK

You can use the 33 strategies to consistently publish on your blog, finally finish writing your book, and balance writing with the rest of your life.

To help you get out of your creative jams, I've included proven writing prompts you can use to kick-start your writing projects.

I wrote each of these strategies as stand-alone chapters with steps you can put into practice today. Although there's a natural order to this book, you can dip in and out of each strategy and apply it to whatever you're writing.

You can read this book from start to finish, use it as a companion guide or apply the individual strategies most relevant to how you like to work or write. This book isn't specifically about fiction or non-fiction writing, but I reference both kinds of creative work.

Whatever your interests, I hope this book helps you become a more confident and successful writer.

Using these 33 strategies, you'll be able to write every day, create a writing habit that sticks and finish what you started.

You will become *the productive writer*.

LEAVE YOUR INTRODUCTION
TILL LAST

L et me tell you a secret.
Productive writers create their introduction last.

The purpose of the first sentence is to convince a reader to continue to the second sentence. The purpose of the first paragraph is to convince the reader to continue to the second. The purpose of the first chapter…and so on.

Think about it: What's the first thing a customer in a bookshop looks at when they open a new book? Unless you're one of those crazy types who likes to read the ending, it's the first line.

Almost every writer I've met writes their first paragraph and their first sentence last.

No matter if you're writing a book, article, blog post or copy for a webpage, you must capture and hold the reader's attention, which is a valuable commodity.

Writing a solid first line or a good opening is hard work. If you don't know what the subsequent sentences, paragraphs and chapters are about, writing a great opening is impossible.

During your next writing project, don't worry about the beginning until you reach the end. Then read through your work and summarise it in a sentence or two. If you can come up with a good hook or metaphor to draw the reader in, even better.

Once you're happy with your introduction, reread your conclusion and explore how you can link the two together.

Perhaps you have an idea or a metaphor you can return to.

Maybe you can use similar language to answer a question you raised in the introduction.

A book's introduction and conclusion are like sign-posts. They let the reader know what lies ahead and where he or she just visited.

Whatever your approach, work hard on your opening and even harder on your first line. Smooth, buff, polish and make it shine. The reader should find your opening line irresistible.

Your first line can and should make the reader feel inspired, curious or motivated for your next line.

Whatever you do, don't bore them with a long, ponderous sentence. Make your reader feel something, and they'll keep reading.

Whenever I'm struggling to find an opening, I go back and read great first lines for inspiration.

With this in mind, here are ten of my favourite opening lines of all time. Each of these succeed because they make the reader feel something.

- "Call me Ishmael." – Herman Melville, *Moby-Dick* (1851)
- "It was a bright cold day in April, and the clocks were striking thirteen." – George Orwell, *1984* (1949)
- "It was the best of times, it was the worst of times, it was the age of wisdom, it was the age of foolishness, it was the epoch of belief, it was the epoch of incredulity, it was the season of Light, it was the season of Darkness, it was the spring of hope, it was the winter of despair." – Charles Dickens, *A Tale of Two Cities* (1859)
- "Lolita, light of my life, fire of my loins." – Vladimir Nabokov, *Lolita* (1955)
- "Happy families are all alike; every unhappy family is

unhappy in its own way." – Leo Tolstoy, *Anna Karenina* (1877)

- "It is a truth universally acknowledged, that a single man in possession of a good fortune, must be in want of a wife." – Jane Austen, *Pride and Prejudice* (1813)
- "It was a queer, sultry summer, the summer they electrocuted the Rosenbergs, and I didn't know what I was doing in New York." – Sylvia Plath, *The Bell Jar* (1963)
- "If you really want to hear about it, the first thing you'll probably want to know is where I was born, and what my lousy childhood was like, and how my parents were occupied and all before they had me, and all that David Copperfield kind of crap, but I don't feel like going into it, if you want to know the truth." – J.D. Salinger, *The Catcher In The Rye* (1951)
- "In my younger and more vulnerable years my father gave me some advice that I've been turning over in my mind ever since. Whenever you feel like criticising anyone, he told me, just remember that all the people in this world haven't had the advantages that you've had." – F. Scott Fitzgerald, *The Great Gatsby* (1925)
- "As Gregor Samsa awoke one morning from uneasy dreams he found himself transformed in his bed into a monstrous vermin." – Franz Kafka, *The Metamorphosis* (1915)

HOW TO USE THE INVERTED PYRAMID

Journalists use the inverted pyramid to arrange the key facts of what they are writing.

This concept came about because editors and printers of early newspapers sometimes didn't have enough print space to fit entire stories into their papers.

They needed a way of removing information quickly to make the text of each story fit, and cutting off the bottom paragraphs of news stories was the fastest way to do this.

So journalists started writing the most important point first, the second most important point second, and so on.

Although printing technology has improved, the inverted pyramid still applies because newspaper readers don't always read a story all the way through.

A reader will glance at a headline, and if it's of interest they'll pick up the paper and read the rest of the story.

Today, journalists use the headline, the first sentence, and the first paragraph to answer the following questions in increasing levels of detail:

- What happened?
- When did it happen?
- To whom did it happen?
- Where did it happen?
- How did it happen?
- Why did it happen?

Writers also use the inverted pyramid for web pages because the average visitor doesn't stay for more than 10 to 20 seconds on a webpage.

So an online writer has to capture the reader's attention by putting the most important information first and writing for people who scan digital copy.

The inverted pyramid works for short, non-fiction writing projects. You can apply it to newsletters, social media posts, copy for web pages, blog posts or articles.

If you are writing for the web, you can use the inverted pyramid to get to the point faster. Say what is most important first and induce the reader to stay a little longer.

The inverted pyramid isn't as effective when your writing has more room to breathe and when you can count on the reader's attention for a thesis or an article of more than 3,000 words, for example.

Then you have the time and space to expand on your arguments or tell a story.

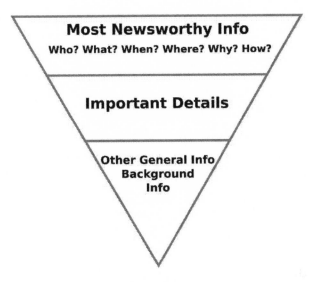

The Inverted Pyramid, via Wikimedia and The Air Force
Departmental Publishing Office (AFDPO, 2011)

OPEN WITH FLAIR

The introduction is the hardest part of any article or story to write. If you're struggling to create a compelling opening, leave it till last. When you're finished writing, you'll have a better idea of how to begin.

If you're still stuck, open like a journalist. They write their articles with the end in mind. Journalists know what their news story is about and understand what they're saying before they start writing.

A journalist doesn't begin a news article hoping by the time they reach the last paragraph they will have said something important or newsworthy.

Neither does the productive writer.

WARM UP LIKE A PRO

"I f you want to be the best, you have to do things that other people aren't willing to do." – Michael Phelps

Do you warm up before you write?

The Olympic swimmer Michael Phelps begins exercising in a pool separate to the competition for 45 minutes before a big race.

The world's fastest man, Usain Bolt, practices sprinting near the track before he competes. And tennis champion Roger Federer skips, jumps and stretches before a match.

Writers who want to become more productive should apply the same approach to their craft.

It takes five or 10 minutes of writing to forget the distractions of the day, warm up and pay attention to whatever you're supposed to be working on. These first few minutes of writing might not produce anything of merit.

The first few minutes of any writing session should help you focus on the task ahead.

Warming up will help you overcome procrastination. If you do it regularly, those first few minutes of writing will feel less painful.

You can warm up in many different ways before you write.

Reading poetry or listening to music can fire up the left side of your brain for more creative work. Reading a passage from a book or an article can engage your critical faculties for non-fiction writing.

Printing out, reading and annotating the entirety of the previous day's work is also useful if you're about to embark on an editing session.

You can use a writing prompt to warm up today too.

JUMP-START YOUR WRITING

These writing prompts aren't meant as final first lines for your work.

Instead, you can use them as a jumping-off point into your work or for freewriting.

Take one of these lines, write it down and then freewrite whatever comes to mind for at least 30 minutes. I suggest using a kitchen timer.

This is long enough to accomplish something on the blank page but not so long that it feels overwhelming.

Later when you've written something more polished, go back and delete the writing prompt.

If you dislike my selection of prompts, take a great first line from your favourite book, poem or story and use that.

Whatever your choice, writing prompts will help you stand on the shoulders of giants. And up there, you can see for miles.

- "I remember the last time I..."
- "I remember the first time I..."
- "The next time I..."
- "It tasted like..."
- "It felt like..."
- "It sounded like..."
- "We were wrong about..."
- "We were right about..."
- "That was the day we..."
- "This is our new..."

- "It's here."
- "I learnt that…"
- "I made a terrible mistake when…"
- "Nobody expected us to…"
- "Do you know why…"
- "It's always important to…"
- "Most people don't know this but…"
- "I probably shouldn't be telling you this, but…"
- "Here's a secret nobody knows…"
- "I do this because…"
- "Admit it."
- "I found out that…"
- "He gave us a…"
- "She took a…"
- "We found a…"
- "I was in pain."
- "We discovered…"
- "Today is a good day for…"
- "Tomorrow is a bad day for…"
- "This time it will be different."
- "We need to talk about…"
- "You need to face up to…"
- "Our only hope is…"
- "On my desk I can see…"
- "Outside the window…"
- "I ate…"
- "If I was…"
- "When I'm…"
- "Go to…"
- "Now that we…"
- "We argued about…"
- "Being wrong is hard because…"
- "Being right is lonely because…"
- "Together we can…"
- "Apart we are…"

- "Let me guess."
- "If I understand you correctly, you think…"
- "My friend is…"
- "I love her because…"
- "I hate him because…"
- "We're going to…"
- "Let's take a trip to…"
- "My favourite…"
- "I'm lost."
- "We want to get to…"
- "The weather is…"
- "We're going to eat…"
- "Food is…"
- "Water is…"
- "Money is…"
- "Help is…"
- "Sex is…"
- "Last night I dreamt of…"
- "I slept for…"
- "I'm working for…"
- "I failed at…"
- "I succeeded at…"
- "You showed me how to…"
- "He explained that…"
- "She made us laugh when…"
- "My hero is…"
- "My enemy is…"
- "I regret…"
- "This time we went too far."
- "I told him…"
- "She told me…"
- "I looked in the mirror and saw…"
- "Black."
- "White."
- "I awoke at 3:00 a.m. and realised…"

- "I should have listened."
- "He won't do that again."
- "It was the first storm of the year…"
- "Her eyes are…"
- "His hands make me want to…"
- "She tastes like…"
- "He feels like…"
- "Danger."
- "How can we…"
- "Open your…"
- "Keep it safe."
- "It's a new day."
- "It's later than we think."
- "If I ever see another…"
- "The best day of my life was…"
- "The worst day of my life was…"
- "When I'm king…"
- "You could be a queen of…"
- "Looking back…"
- "They caught me."
- "I was crushed because…"

If need more help with writing prompts, please see book one.

HOW TO FREEWRITE

Freewriting is simple to learn, and every productive writer should have this skill in their toolbox.

All you have to do is sit at your desk and write about anything that comes to mind without interruption for five, 10 or 20 minutes. If you write nothing but gibberish, whatever you do, don't stop writing.

When you freewrite, you're not trying to accomplish or complete anything on the blank page.

Author Mark Levy wrote in his book *Accidental Genius,*

Freewriting...pushes the brain to think longer, deeper and more unconventionally than it normally would.

Freewriting can help you clear mental blocks, come up with better ideas, write more honestly, think differently from your peers, and find a new perspective for your writing.

You can freewrite a cover letter for a job application, copy for your website, a blog post, a magazine article or a chapter for your book.

If you want to try freewriting as a warm-up exercise for your current writing project, don't worry about capturing fully formed ideas.

Instead, just type or write about anything that comes to mind.

It's OK if you jump from one idea to the next. Document your thoughts as they arise without holding back. Don't edit or censure yourself.

If something daft comes, like the sound of a dog on the street, write that down too. And if someone interrupts your train of thought, record that you were interrupted.

If you keep freewriting, you will overtake your brain's ability to edit, and you'll break past your internal critic.

You will reach a place where you can write about wild ideas and make connections that otherwise wouldn't have been possible if you'd held back.

Your word count will shoot up, sure. And if most of what you write is rubbish, at the end of your freewriting session, you can extract one or two good ideas and then spend time developing these into something more usable for your current writing project.

WRITE WITHOUT EDITING YOURSELF

Freewriting works only if you don't question or criticise every sentence, idea and story you put down on the blank page.

Instead, let the words flow freely through your fingers onto the page without pausing or questioning what you're writing.

Then when you've finished your freewriting for the day, spend time polishing, buffing and making your prose shine.

WRITE WHATEVER COMES TO MIND

Freewriting enables you to follow a train of thought in new and exciting directions.

When you're freewriting, record what you're thinking or if you feel distracted. It doesn't matter if it's unrelated to the topic you're writing about. This could mean recording the the colour of a plant on your desk or a swear word.

Don't hold back.

TIME YOUR FREEWRITING SESSIONS

Get a clock or open the timer on your computer. Set it for 25 minutes and write. When the buzzer sounds, take a short break and repeat. Do this two to four times before taking a longer break.

FREEWRITE FOR AN HOUR OR LONGER

If you're struggling to make a breakthrough, freewrite for an extended period without taking a break.

Yes, this is mentally and physically demanding, but you don't have to do it very often. It will help you overcome those difficult barriers every writer faces at some point.

KEEP YOUR HAND MOVING

This tip is straight from the pages of Natalie Goldberg's excellent book *Writing Down the Bones: Freeing the Writer Within.*

An advocate of freewriting, or "writing practice" as she calls it, Goldberg recommends "keeping your hand moving."

If you're a typist, don't take your fingers from the keys until you've finished writing.

If you prefer a pen, this means keeping the pen pressed between your fingers. And if you like to dictate your writing, keep the dictation machine recording until you're done.

KEEP A LIST OF TOPICS

I use Evernote to organise my writing. Inside, I keep a notebook full of topics that I want to freewrite about.

Examples include ideas for short stories, sentence fragments, blog posts, and ideas that I want to expand on.

Then, when I want to freewrite, I pick one item from my notebook and go with it. Keeping these kinds of lists means I spend less time looking for a topic and more time freewriting.

USE OTHER WRITING TECHNIQUES

Freewriting is just one writing technique you can employ to advance your work.

Sometimes, it makes more sense to plan your writing in advance or to aim towards a target word count.

Combining freewriting with other kinds of writing sessions such as editing, outlining chapters etc. It will help you mix things up during the week, test your boundaries and avoid becoming bored with the process.

KEEP YOUR CAST-OFFS

Freewriting produces a lot of leftover ideas that don't immediately belong anywhere. Don't throw this writing in the bin or delete it.

Instead, keep your cast-offs in your journal or a file on your computer.

A time will come when it makes sense to return to your leftovers and extract something useful. These leftovers also serve as markers for your progress as a writer.

Don't worry though. I address how to do this more in chapter four.

EXPAND ON IDEA

I read a lot of non-fiction books, and I regularly come across ideas that surprise, inspire or confound me.

Sometimes I take these ideas and expand on them during freewriting sessions. Freewriting about ideas helps me internalise them and figure out how I can use them.

If you want to do the same, underline key passages in the books you're reading, write notes in the margins and review these when you've finished reading The Kindle is ideal for this.

Then pick one or two ideas and use them as topics for your next freewriting session.

FREEWRITE A PROBLEM UPSIDE DOWN

Are you having trouble with a particularly difficult writing project?

Perhaps the feedback from a client wasn't helpful.

Or maybe you can't figure out the right arc for your story.

Write down this problem at the top of your page.

Then freewrite everything about the problem that's bothering you and what you're afraid of. Freewrite all the solutions you can think of.

If you get lucky, you'll make a breakthrough. If you don't, you're still venting your frustrations and practice writing at the same time.

Think of it as therapy and writing practice rolled into one.

WHY YOU SHOULD FREEWRITE FOR FUN

Sometimes you need to hit a word count, and press publish. Other times, writing is supposed to be fun, you need to try something different or go in a new direction.

For the latter, freewriting is the perfect writing technique. This week, allocate 30 minutes of time for freewriting. Use it to write about whatever you want. It's your guilty pleasure.

Are you still unsure about freewriting? Why not freewrite about the ways it can help you finish what you started? Who knows where you'll end up?

STOP WAITING FOR INSPIRATION
(IT'S NOT COMING)

"Don't be daunted. Just do your job. Continue to show up for your piece of it, whatever that might be." – Elizabeth Gilbert

What would happen if a professional athlete stopped training for an event because they were tired of their sport?

If he or she made a habit of not training, they'd lose their next event.

What would happen if an engineer stopped working on a construction project because he didn't feel excited about plans for the project?

He'd lose his job.

What happens to the writer who waits for inspiration to arrive?

She doesn't write at all.

Writing is hard work. It's demanding and time-consuming, and it requires you to sit in one place and concentrate for extended periods of time. If you want to write professionally, treat the work seriously.

Like any profession, it's your job to turn up in front of the blank page each day and not just when inspiration arrives. It's your duty to write when you don't feel like writing, when you're tired, angry, anxious or afraid.

Leave divine moments of inspiration for the creative geniuses.

American short story writer and author John Updike wasn't one for waiting around for inspiration. He wrote for several hours each day.

Updike published his first work, a collection of poetry called *The Carpentered Hen,* in 1958. Thereafter, he published a book almost every year.

"I've never believed that one should wait until one is inspired, because I think that the pleasures of not writing are so great that if you ever start indulging them, you'll never write again," he said.

Stop waiting around for an idea or solution to whatever causes you problems. Force yourself into the chair and start to write.

The first few sentences might not make much sense, but several sentences in you'll realise you're not as tired or devoid of ideas as you thought; you were just procrastinating.

Even if you turn up and produce nothing of value, at least you put in a morning or an evening's work. Take heart from author and speaker Elizabeth Gilbert. She said,

> Creativity itself doesn't care at all about results - the only thing it craves is the process. Learn to love the process and let whatever happens next happen, without fussing too much about it. Work like a monk, or a mule, or some other representative metaphor for diligence. Love the work. Destiny will do what it wants with you, regardless.

ACCEPT YOUR SUBCONSCIOUS

The subconscious is a powerful beast.

It needs food and attention.

Take notes, turn up every day in front of the blank page and make a concerted effort to finish what you're working on. The writer who does this understands how important it is to feed his or her inner beast.

If you write sales copy, your subconscious is hungry for the words that sell, for words written by talented copywriters.

If you write articles for magazines, your subconscious is waiting for exotic, fresh and colourful stories.

If you write blog posts, the subconscious wants to devour in-depth, meaningful posts so it can present you with new ideas.

If you write fiction, your subconscious craves anecdotes, stories, characters and dialogue.

Keeping the beast happy also means giving it time and space to roam free through your mind.

I'm talking about daydreaming.

Most creative people are familiar with those small eureka moments of life whereby a solution suddenly presents itself when you're working on something else entirely. These ideas can turn up when you're in the shower, eating a meal, watching television or out for a walk.

Of course, it would be more convenient if we could summon these ideas at will in front of the blank page, but the subconscious is a wild animal; it can't be tamed.

French artist Henri Matisse gave his subconscious time and space while painting landscapes. He sometimes stopped working to meditate on the environment around him. He did this at length before returning to his canvas with a new perspective.

Matisse did pretty well for himself in the end. As one of the greatest and most productive painters of the twentieth century, he finished several dozen masterpieces during his lifetime. So, don't be afraid to pause what you are doing.

Let the beast run free.

LEARN FROM ALBERT EINSTEIN

Are you still procrastinating?

Do you need just a little bit more encouragement to pick up the pen?

Are you still thinking, "But I could accomplish more if I didn't have to do all these other things?"

Take some productivity lessons from Albert Einstein.

He is one of the most famous scientific writers of all time. Although he is more famous for his mathematical equations than his writing, Einstein's life shows writers can succeed because of life's day-to-day struggles and not in spite of them.

Einstein's Peers Rejected Him

During his early twenties, Einstein spent several years seeking employment as a teaching assistant. He struggled to find meaningful work, and he couldn't get his dissertation published as part of an application for a doctorate.

Einstein even sent professors copies of his dissertation with a postage-paid card, to encourage them to reply and offer feedback (sometimes we take email for granted!).

Numerous leading professors and employers in Germany, Austria, Italy and Switzerland rejected Einstein repeatedly. At one stage, Einstein became so despondent about his career that he contemplated abandoning science for engineering.

His father, an engineer, wrote to Wilhelm Ostwald, the Professor of Chemistry of Leipzig, and implored Ostwald to read Einstein's paper and write a few words of encouragement.

Ostwald didn't reply (although much later he did nominate Einstein for the Nobel Prize).

Later Einstein published a series of landmark papers that over-turned the basics of physics, but he spent several more years waiting for the academic and professional recognition he deserved.

Today, writers have much more opportunities than Einstein to make their voices heard. If a gatekeeper refuses our work, we can use a blog to build a platform, enter contests or self-publish a book.

Today, it doesn't take a genius to find an audience.

Einstein Pursued Many Interests

Einstein loved music since he was a child, and he became an accomplished violinist. He often entertained dinner party guests, academics, friends and his family by playing Mozart.

He didn't care much for material possessions or appearances, but he did bring his violin almost everywhere.

Einstein once played with noted Russian violinist Toscha Seidel and afterwards explained his theory of relativity to Seidel.

He stopped playing later in life only when his fingers struggled with the violin strings.

Einstein's first love was science, but he still made time for other passions and interests. Writers don't have to pursue their craft at all costs; if anything, your writing will improve if you make time for other passions.

Einstein Challenged Himself

Einstein saw himself as a nonconformist and a rebel. This belief system was both a result of the times he lived in and his personal character.

Einstein lived through two World Wars, and he had to leave Hitler's Germany for America because he was Jewish.

As a younger man, he suggested academic life wasn't conducive to great work, and according to his biographer Walter Isaacson, he took delight in challenging the prevailing wisdom of his academic peers.

From the 1920s onwards, many of Einstein's theories were challenged or overturned by a new branch of physics: quantum mechanics. This branch of physics described randomness in nature, but Einstein dismissed it saying, "God does not play dice."

He spent the later part of his life researching a way of unifying his general theory of relativism with electromagnetism.

Einstein's contemporaries, who were more concerned with quantum mechanics, regarded his quest as rather quaint and even as a waste of Einstein's time.

Einstein didn't care.

Always the rebel, he felt he'd achieved enough status and security in life to spend time researching areas of physics that his younger peers would have been discredited for.

For Einstein, pursuing a passion was more important than what others thought of him or how he spent his time.

Don't seek success for its own sake. It's more important that you challenge yourself, publish your work and avoid complacency.

He Didn't Regard His Craft as Work

In 1955, a 76-year-old Einstein died in hospital from a long-standing stomach ailment.

On his deathbed, he left 12 sets of equations that formed parts of Einstein's search for a unified field theory. He also left an undelivered speech, which he had just written for Israel Independence Day.

I'm not suggesting writing on your deathbed, but Einstein's story demonstrates a life's work can take on a greater meaning if we're passionate enough about our craft.

At the very least, remember Einstein's advice for scientists and by extension writers, "If you can't explain it simply, you don't understand it well enough."

FAIL LIKE A GENIUS

Genius or not, Einstein had many personal flaws.

Einstein married Marić Mileva in 1903, and he divorced her in 1919 after a difficult and unhappy marriage. He also rarely saw his son Eduard Tete, who had schizophrenia and had a more difficult life in various mental health institutions.

Einstein married his second wife Elsa Löwenthal in 1919 and, although they were married until her death in 1936, he had several affairs.

After Elsa's death, Einstein praised a friend for managing to live in harmony with a woman, saying this was one thing he failed at.

He could also be cold and distant. As a younger man, he often made life harder for himself by deliberately antagonising and challenging his peers.

Einstein overcame many personal and professional obstacles, but he also failed and failed often. He experienced the same pain and suffering many of us go through.

FUEL UP ON IDEAS

"The knowledge of all things is possible." – Leonardo da Vinci

You can't drive a car without fuel, and you can't write if you haven't got any ideas.

The good news is that unlike fuel, ideas are everywhere. All you have to do is get into the habit of regularly filling up your creative tank, and you will always have what you need to write.

This creative habit is one accomplished writers, artists and even inventors cultivate.

When Leonardo da Vinci died in 1519, he left behind dozens of notebooks filled with ideas for new art projects, paintings and inventions. Some of these ideas, such as his initial concept for the helicopter, informed future inventions.

Da Vinci's journals and notebooks are a reminder of the importance of generating ideas every day. His ideas showed us how we can better understand the world around us.

Scholar Michael Gelb studied da Vinci's notebooks and his life.

Gelb recommends anyone who wants to become creative like da Vinci should make a habit of recording new ideas every day.

In *How to Think Like Leonardo da Vinci*, Gelb wrote:

> Busy lives and job responsibilities tend to drive us toward hard conclusions and measurable results, but the exploratory, free-flowing, unfinished, non-judgmental practice of keeping a da Vincian notebook encourages freedom of thought and expansion of perspective. In the manner of the maestro, don't worry about order and logical flow, just record.

You too should just record. Don't worry about being logical, tidy or organised, at least at first. Writing (and creativity) doesn't fit into tidy little boxes, so get into the habit of making a mess.

Leonardo da Vinci's Vitruvian Man is one of his most famous
journal entries, via Luc Viatour / www.Lucnix.be (2007)

RAISE THE BAR

Get a pen and paper and write down 10 or even 100 ideas for whatever you're working on.

Don't judge, dismiss or censure whatever comes to mind. Instead, record your idea and progress quickly to the next one. The task of generating so many new ideas will force your brain to make new connections and mash up old ideas.

If you're struggling to come up with ideas, try writing down at least 10:

- Reasons why something will work/won't work

- Arguments why you're for/against something
- Ideas you can combine
- Things you need to do next
- Interviewees you could source
- Headlines
- Ways to open or close your story with a bang
- Questions you need answers to
- Unusual facts or pieces of information you possess
- Strengths/weaknesses of your chosen topic

Much like freewriting, don't worry about the quality of your ideas. Aim for quantity over quality. It's easier to generate 100 ideas of variable quality than it is to think of one perfect idea.

After you've captured 35 bad ideas, you stand a better chance of coming up with one great idea. Conversely, if you try to come up with one great idea for your writing project, you will struggle.

Raise the bar impossibly high and you will surprise yourself with what you can achieve.

At the very least, if you have more ideas to write about, you will find it easier to sit down in front of the blank page.

Every day, I write down 10 ideas for blog posts, articles, short stories or book chapters in my notebook.

Some of my ideas are terrible, and others never make it beyond my notebook. However, by the end of the week I have lots of new ideas I can sift through, and at least one always holds some value.

I might sound borderline obsessive about generating new ideas each day, but I don't want to run out of fuel when the time comes to write.

REVIEW YOUR IDEAS

After you get into the habit of generating new ideas, you'll have more than you can write about. The day lacks enough hours, and life carries too many commitments for you to write about everything you want.

Here's the thing:

Acting on an idea carries an opportunity cost. When you write about one idea, you're spending time that could be spent writing about something else.

For example, if I've got an idea for a blog post and an idea for a book chapter, I can only focus on one at a time. So, do I write the book chapter or the blog post?

The answer depends on my priorities and how good the idea is. If you want to decide what ideas are best to spend time on, ask yourself:

- Is this something I'm passionate about writing?
- Can I say something in a unique way about this topic?
- Is this idea newsworthy or popular online?
- Am I prepared to give up working on another idea to work on *this idea?*
- Do I have enough knowledge and research to hand to write about this idea in detail?

BE HONEST WITH YOURSELF

Several years ago, I spent a lot of time reviewing products, games, services and music for Irish newspapers. These articles were easy to write, I got to keep what I reviewed, and I enjoyed the process, at first.

Later though, I recognised I was criticising ideas other people had created and worked on, and it's almost always easier to criticise than it is to create.

So, I told my editor I didn't want to review games, films or music albums anymore. I wanted to concentrate on writing news stories and feature articles. At least this kind of writing would give me room to come up with ideas and make better mistakes.

I'm not a journalist anymore, and I review products on my blog only if I'm passionate about the product or service and it can help writers accomplish more. I prefer spending my time writing longer, more involved articles that are challenging.

This pursuit is harder and more time-consuming, but it's also more satisfying.

Becoming a more productive writer means coming up with ideas every day and then spending time refining your ideas to an essential few. It means being honest about how you spend your precious creative time.

BUILD A PERSONAL LIBRARY OF
GREAT IDEAS

"We judge it is of great service in studies. . . to bestow diligence and labor in setting down common-places; as it affords matter to invention, and collects and strengthens the judgment." – Francis Bacon

Productive writers keep a personal library where they store their best ideas, what they've learnt, information about what they've read and even notes on what they'd like to write next.

I'm not referring to building a spare room in your house that you fill with shelves and books.

Instead, you can create your personal library by keeping a commonplace book and a swipe file. You can also build one by annotating your favourite books and articles and writing down your ideas.

HOW TO KEEP A COMMONPLACE BOOK

A commonplace book will help you marshal research for your writing projects. Before the digital age, commonplace books were popular.

They were a kind of personal, pre-internet repository of letters, medical information, quotes, facts, experiences, anecdotes and personal histories. They were also a way for individuals, families and communities to sort and store knowledge about their lives.

Historical figures, authors and poets such as Marcus Aurelius, Napoleon, Thomas Jefferson, Francis Bacon, John Milton and W.H. Auden all kept or published commonplace books.

More recently, American author Ryan Holiday explained how he uses a commonplace book to write his books.

He said,

> The purpose of the [commonplace] book is to record and organise these gems for later use in your life, in your business, in your writing, speaking or whatever it is that you do.

A commonplace book will help you become a more productive writer because when the time comes to write your next book or article, you will already have a resource of relevant information to draw on. You will be the kind of writer who is always researching, learning and on the hunt for new ideas.

You won't need to spend hours researching because you will already know what you want to write about. Your research will form part of your creative life.

A commonplace book works only if you read widely and mark what's relevant as you go. Then you must extract useful information and put it in your commonplace book. You can use a paper-based or digital system to store this information in your commonplace book.

Whatever your preference, categorise entries in your commonplace book with terms that apply to your work and your life.

For example, I use the term "blog" for ideas and articles that are relevant to blog posts I want to write. I use the term "journal" to record ideas and information for entries in my journal.

When I was writing this book, I categorised various entries in my commonplace book by terms related to each strategy.

To get value from your commonplace book, make a habit of regularly reviewing and reorganising your entries. This way, the wisdom you're gathering will sink into each of your writing projects.

HOW TO KEEP A SWIPE FILE

A swipe file is a place where you store facts, figures, sentences and ideas relating to your work. It's a repository of information that if not relevant to your current writing project,will be of use at some point in the future.

Copywriters and advertisers use swipe files all the time to keep ideas, research and information they can use for future campaigns.

Dan S. Kennedy is a legendary business author, copywriter and salesperson. He writes about swipe files,

> I built up huge "idea files"—samples of ads, mailings, and sales letters…You do not need much creativity to write letters; you only need to be adept at recycling and reorganising ideas, themes, words, and phrases.

I don't know about you, but I'd rather become adept at this craft than be the kind of person who grinds it out, project after project. If you're interested in learning more about copywriting, I explain how to write words in chapter 13.

If you keep a swipe file, the next time you have to write copy for a website, blog post, email or social media campaign, you can take information directly from your swipe file instead of having to come up with fresh ideas.

Maintaining swipe files means you can spend less time staring out of windows and more time accomplishing your non-fiction projects.

Don't think of swipe files as cheating. Lawyers keep boilerplate legal text they can use for future contracts and agreements.

Professional software developers store snippets of code that can be used for future projects. Even journalists keep quotes from interviewees that they can use for future news stories.

As with a commonplace book, you can keep a paper or digital

swipe file. A paper swipe file could consist of newspaper and magazine clippings, as well as your notes that you store in a drawer next to your desk, or you could keep a digital swipe file using a tool like Evernote.

Here are some of the more popular kinds of information productive writers keep in their swipe files:

- Headlines
- Quotes
- Interviews with people in your area of interest
- Inspiring videos and pictures
- Random facts and figures
- Sketches
- Phone numbers
- Angles for blog posts
- Emails
- Writing prompts
- Great first lines
- Advertisements
- Social media posts
- Presentations

To get the most use from your swipe file, take time at the end of the week or before you're about to start a new writing project and see if you can extract useful ideas and turn them into something fresh.

ANNOTATE WHAT YOU READ

If you've ever picked up a dog-eared book from six or 12 months ago, you've probably had the experience of looking for half-remembered passages, quotations and arguments.

Annotating your favourite works means you can spend less time researching your current writing project and more time writing. This practice will help you critically engaging with whatever you're reading and ensure this information seeps deeper into your subconscious.

I annotate books by highlighting passages on my Kindle. I also record observations about what I've read in digital apps like Evernote.

There's nothing wrong with making notes using pen and paper. You can do this in a journal, or you can underline favourite sentences in books.

These highlights, bookmarks and annotations can become food for future works. They enable you to connect the concepts in one book to another and examine how the author's writings relate to your life or your work.

Some experts recommend writing a brief summary after finishing a chapter so you can assess the value of a book later. I use this method when I want to remember something–for an exam, for example–but I rarely do this when I'm reading for relaxation.

When I'm writing an article or blog post, I return to my annotations for inspiration, advice and sometimes to back up a point.

Prior to making annotations, I spent a lot of time searching old books for quotes that I half-remembered and points I wasn't sure about. Now I can save time on research and spend more time writing.

Getting into the habit of annotating what you read and love is a great way of emulating and learning from the writing techniques of more accomplished writers.

At the very least, annotations will help you consider what makes for a good sentence or argument and what makes for a poor one.

WRITE DOWN YOUR IDEAS

Many accomplished writers are fastidious about recording their ideas throughout the day.

Mark Twain carried a pocket notebook with him at all times to record his ideas.

Thomas Jefferson jotted down notes about everything from the growth of plants and flowers to observations about daily life.

Even George Lucas keeps a notebook with him when he's shooting a film.

The children's author Roald Dahl valued writing ideas down too. He said about his work, "A writer of fiction lives in fear. Each new day demands new ideas and he can never be sure whether he is going to come up with them or not."

Dahl famously wrote down the word "chocolate" into the dirt on his car, while stuck in traffic. He later turned this idea into the book *Charlie and the Chocolate Factory.*

Whether you use a commonplace book, a swipe file or just a notebook, get into the habit of writing your ideas down every day.

You can keep a portable notebook for recording ideas on the go. You can use digital tools like an app on your smartphone, or you can buy a small notebook that fits in your pocket.

Whatever your tool, your notebook should become an extension of yourself.

HOLD YOURSELF TO ACCOUNT

"When the beginnings of self-destruction enter the heart it seems no bigger than a grain of sand." – John Cheever

Holding yourself to account means taking time to see how your writing is progressing and if you are working on the right things. To follow this strategy, you must be realistic about your progress and growth as a writer and find a way to keep yourself honest.

Productive writers can use two great methods to hold themselves to account.

The first is to **set clear goals** for your writing projects that you track and make progress towards each week. This method is suited to people who like lists and clearly defined boundaries.

The second method is to **keep a journal** where you write introspective entries about your writing. This method is best suited for writers who dislike the confines of a To Do list but still require a way to review how their work is progressing.

In this chapter, I'll explain how you can use either method to hold yourself accountable.

SET GOALS FOR YOUR WRITING

Setting goals will give you something to work towards and help you eliminate nonessential tasks from your life. I like goals because they give a clear marker that I can make progress towards. In other words, I can either achieve a goal or miss it.

You can set goals for your writing easily. All you have to do is make sure they are SMART. That is:

(S)pecific: Be clear about what exactly you want to achieve. "I want to write a book" is not specific. "I want to publish a collection of children's short stories" is.

(M)easurable: Have a system for measuring your progress towards your goal each week or month.

(A)chievable: Pick a goal that you can accomplish. If you haven't written much before, you're unlikely to write a novel in three months no matter how productive you are.

(R)ealistic: You must have a reasonable chance of accomplishing your goal. Winning the Nobel Prize for Literature is an unrealistic goal for most of us.

(T)imed: Set a deadline for yourself that you can meet.

Here is one of my creative SMART goals:

I will self-publish (realistic) and sell (achievable) a short story collection (specific) by my birthday (timed, measurable).

Here's another SMART goal:

I will write 1,000 words a day or write 10 hours a week (measurable and specific) every week (achievable, realistic) before June 31 (timed).

KEEP TO DO LISTS

Now comes the nuts and bolts of doing your work.

Each of your creative projects should have an **outcome**, that is a statement of how you want things to turn out.

Next, write down all the actions that you need to take on a list to achieve this outcome.

You can keep a separate list for each project or you can keep one master list with your tasks organised by context.

When writing your "To Dos", use clear and specific active verbs so you don't have to think when you read them later on. Set deadlines for each of these actions in your calendar so you track what's coming up.

For example, when I'm planning my writing for the week, one of my action items will say, "Write a 1,000-word scene set in a restaurant on Thursday."

When I finish my blog post about productivity, my action item will say, "Email my latest blog post about productivity to my list by Wednesday."

Remember, you don't need to do everything on these lists. Instead, simply get everything down in one place so you don't waste mental energy thinking about what you need to do during the week.

Then, once a day, once a week or as often as is necessary, pick the most important tasks from these lists and do them.

At the end of each day, I pick the three most important things I need to do the following day and focus on accomplishing those tasks first thing.

So stick with the task at hand without overthinking what you're doing.

USE JOURNAL WRITING

Don't like goals or To Do lists?

Don't worry, lots of writers find them confining. You can use a simple writing practice to gain an insight into how your writing is progressing.

Keeping a journal will foster your creativity and help you write more often. It's also a great way of holding yourself to account.

Why?

Writing a journal can help you turn thoughts and feelings into words and ideas. Because a journal is private, you're less likely to censure yourself.

This kind of honest writing is key to improving your craft and expanding the boundaries of your writing. If you keep a journal for several years, older entries serve as signposts for how your writing is progressing.

You can keep a journal in a paper notebook, in a password-protected file on your computer or by using one of the many journal apps available for smartphones.

In it, you could describe how your current writing project is progressing, what's holding you back and your plans for future. You could also use your journal to note sentences that you'd like to use and to tease out ideas for your writing projects.

American novelist and short story writer John Cheever kept one of the best journals of the 20th century, and he wrote like one good friend talking to another. Throughout his life, he chronicled his difficult marriage, his loneliness, sexuality, alcoholism and decline.

Virginia Woolf was also fastidious about her journal writing as a means of holding herself to account. In an entry dated 1919, she described how journal writing encouraged and improved her craft.

> I believe that during the past year I can trace some increase of ease in
> my professional writing which I attribute to my casual hours after tea.

My life isn't much like Cheever's or Woolf's, but I learnt a lot about the art of journal writing from both authors.

Keeping a journal doesn't mean recording a daily summary of one's life. Anyone interested in writing a journal should expose themselves entirely in their journal and seek out brutal honestly.

I write about what I accomplished and failed at recently and what I'm thinking about. I also write about ideas for future writing projects. Some of my journal entries are only one or two lines long.

My shortest entry simply reads "Exhausted" (did I mention that I have two small children?).

Others run several paragraphs or even pages in length.

The journals of Cheever and writers like Vladimir Nabokov taught me that keeping a journal helps identify negative patterns, thoughts and behaviours. In a way, journal writing is like the all-seeing eye of Sauron in *Lord of the Rings*. You can't hide, and you can't run from it.

Woolf writes about her depression at length in her journals. In 1934, she describes the period after she finished her experimental novel *The Waves*. "I was, I remember, nearer suicide, seriously, than since 1913."

Cheever chronicles his alcoholism at length in his journal, and I felt a sense of relief when he writes about finally becoming sober.

I don't want to be too morbid here.

The journals of these authors aren't all filled with dark life lessons and lamentations.

Nabokov, the author of *Lolita*, writes at length about his love for his mother and father, his son and Russia of old. And I've yet to read a more powerful personal mission statement than Cheever's aspiration for the blank page.

> To write well, to write passionately, to be less inhibited, to be warmer, to be more self-critical, to recognise the power of as well as the force of lust, to write, to love.

KEEP A SENSE DIARY

Keeping a sense diary or journal is a useful practice for more creative writers who want to hold onto their experiences and ideas. In this diary, record experience that triggered your senses of touch, taste sound, or smell per day.

You could write about how a meal tasted or what a person's voice sounded like. You may also notice the stickiness of sweet tea, the coarseness of an unvarnished floor and the pain behind your eyes when you're tired. The world is your source material.

Then see if you can remix your sense diary to describe how a smell tasted or what a sound looks like. This may sound daft, but it's an unusually effective creative trick.

Synaesthesia is an accepted process for perceiving one sense in terms of another. It is also common practice for creative writers to remix and play on readers' perceptions of the five senses in their works.

Nabokov described to the BBC in 1962 how he could hear colours in different languages.

He said, "The long 'a' of the English alphabet has for me the tint of weathered wood, but a French 'a' evokes polished ebony."

GOING WITH WHAT WORKS

I set goals for each of my writing projects, and I keep a journal. I set goals because this keeps me honest and I find some comfort and security in having a To Do list that I can review, tick off and manage.

I also keep a journal. I like journal writing because it allows me to practice writing when I want to do anything but, and when I reread older entries I can unearth problems in my creative and even my personal life.

Use what works for you and abandon what doesn't.

STUCK? KEEP READING

"Either write something worth reading or do something worth writing." – Benjamin Franklin

German blacksmith Johannes Gutenberg invented the printing press sometime before 1450. His invention enabled the printing of lengthy texts that people used to spread their ideas.

In 1518, theologian Martin Luther used Gutenberg's invention to print German copies of his Latin book *95 Theses*.

The subsequent popularity of this book across Europe became a driving force of the Protestant Reformation.

Gutenburg's printing press enabled the dissemination of ideas that opened people's minds to new ways of thinking and looking at the world, and it's a classic example of just how powerful ideas and books are.

If you want to become a better and more productive writer, read frequently and outside of your comfort zone.

Reading and writing have a symbiotic relationship. Through reading, you will discover stories, facts and arguments for your work, and you will find new ideas and make connections that improve your writing.

Bulgarian writer and critic Maria Popova described this process as "combinatorial creativity." She wrote:

> ...in order for us to truly create and contribute to the world, we have to be able to connect countless dots, to cross-pollinate ideas from a wealth of disciplines, to combine and recombine these pieces and build new castles.

Even if you read for pleasure, every time you open a book, you make an unconscious deposit in your memory bank of ideas.

However, if you don't read at all, the next time you turn up in front of the blank page your memory bank of ideas will be empty, and writing anything meaningful will feel almost impossible.

HOW BENJAMIN FRANKLIN WORKED

Benjamin Franklin is famous productive genius.

As one of the United States founding fathers, he used the printing press to spread his ideas, and he even invented a more modern version of this device to grow his printing business.

Alongside work, Franklin put aside several hours every morning and evening for reading and self-examination.

Each morning he asked himself: "What good shall I do today?" Franklin also advocated a daily 'air bath' instead of bathing in cold water.

He said about air baths,

> I rise early almost every morning, and sit in my chamber without any clothes whatever, half an hour or an hour, according to the season, either reading or writing.
>
> This practice is not in the least painful, but on the contrary, agreeable; and if I return to bed afterwards, before I dress myself, as

sometimes happens, I make a supplement to my night's rest, of one or two hours of the most pleasing sleep that can be imagined.

Air baths won't help you write (or keep clean for that matter), but Franklin's life demonstrates how we can manage our downtime and incorporate important activities like reading and self-examination into our busy days.

For example, many people read at the end of the day. That's fine, but if you have a job and family commitments, you may lack the energy or patience for a challenging read.

This, perhaps, is one reason why Benjamin Franklin made time for reading in the morning and afternoon. Remember, as a productive writer it's smart to be mindful of your energy levels.

The morning question, What good shall I do this day?	5	Rise, wash, and address *Power-*
	6	*ful Goodness*; contrive day's busi-
	7	ness and take the resolution of the day; prosecute the present study; and breakfast.
	8	
	9	Work.
	10	
	11	
	12	Read or overlook my accounts,
	1	and dine.
	2	
	3	Work.
	4	
	5	
	6	
	7	Put things in their places, sup- per, music, or diversion, or con-
	8	versation; examination of the day.
	9	
Evening question, What good have I done today?	10	
	11	
	12	
	1	Sleep.
	2	
	3	
	4	

Benjamin Franklin's original daily routine via http://www.usgennet.org/

FIND TIME TO READ

Some people say they'd like to read more, but they don't have the time or energy.

If you're having this problem, carve out small parts of the day when you have the energy or time to read, such as first thing in the morning.

You can also take advantage of those random blocks of free time that life sometimes presents, such as the unexpected 20-minute wait in the doctor's office, railway station or airport.

If you get into the habit of carrying a book or e-reader, you can read during a lunch break, over breakfast, after dinner or while waiting for an appointment.

Committing to read at least 20 pages every day is another great way of setting yourself up for success. After all, if you can't find time to read 20 pages, then how can you find time to write? Similarly, if you drive to work, you can read more by listening to audiobooks during your commute.

I love reading, but like many people I browse the internet when I should be reading, or I end up reading the wrong book altogether.

Let me explain.

When I read about a book that sounds interesting, this thought leads to an "I'd love to read that book, but I have to read this book first" moment.

Then I invariably forget the name of the interesting book. Keeping a running list of books I want to read helped me overcome this problem.

If you do this, when you're stuck for something to read, you can consult your list before you buy. Such a method shortcuts wandering around a virtual or bricks and mortar bookshop and buying a book because the cover, reviews or discounts are impressive.

STOP AFTER THE FIRST 50 PAGES

Oprah Winfrey advises if you're 50 pages into a book and not enjoying it, put the book down.

The world contains so many good books – and more than anyone can read in one lifetime – so why waste time reading a book because you feel like you should?

You can take Winfrey's advice farther by reading samples that Amazon and other stores offer for free before you buy a book.

Some heavy readers advise concentrating on one book at a time because this increases your chances of finishing one book and moving on to the next.

I disagree.

Reading several books at once means you can alternate books when one becomes tiresome or a slog.

Then, you can return to the first book when you feel refreshed. For this method to work, read books from several different genres or combine fiction and non-fiction.

Personally, I find non-fiction books are best suited for daytime reading while fiction books make for ideal nighttime reading. I've also found reading three books at once feels about right; any more becomes overwhelming.

WAIT FOR A GREAT SENTENCE

Sometimes, I read several books at once over the course of a week or two. On other occasions, I go several weeks without reading any long-form works. This drought isn't because I don't want to read; it's because the challenges of a day-to-day life get in the way.

I used to feel guilty about these breaks from consuming the written word, but now I accept them because I know I will return to a bookstore with my list and a belief that a great sentence is waiting.

Reading, like any activity, has its peaks and troughs, and rather than beating yourself up about not reading, accept you won't always have free time to read. And if you hate the damn book, put it down and start something new, something better.

As a productive writer, you must read books that fall inside and outside your comfort zone.

You can do this by carving out reading time in your day, making the most of those random blocks of free time we all have and by keeping track of what you want to read.

GET PERMISSION LATER

"Never ask permission, ask for forgiveness later." – James Altucher

Many people say they to want write, but then they make excuses. They say things like:

"I'm not good enough to write a book. Nobody will ever want to read it."

Or

"I've got nothing to write about. I need to find more ideas and do more research."

Or

"Writing is just too hard. I was always bad at English in school and I've no idea how to become a good writer."

Instead of waiting for some anointed writing guru to give you permission to write, start today.

You already have what you need.

START NOW

School teaches almost nothing about writing beyond how to read and spell. You can learn many things about writing by reading voraciously.

You don't need years of life experience either; American disability activist and author Helen Keller published *The Story of My Life* when she was 22.

If you pick up the pen and sit down in front of the blank page, you are good enough simply because you've moved past the point of procrastination. This act is no small feat.

Today, successful writers don't need as much talent or luck as writers like Updike or Hemingway had.

We can write a blog post, article or book and then self-publish it. If we write, we can take advantage of the digital tools that our predecessors didn't have and share our work almost instantly with an audience.

You can write for someone's website, start your blog or self-publish a book on Amazon.

Don't wait for someone to give you permission.

Writing consumes a lot of time, but you can recover this back eliminating passive activities in your day. Television, casual internet browsing, social media and staying up late into the night—I'm looking at you.

After you eliminate time-wasters and get into the habit of regularly writing, your mind will fill the vacuum with new and more fantastic ideas clamouring for space on the page in front of you.

If something you have to do is more important than writing, ask yourself why you want to write in the first place and then decide what's more important. It's going to be hard work, but most worthwhile things are.

As soon as you turn up in front of the blank page with a desire to say something, anything, you're already ahead.

Stop making excuses and pick up the pen. Later, if you find the whole process a waste of time, you can cross writing off your list and move on with your life.

LEARN TO WRITE FOR YOURSELF

Writing isn't a shortcut to celebrity or riches.

If that's your goal, you will find rewards far quicker by concentrating on other professions. I'm not suggesting writers should starve, but you must be passionate about your work.

A love of the craft will sustain you when others criticise and reject your work.

This passion will drive you when you're struggling to make money from your words. And if you are passionate enough, you will keep seeking ways to improve even when you're exhausted, frustrated and broken.

If, on the other hand, you're not passionate about your writing, why should your readers care?

Write for yourself first, write something you enjoy reading and write something that makes you regard a page of wet ink (or a screen of pixels), a page you filled, with pride.

Use the life of J.D. Salinger as an example.

After the success of *The Catcher in the Rye*, Salinger withdrew from public view. In 1953, two years after the publication of his famous book, Salinger left New York and moved to a remote, 90-acre place in Cornish, New Hampshire.

He continued to write, but this time for himself, and some of these stories were published only after his death in 2010.

Others remain unpublished.

Salinger loved what he did, and he didn't care if people read his works.

DON'T WAIT

I once coached a non-fiction writer about how he could focus on his work and write 1,000 words a day.

We talked about how he could use a productivity strategy to eliminate distractions and increase his daily word count. I asked this writer to eliminate distractions for where he works and hold himself to account (see chapter six).

I think the writer was happy with how our coaching call went because afterwards he emailed me to say thanks.

At the bottom of his email he wrote, "The other helpful thing was the sense of legitimacy as a writer I got from talking with you."

I was happy to get positive feedback like this – I'm human after all! – and to know I was able to help him.

But something didn't sit right with me. The more I thought about our conversation, the more I realised I'd missed an important point. This writer was already doing his most important work before he had ever talked to me. He is well on his way. If you wrote today, you are too.

Whatever kind of writer you are, you don't need affirmation from me or anyone else to call yourself a writer or to feel like what you are doing is worthwhile.

If you have the guts to turn up every day, sit down in the chair and do the hard work of putting one word after another onto the blank page even when you know what you're saying might not be any good, then you are a writer.

Don't ask for permission.

Don't wait for someone to tell you what you're doing is worthwhile.

And don't do it just for the money.

I spent most of my early twenties looking for affirmation from accomplished writers and professional editors. I paid for writing courses and I made a point of getting closer to editors who I knew were better than I. Sometimes I got the affirmation I was after, but more often than not I didn't.

Either way, I still had to sit down in front of the blank page alone, get the words down and figure out a way to get better.

Every day, I try to do what writers like Natalie Goldberg recommend. "Write what disturbs you, what you fear, what you have not been willing to speak about. Be willing to be split open."

I still feel like giving up some days. I almost gave up last week.

I'm still trying to figure out this strange job of ours.

Writing is often a lonely craft, and it sometimes helps to talk to other writers about a problem you're having on the blank page.

We all need support and critical feedback to overcome our problems from time to time. Being recognised by other writers feels great when your motivation is waning. Similarly, hiring an editor is a sure-fire way to improve your craft.

I love getting comments and emails from readers who have opinions and even nice things to say about my work.

I keep them in a file in my computer and reread them when I feel like quitting.

I'd like to tell you I don't feel like quitting very often, but I'd be lying.

These comments and emails keep me going when I want to stop. And I must keep putting one word after another because this is what we do.

To become a productive writer, turn up for, write and go after what you want day after day.

Even if you win the lotto tomorrow, and your money worries disappear, even if you're the lone survivor of a nuclear holocaust, sit down and do your most important work.

Do it because there's an ache inside you that only writing can soothe.

Do it because you can't imagine doing anything else.

Do it because to write is to create and to create is to live.

Anything else isn't an option.

STEAL FROM THE GREATS

"Good artists copy, great artists steal." – Pablo Picasso

Are you a thief?

If you're a writer or in any way creative, you should be.

More than seven billion people are alive on this planet today, to say nothing of those who went before us. To think your idea is original is to ignore the weight of history. *The Bible* has been done, *War and Peace* is over, and Moby Dick has been harpooned.

I'm not special. My ideas are far from original. I wrote *The Savvy Writer's Guide to Productivity* because I've read so much good, bad and unusual advice about productivity and writing over the years.

I wanted to put it down on the blank page and remix it with my voice and experiences. I wanted to learn from my idols and create something that would help readers, that would help you.

So I stole.

I'm not the first person to confess this crime.

Take Apple's co-founder, Steve Jobs. He is widely acknowledged as one of the most creative innovators of the past 50 years, but Jobs stole like crazy, and he openly admitted it.

You can see Jobs in a viral YouTube video explaining why creative people steal.

He said, "Picasso had a saying—'good artists copy, great artists steal'—and we have always been shameless about stealing great ideas."

Jobs is widely credited as the inventor of the portable music player or iPod, but he wasn't the first person to invent a portable music player; the boffins at Sony were.

Jobs wasn't the first person to invent a tablet either; BlackBerry and IBM designed dozens of models before the iPad.

Instead, Jobs took ideas already in existence and remixed them with his voice. He took old ideas and transformed them into better ones.

Don't waste time sitting around stroking your chin, gazing at the night sky and trying to come up with something original.

Somebody, somewhere has already written or thought about what you're about to say. Your challenge as a productive writer is to take an old idea, add your voice and transform it.

HOW TO EMULATE YOUR HEROES

The productive writer learns faster by emulating his heroes.

This process is different from stealing or copying from them. When you emulate, you make a conscious decision to take apart the work of writers you admire and reassemble it using your voice and ideas.

This educational process will help you discover how accomplished writers succeed and fail on the blank page, and it will help you finish what you're working on.

"At some point, you'll have to move from imitating your heroes to emulating them," Austin Kleon wrote in *Steal Like an Artist*.

When a mechanic wants to figure out an engine, he or she sometimes spends hours taking it apart and putting it back together. This process helps the mechanic see how the engine works and even what's wrong with it.

If you want to learn from your favourite writer, pick a work you admire. Take it apart sentence by sentence and ask yourself:

- How does the writer make you feel throughout the piece?
- Where does the writer use the first, second or third person?
- Does the writer address you directly or indirectly? How does this make you feel?
- How much of the work is fact, fiction or embellishment?
- How does the writer manage to convey their opinions or arguments?
- How does the writer begin and end each sentence, paragraph or chapter?
- Do you agree with what the author is saying or could you say it differently? If so, how?
- How does the writer introduce a topic and arrive at a conclusion?
- When does the writer repeat and idea and why?
- What kind of journey does the writer bring you on?
- Why has the writer structured his or her work one way and not the other?

You can do this by writing out the stories of your idols line by line, by annotating their work or even by extracting key quotes and ideas and putting them into your swipe file or commonplace book for future use.

Disassembling and reassembling the work of your heroes will help you figure out how they construct their sentences, paragraphs, chapters and ideas.

This creative process is time-consuming, but it will help you develop your voice for writing and give you an insight into how other writers work.

WHAT I STOLE

American poet, novelist and short story writer Charles Bukowski is one of my creative idols.

His brash style of poetry makes me feel like he's picking a fight with me, and I've always been fascinated by his honest portrayals of writing, creativity, the drudgery of work and his relationships with women.

I took his work apart line by line by writing down key lines from his poems and using them as fragments and ideas for entries in my journal. I even used one of his poems as inspiration for a short story.

Short story writer Raymond Carver is another creative idol of mine. I've spent hours reading and rereading his collection of short stories, *What We Talk About When We Talk About Love* and *Cathedral*.

I tried to mimic his manner of writing sparse and clean sentences and studied how he portrays a character, a scene and a major plot point. I used what Carver knew about the art of the short story to expose weaknesses in my work.

My efforts at reconstruction fell short on both counts, but I discovered I'm more comfortable writing in the first person and using everyday language. I found out more about the mechanics of a great story, and I discovered the nuggets of ideas for my fiction and non-fiction.

STEAL RESPONSIBLY

The next time a writer impresses you, read them closely, emulate what they do and steal their best ideas.

I'm not advocating a cut-and-paste job; instead take what they've done and remix it with your voice. If you take only from one writer, it's outright theft, but if you take from the many, it's creative.

Use the creative hard work of your idols to provide a foundation for what you're going to write. Prop your ideas on the foundations of their hard work. Cite your sources and wear your inspirations on your sleeve if you need to.

Don't be ashamed about what you're doing. Creativity exists somewhere between a stolen idea and your inner voice.

You can use that.

DECIDE WHAT'S ESSENTIAL

"You cannot overestimate the unimportance of practically everything." – Greg McKeown

How often do you get the right things done?

By the right things I mean writing your book, articles and stories. Once you've taken care of your family and the bills, it's up to you to write.

It's up to you to decide what's essential.

According to Greg McKeown, author of *Essentialism: The Disciplined Pursuit of Less*, an essentialist removes the trivial and focuses on what adds value.

Essentialists make smart decisions about how to spend their time, energy and resources because they understand this is the best way of contributing more to the people in their lives, their families and society. That sounds a lot like what the productive writer does too.

I've discovered five important questions that are helping me make progress towards getting more of the right things done. And I want to share them with you.

Q. Is this Activity Adding Value to My Life?

Since I was a child, I played and loved video games. When I was in my mid-twenties, I even reviewed them for a popular entertainment website.

The website didn't pay me, but I didn't care. I enjoyed gaming, and I was able to keep the games after I wrote my reviews.

After a year or two, I felt a shift in how I approached games. Instead of looking forward to playing the next AAA title or block-buster release, I began to dread the tedious missions, the walk-throughs, and inevitable write-ups.

So I sold my games, gave my console to my son and abandoned my hobby.

I'm not making a case against gaming; instead, I share this example of how we value our time differently as writers mature.

Perhaps you have old hobbies which you no longer enjoy. Or maybe you could cut back on the hours you spend at the office seeking promotion. If it's not adding value to your life, consider if you can remove it and use this extra time to write.

Q. How am I Going to Fill My Glass?

Consider your entire day as a glass.

As Stephen Covey notes, you can fill this glass with important activities or big rocks, such as spending time with family or working on projects you're passionate about.

Then, you can fill the glass with nonessential activities like answering email or watching television. These are like grains of sand, and they will settle around the big rocks in your day.

If you fill your glass with non-essential activities first, there will be no room left for the big rocks in your day.

Every night before I go to bed, I ask myself what I want to fill my glass with.

My answer is almost always the same: to write.

Unless I act, grains of sand will fill my day and leave no room for writing. However, if I make a conscious decision to write, grains of sand settle around the big rocks in my day.

I'm not going to lie and say I fit writing into every day, but when I do I feel lighter. And if I write first thing – even if it's just a journal entry – I don't have the inevitable moment when I sit on the couch after an exhausting and demanding day and think, "Oh no, I still have to write."

If you're not a writer, you still have big rocks in your life.

Examples include spending time with a loved one, meditating, exercising and work. Your grains of sand might be commitments you've made to others who aren't adding value to your life or passive activities like watching the news or reading social media feeds.

Decide on your big rocks before you go to bed, and you will wake up and fill your day with what matters.

Q. What Clutter Can I Eliminate?

Two years ago, I lost a dream job. I was unemployed for six months and spent my free time figuring out what matters most to me and reading about essentialism.

Essentialism felt like something I could get into, and when you're unemployed, you need something to get into. I learnt the quickest way to get started is to eliminate material goods you don't use, need, love or depend on.

I sold my laptop because I prefer to write using my desktop computer. I donated every book to charity that I promised myself I'd read but had no intention of doing.

I got rid of every item of clothing that I hadn't worn during the past 12 months. And I deleted almost all of the unwatched films and TV shows on my hard drive and cancelled my online subscriptions.

After I found a job, I thought of buying a new laptop and replacing the clothes I'd given away. But I found I didn't miss any of those things.

Eliminating clutter gave me more space, more time and more room for the big rocks in my life.

Q. How Do I Protect Myself?

To be an essentialist is to protect your physical, mental and spiritual health. Each of these areas represents one side of a triangle, and if one is under stress, the other two will suffer.

To look after my mental health, I expose myself to new ideas by reading challenging books and recording 10 ideas every day based on those books. This practice, as recommended by the writer James Altucher, keeps my brain active.

For managing my my physical health, I run up to 20 miles each week. This practice helps me work through stressful problems, and it gives me more energy for other areas of my life.

To protect my spiritual health, I meditate for an hour or two each week, and I write regular journal entries about what I'm struggling with and grateful for.

I find these practices exceptionally difficult, but taking a step back from the trenches of the working week helps me quiet my monkey mind. It helps me sleep better at night. And then I can return to whatever I'm doing with a renewed vigour.

Q: How Often Do I Disconnect?

Several years ago, I went on vacation to a campsite in Italy. The campsite lacked reliable internet access, and I wasn't able to check my phone and my feeds or read the news whenever I wanted.

On the first day of this trip, I felt disconnected and behind. My hands kept reaching for the email app on my phone even though I knew I didn't have access to the internet.

After a day or two this habit died, and I began to enjoy those disconnected few days away from home. I took one lesson home from that holiday.

Being constantly connected kills my opportunity to escape, enjoy a vacation, spend time with the people I'm with and even focus on my work.

It's been awhile since I've gone a week without email, but I've removed the email app from my phone and check it only at predefined periods during the day.

I've also disabled as many notifications as possible on the devices I use. And I regularly work without being connected to the internet.

If you take regular time out to take care of yourself, you will be better able to focus on what matters.

LIVE YOUR WILD AND PRECIOUS LIFE

Essentialists avoid spending time on tasks they can say avoid, people they should say no to, and compromises that aren't worth making.

They are committed to working on what inspires them, what they're talented at, and pursuing their contributions to the world.

I'm still working on becoming an essentialist and eliminating the trivial from my life. I find the practices of essentialism difficult, but I know the productive writer can live their wild and precious life if they're brave enough.

LEARN TO SAY NO

"It takes determination, it takes a willingness to say 'no' and it can take time. But it will pay off in so many ways, for the rest of your life." – Leo Babauta

What's the biggest barrier between you and a finished piece of work?

Look in the mirror.

The day never seems to have enough hours. If you're like most people, you probably have too many personal and professional commitments to balance writing with other ambitions.

The vast majority of us have far more going on in our lives than we realise. All these commitments and projects carry a psychic weight.

This mental fatigue slows your progress and complicates reaching the end of whatever you're working on.

For example, can you concentrate at length on your novel or book if you also have to manage a large DIY project?

If you attend a late dinner with friends and go for drinks afterwards, will you be able to rise early in the morning to write?

How productive will you be on the blank page if you've already worked overtime to pay for a new television?

Learning to say no to internal and external commitments is key to becoming a more productive writer.

If you decide to learn a new language, develop a new skill or take up a new hobby, you are taking time away from writing.

These new hobbies and skills might add value to your life, and you might be able to juggle your commitments, but writing is a demanding mistress who needs your attention. Can you afford to spend your valuable free time elsewhere?

Every new project you begin represents time you won't spend in front of the blank page. These new commitments can clog your creative bandwidth and reduce your ability to focus on the blank page.

By saying no, you can protect the parts of your day that you spend writing and concentrate on finishing what you started.

In *Daily Rituals: How Artists Work*, Mason Currey describes how French novelist Marcel Proust "made a conscious decision in 1910 to withdraw from society" and concentrate on his work.

Curry notes Pablo Picasso and his girlfriend, Fernande Olivier, regarded Sunday as an "at home" day, free from the obligations of friendship.

You don't need to be a recluse to become a more productive writer. Instead, consider how you're spending your time and if the result is worth the effort.

APPLY PARETO'S PRINCIPLE

In 1906, Italian economist Vilfredo Pareto found that 80 percent of the land in Italy was owned by 20 percent of the people.

Today, Pareto's Principle is the approach that anyone, including writers, can use to become more productive. It states that 20 percent of what we do provides 80 percent of the value we experience in our lives.

As described in chapter 10, consider what activities in your life are meaningful and what you can eliminate or reduce.

Your goal should be to concentrate on those 20 percent activities that give you 80 percent of the value you experience.

For example, it's more productive to spend an hour every day writing than spending this hour promoting your work on social media.

Look for secondary activities you can eliminate from your life too.

Examples include: watching television, browsing social media sites, comfort eating, online shopping and so on.

Indie authors Johnny B. Truant and Sean Platt address this point in their self-publishing guide *Write. Publish. Repeat: The No Luck Required Guide to Self-Publishing Success.*

> Eighty-percent activities are writing more and better books, building a moderate amount of reader engagement (efficiently, not via long emails), creating solid calls to action that lead people to your next books from the backs of those they've just finished, completing bundles and product funnels...and so on.

When I'm writing, I reduce the amount of time spent watching television, gaming and browsing my favourite websites so I can spend more time writing.

I don't always succeed, but Pareto's Principle helps me refocus.

For example, when I began building an online platform for my writing, I became preoccupied with learning to code. I spent hours teaching myself HTML, CSS, JavaScript and the backend of WordPress.

I also took online classes in Illustrator, Photoshop and other design applications. I wrote reviews about my experiences and even considered started a blog about coding.

What happened?

I learnt something of effective design, but I also had less time to write the kind of prose that inspires me, and I produced fewer blog posts and articles.

I was putting more time and effort into design and coding activities and experiencing less meaningful results. I've never had ambitions to become a serious coder or designer and these activities were side attractions.

Now, I outsource any technical aspects to my blog on sites like Upwork. I also spend less time concerning myself with the design of my site.

Instead, I rely on premium WordPress themes and plugins that take care of the hard work for me. This way I can spend more time writing and finish what I started.

Before you say yes to your next project, consider if the project is part of the 20 percent that will provide real value later on.

USE NO TO GET MORE DONE

If you want to become a more productive writer, make friends with the word no.

Using this word will help you avoid getting distracted, get out of unnecessary commitments and spend more time writing. Saying no to nonessential tasks will enable you to become a more productive writer.

So what should you say no to?

The Wrong Writing Projects

For several years, I reviewed products and services I had no interest in because a newspaper paid me for the work. This mindless writing stopped me creating the kinds of fiction and non-fiction that inspires me.

As a writer, you'll have many chances to exercise your creative muscles.

It might feel good to write an email, a page of copy or even an article, as we all need to get paid. However, what are your larger ambitions for the blank page?

Is your current writing project going to help you achieve your goals?

So-So Ideas

THE SAVVY WRITER'S GUIDE TO PRODUCTIVITY

The more often you write, the more connections your brain will make between pieces of information you pick up during the day.

Your brain will spit out topics to write about, projects to take on and opportunities to purse. Some ideas will be good and some terrible.

It's easy to refuse a terrible or a daft idea, but it's harder to refuse a good idea.

If you pursue every good idea, you won't have time or space for the great ideas.

The next time you've got a good idea, ask if it's worth pursuing and if it's something you should be writing about.

New Writing Tools

Confession: I love new writing tools.

I've spent hours testing writing apps, online services and even the perfect desk and chair.

Like many new writers, I find the tools of the craft exciting to discover.

Some tools help me become more productive, but when I start using a new tool for the first time, it interrupts the flow of writing.

These tools are side attractions that distract from the main event.

Boring Books

Are you reading a boring book? Are you past page 50? Put it down and move onto something more exciting.

Get out of the genres that make you feel at home and away from your old reliable authors.

They have their purpose, but creative people go in search of fresh and challenging ideas. They find them in unexpected places, by reading challenging genres for example.

Unproductive Habits

Do you stay up late at night watching television? Is Facebook taking up your time. Or perhaps you're spending your attention checking emails on your phone.

These unproductive habits are draining your mental energy.

Consider using social media only at predetermined periods and removing email entirely from your phone and making a commitment to your creative work over all else.

HOW TO SAY NO LIKE A PRO

Now you have an idea of what to say no to, but how can you do it without offending your spouse, boss or friend?

If you're a professional writer, part of your job is to tell your editor about your commitments.

Then if your editor asks you to work on something you can politely decline and point to your commitments.

Do less but better.

If what you're writing is more personal, communicate clearly to friends and family members that you write at a certain time every morning or every night.

Stephen King describes this in *On Writing: A Memoir of the Craft*, saying writers must "write with the door closed."

At first, family might come to you during these times to ask a question or make a request, but if you explain your passion and they see your commitment, the people close to you will respect the time you're spending writing.

GUARD YOUR TIME

As a productive writer, the word no is your most powerful weapon against the time-consuming demands of daily life.

You can use the word no to keep meaningless activities from filling your day and to prioritise what's important in your life. Saying no will help you become the productive writer you're meant to be.

WRITE WITHOUT FEAR OR FAVOUR

"I wrote and wrote without pause without consciousness of my surroundings hour after hour. I felt a different person...I didn't feel frustrated or shut up anymore. I was free, I could think, I could live, I could create..." – Christy Brown

Some people love you.

Other people hate you.

Most people don't care.

Readers have so much to pick from, and your voice is just one of many shouting, "Choose me."

The glut of information is why you should never hold back when you write.

If you tone down an article because you're afraid of what people will think, remember that most people are too wrapped up in their lives to care about one more blog post, article or book. Yes, some of your friends and family might take issue with what you've got to say, but you're not writing to impress them.

You could take the easy road and try to convince people that good or honest person, but if this results in a bland, generic ., you've wasted your time.

If you convince a reader to spend time with you, respect that they're giving finite hours of their life to you.

Whatever you have to say, it better be damned good.

The next time you sit in front of the blank page or screen, forget your reader's reactions. Write without fear of what your reader will think of you. If you find this difficult, you could:

- Write about your fears and use this as an entry point into your work.
- Accept fear as a form of perfectionism that must be confronted.
- Acknowledge your fears, accept them and write what you want.
- Write a letter to a friend explaining what you're afraid about and then burn it.
- Remember what the goal of your writing project is. Then move towards this goal one action or sentence at a time.

If you come across as compassionate and caring, so be it. If you come across as angry and insensitive, so be it. As a writer, you must call out to readers and convince them to spend time with you.

If your writing is honest, it will be far more engaging than a piece where a writer holds back on revealing some essential truth because they're worried what others will think.

DON'T HIDE

If you use writing to hide yourself, then why should I spend time with you?

You know the kinds of writing I'm talking about.

You can find it on the promotional materials that came with your last bank statement or utility bill. You can read it on government documents and healthcare informational leaflets. It's there on thousands of corporate and institutional websites.

I've nothing against words that sell (see chapter 13). I'm criticising joyless, staid writing that's full of passive verbs, awkward nouns and which doesn't speak to readers or customers.

It comes from a world where nobody does anything to anyone and no one cares. Bland writing tells me things firstly, and secondly, in hindsight, in conclusion, and after further deliberation.

These kinds of writing won't entertain, inform, inspire, educate or sell.

All of it belongs in the bin.

I want to hear the writer's problems and how they overcame them. I want to taste blood and feel the grit between my fingers. I want to take the author's outstretched hand and go on a journey. As a customer, I want you to speak to my problems.

I'm going to give you my time; don't waste it.

The best writers reveal some essential truth about the human condition; the rest of us aspiring authors can at least reveal some truth about ourselves.

I'm not asking you to slip into the confessional mode for every piece of writing; just don't make excuses for producing senseless copy that's devoid of life.

Even if you're writing copy for your business, don't bore me with paragraphs about your product's technical features. Don't expect me to sit through a thousand words of passive verbs, adjectives and nouns nobody ever says.

How are you going to solve my problems? Can you save me money or help me spend more time with my family?

Show me how I can become rich or successful like you.

Tell me something true.

WITNESS WHAT CHRISTY BROWN DID

Christy Brown is one of Ireland's most famous writers and artists.

He grew up in inner-city Dublin during the middle of the twentieth century, and he had cerebral palsy.

Brown was depressed for much of his life because of his disability and subsequent alcoholism.

He grew up in a large family where he struggled to get attention because of his disability.

So with his mother's help, he learnt to write with his left foot. Later, as a young man, Brown wrote the famous memoir *My Left Foot.* He also published his groundbreaking novel *Down All the Days.*

In *My Left Foot* Brown abandoned himself entirely to portraying what it was like to grow up with cerebral palsy and how his real disability lay in the reactions of those around him.

In *Down All the Days,* Brown abandoned himself entirely to portraying how cruel, illogical and hard life was in Dublin during the mid-twentieth century.

Today, the significance of *My Left Foot* and *Down All the Days* might be understated, but their power and honesty remain intact. They are essential reading for anyone concerned with disability or Irish literature.

Brown offers more than just a glimpse of how he lived with disability; he expands our view of the world, and he reveals a fundamental part of the human condition.

When Brown picked up his pen with his left foot, he abandoned himself entirely to the written word.

Both works contain a big idea, and even if you, the reader aren't prepared to climb on board, Brown commits himself entirely.

Although he never quite overcame his depression, he found a new, inner life through his creations and expressions on the blank page. Today Brown's readers can continue share in his life long after his death in 1981.

Any aspiring writer can think and live and create on the blank page. We can stop making excuses and abandon ourselves to an idea. We can all learn from Brown.

MY STRUGGLE WITH FEAR

When I was in my early twenties, I told people I wanted to write a book. There was just one problem. I wasn't writing anything, at all.

I believed I wasn't ready to write and that I needed some anointed mentor to pull me aside and say, "Bryan, now is your time."

I became jealous of the success of people around me and grew sick of my lack of progress. So I joined a fiction and non-fiction writing workshop in Dublin. On the second evening, the instructor said every student had to submit a short story.

I was afraid.

I hadn't written a short story in years, but I didn't want the class or the instructor to know.

A writer in a writing class who doesn't write is a fraud.

I used fear as fuel.

I wrote that night and the night after that. And I wrote until I finished my first story. It was terrible. The instructor told me this later on, but it didn't matter.

I had taken the first step towards facing my fears.

I don't recall one moment where I conquered my fears though. Instead, I got a job as a journalist writing for a newspaper.

There, I had to finish my articles by a deadline because if I didn't the editor would fire me.

I know this because he called me into his office after I missed a deadline and told me.

I was more afraid of the unemployment line than reaching the end.

So I stopped polishing my articles until they were perfect and started finishing them. On more than one occasion, my editor sent the articles back to me saying I'd left out an important paragraph or that my introduction needed reworking.

This criticism made me want to quit.

On other occasions, the subeditors of the paper reworked my article entirely. Having my work taken apart like that felt like an interrogation, but at least I was getting paid to write.

I still struggle with fear today.

While writing this book I was afraid others would ask, "What right do you have to explain how to be productive?"

I still think that.

I also knew I'd spent hours researching productivity methods and studying how artists work. I'd read dozens of books by authors explaining how they work.

I knew enough to organise my thoughts into a book. Although I am nobody, I gave myself permission to write a book because writers must start somewhere.

Even if feels terrifying.

I don't like personal writing like this. It's hard work, and it reveals more of me than a guide to the writing tools I use. I almost deleted this chapter several times before I hit publish.

What's to enjoy about revealing a job didn't work out, that I was lazy and that my work failed?

Stephen Pressfield made me do it.

In *The War of Art*, he said, "Write with the door closed, rewrite with the door open."

Are you paralyzed with fear? That's a good sign. Fear is good. Like self-doubt, fear is an indicator. Fear tells us what we have to do. Remember one rule of thumb: the more scared we are of a work or calling, the more sure we can be that we have to do it.

PRESS FORWARDS

Give yourself permission to start and make messy mistakes.

Remind yourself everyone who wants to become a successful writer must start somewhere and now is your time. Once you begin, you're already ahead of the writer who said, "No, not today. I'm not ready."

Spend more time creating than consuming. You already know more than enough and, like a snowballing rolling downhill, you just need a little momentum.

If you're having trouble finishing your work, set artificial deadlines and stick to them.

When the time comes and even if your work isn't quite ready, show it to a group of people you trust like a writing group. Ask for their help. Then go and fix your writing.

As you get into the habit of finishing your work, you will win more opportunities to gain feedback.

Later, show the world what you created. Enter contests and submit your articles to magazines or websites. Let them judge it in all its ugly imperfections. Respond if you need to or move on. Judgment is better than being ignored.

Anne Frank wrote her autobiography when she was just 15.

Helen Keller wrote the story of her Life at aged 22.

Franz Kafka finished his first novel in his twenties.

Christy Brown used what he lacked as fuel for his books rather than as excuses not to write (see chapter 12).

Charles Bukowski wrote in obscurity for much of his life, until the publication of his novel *Post Office*, when he was 51.

These are extreme examples.

I'm an extreme kind of person.

Are you?

WRITE IN THE FACE OF FEAR

I was rejected three times while writing this chapter. I contacted five authors I admire with interview requests.

Four of them said no. I asked several podcasting experts to share their advice for a guest blog post. Half of them didn't reply. I pitched guest posts at the editors of three big blogs, two of whom said no.

These rejections are tough, but they are normal experiences for the productive writer.

If you want to become a more productive writer, rejection waits for you at the beginning, in the middle and at the end of your work.

Everybody who succeeds gets rejected at some point during their careers.

By turning up and creating, you cut through your fears. Even if some people reject your work, others will embrace it. The next website you pitch might accept your ideas. Your next interview request might be granted.

You must write today. You must write now. You must write like your life depends on it.

Because it does.

USE PROVEN FORMULAS

"Always enter the conversation already occurring in the customer's mind." – Dan S. Kennedy

Copywriting is writing that sells a product or service.

If the reader is unconvinced by the last paragraph, or if they don't read that far, the copywriter has failed.

Great copywriting captures the readers' attention and persuades them to take action. It convinces them to buy or sign up.

As a writer, you might not always be persuading your reader to buy a product or service, but you certainly are persuading them to do something.

You want them to give you their attention, believe that your ideas hold value and take action on your advice.

Copywriting excels at this kind of persuasion. And while great copywriting is part art, the highly persuasive writing on countless billboards, magazine advertisements and online marketing campaigns is driven by tried and tested formulas that have worked for decades.

If you learn copywriting, you will learn how to sell with your words and find the success your writing deserves.

The copywriting formulas in this chapter will help you master the basics faster.

HOW TO USE PAS FORMULA

The simplest and most effective copywriting solution is the Problem-Agitate-Solution Formula or PAS. Copywriters have used this for years to put food on the table because it works.

Let's break down this three-part formula:

- **Problem**: Offer a problem the reader is experiencing.
- **Agitate:** Use emotional language to intensify the problem.
- **Solution**: Provide a credible solution to the problem.

New writers who start a blog often complain about a lack of website traffic. As a result they feel frustrated and anxious about how they're spending their blogging time. Let's tackle this problem for these new writers and illustrate this formula.

[Problem]

Are you sick and tired of writing articles and blog posts that nobody reads?

Now let's whip up our reader's emotions:

[Agitate]

Millions of aspiring writers just like you publish posts every day, worry about SEO and wonder if they should spend hundreds of dollars advertising on Facebook.

But unless you spend your time in the right places, you're never going to build the kind of audience you need to grow a successful blog.

Now we offer the reader a lifeline:

[Solution]

What if I told you there's a better way? What if I told you guest blogging could help you attract thousands of new readers?

See how this formula uses a problem to draw the reader in?

HOW TO USE THE APPROACH FORMULA

Copywriters adapted this approach from a template often used by door-to-door salesmen. It's a soft sell where the writer works hard to make the right initial impression on the reader. You can easily learn this six-part formula.

- Arrive
- Propose
- Persuade
- Reassure
- Make an offer
- Ask for the order

To use the Approach Formula, say something the reader will agree with – something non-threatening that shows you're both on the same page. Then, propose a course of action, something most people who agree with the arriving statement would find reasonable.

Next, gently persuade the reader that this course of action is the correct one. Finally, reassure the reader by overcoming any possible objections. Below, I've used this formula to convince new writers that they can master their chosen craft if they know where to start.

[Arrive]

Becoming a great writer doesn't happen overnight.

[Propose]

You know there's no quick fix or great secret to writing mastery. It simply takes practice. In fact, in his popular book *Outliers*, Malcolm Gladwell suggests a person must commit to 10,000 hours of practice to master a craft. But unguided practice is a terribly inefficient way to learn. That's why it could be time for you to hire a coach.

[Persuade]

A writing coach will allow you to combine practice with the experienced feedback necessary to hone your skills in the fastest possible time. A writing coach will guide you past obstacles that will block you for hours, days or weeks working alone.

[Reassure]

But if engaging a writing coach sounds complicated and expensive, don't worry—I'm going to keep this simple. I'll share the five things new writers should look for in a coach. I'll even show you how to get coaching for free.

New writers who are ready to get help should look for five things from their next writing coach.

(Now the copywriter should go into specifics about what to expect from a good writing coach).

[Make an Offer-Ask for the Order]

If you need help with writing, it's time to act. We'll spend three months working one-on-one, so you can finally go from the first page to the last page. There's just one problem: places are limited.

Sign up now.

SELL YOUR PRODUCT OR SERVICE

Whatever you're selling, you must be able to tell a compelling story about your product or service and how it's going to improve the lives of customers.

Even if you're writing copy for a boring product or service, you can still bring a sense of passion or excitement to a salespage.

Famous copywriter David Ogilvy wrote about the Rolls-Royce, "At 60 miles an hour the loudest noise in this new Rolls-Royce comes from the electric clock."

What's compelling about this example is Ogilvy's use of small details to bring this statement to life. He puts the reader right in the car.

Here's another example:

Taking piano classes isn't the most glamorous way to pass time, but in 1926, John Caples wrote one of the most famous advertorials of all time about piano classes for the U.S. School of Music.

The headline for his famous advertorial reads, "They Laughed When I Sat Down At the Piano But When I Started to Play!"

Caples goes on to describe how, thanks to a course by the U.S.

School of Music, he surprised his friends and family by playing the piano.

> I played on and as I played I forgot the people around me. I forgot the hour, the place, the breathless listeners. The little world I lived in seemed to fade—seemed to grow dim—unreal. Only the music was real.

This advertorial blurs the line between art and copy. This ad isn't just about learning to play the piano; it's about the power of music and how we all aspire to become better people.

Caples's ad also demonstrates how a copywriter can use an emotional benefit of a product or service, tell a story and win over customers and readers.

Whether you're writing about consumer electronics, sports cars or a more boring product like an insurance product, the basics remain the same.

GRAB THEM BY THE EYEBALLS

Your readers and customers won't click on boring, bland or unsexy headlines.

So grab them by the eyeballs with an engaging headline.

If you're struggling to find a good headline for your article, take a look at magazine covers like *Cosmopolitan*.

The writers for magazines like *Cosmopolitan* are well-paid pros, and you can easily rework any of these proven headlines to suit your copywriting.

For example, I recently found the *Cosmopolitan* headline "10 Sex Myths Busted!" and turned it into "10 Writing Myths Busted!" and I used the latter for a blog post (see chapter 19).

Write at least 10 headlines for every article, salespage or book chapter you write and you will get better at the art of headline writing.

USE EVERYDAY LANGUAGE

Author and salesperson Dan Kennedy best explains why words that sells must be simple and easy to read.

"I think sales letters should be reader-friendly. That means the letter appears easy to read, is easy on the eye, uses everyday language, and doesn't require you to be a Harvard grad or a determined masochist to get through it," he wote in *The Ultimate Sales Letter.*

I think of this sentence every time I pick up an indecipherable pamphlet from the insurance company, a jargon letter from the bank or a detailed brochure from my electricity provider.

Most of the time these documents are impossible to read, and they almost always end up in the bin.

The next time you write copy for your audience consider if you use use everyday language.

ACTIVATE YOUR VERBS

One of the best ways to give your copy about a product or service more life is to shun the passive voice in favour of the active voice.

In the passive voice, the subject (you) is acted on by a verb. It sounds weak, and you can usually spot the passive voice if a verb ends with -ed.

For example:

- It was decided . . .
- The product was revealed . . .
- A product is going to be . . .

In the active voice, the subject (you) performs the action. For example:

- We're releasing . . .
- We're announcing . . .
- We've just updated . . .

I'll cover the active voice in more detail in chapter 31. However, if you're writing copy, remember the active voice will help your writing sparkle and capture your readers' (or customers') attention.

INCLUDE A CALL-TO-ACTION

When you finish your copy, always call on your readers to act.
You could say:

- If you enjoyed this post, share it on Facebook/Twitter/LinkedIn.
- Share your tips for [insert topic] in the comments sections.
- Watch this free video/download this free resource to learn more about [insert topic here].
- Join the Insider list and get exclusive tips for [insert benefit here].
- Begin your 30-day free trial of [insert product] here.

SELL LIKE A PRO

Copywriting is a skill like any other, and you've got to practice to improve. You can use the PAS or Approach formulas to sell products, ideas and services to your readers.

I recommend saving great examples of copy in your personal file so you can see what works.

If you make a habit of writing copy and studying how the experts sell with words, you'll naturally discover what sells and what doesn't work.

You'll become the kind of productive writer who knows how to build lasting relationships with readers and customers.

SELL WITH POWER WORDS

Below, I've provided fifty top power words which many marketers and copywriters use. These words will help you invoke emotion in the reader and accomplish more with your writing or sales copy.

- Agony
- Astonishing
- Announcing
- Alert
- Beware
- Confidential
- Compare
- Devoted
- Download
- Evil
- Excited
- Extra
- Fearless
- Fortune
- Free
- Fulfil
- Genuine
- Gift
- Growth
- Guaranteed
- Happy
- Hero
- Insider
- Introducing
- Immediate
- Improved
- Important
- Jail
- Mind-blowing

- New
- Obsession
- Practical
- Private
- Prize
- Refundable
- Sale
- Security
- Sex
- Silly
- Strange
- Slaughter
- Sleazy
- Strong
- Tax
- Urgent
- Ultimate
- Unusual
- Valuable
- Zero

There are hundreds more power words like these.

If you write online, use Twitter to research the power words that work best for your ideas. You can do this by tweeting different headlines to the same piece of writing several hours apart and determining which headlines perform best.

If you don't have a large Twitter following, study the most popular social media posts and blogs in your industry and take note of the emotional words writers use in their headlines.

I also recommend visiting BuzzFeed. The headline writers of this popular entertainment and news website are masters of using power words and emotional language to encourage more people to click on their headlines.

Whatever your approach, a swipe file is an ideal place to store power words that work for you. It will save you hours of writing time.

KNOW WHAT YOU'RE WRITING ABOUT

"We may be very busy, we may be very efficient, but we will also be truly effective only when we begin with the end in mind." – Stephen R. Covey

The productive writer understands great writing does at least one of four things. It informs, educates, inspires or entertains readers.

A news story is informative because it tells the reader something important about a current event. A tutorial is educational because it explains to readers how to accomplish a task.

A short story is entertaining because it gives the reader a place to escape their troubles. A self-help book is inspirational because it shows readers how they can improve their lives.

Before you start writing, decide if you want to entertain, inform, educate or inspire your reader. You don't have to achieve all four, but your writing should tick at least one of these boxes. If you don't, your reader will lose interest in your writing.

The good news is, you can easily give your readers what they want and hold their attention.

HOW TO INFORM YOUR READERS

Informing your readers means peppering your writing with research and facts that build credibility.

If you're writing for a publication, your editor will provide clear directions about what your writing should achieve and how you can give your readers what they want.

When I worked as a freelance journalist, I often received detailed briefs from editors explaining the topic I should cover, whom I should interview and how long the piece should be.

Even if you're not working for an editor, consider yourself a journalist who must examine a single topic with an unblinking gaze. You must be clear and level-headed in your writing.

You must put some distance between your feelings and the facts. Informative writing means you'll be spending time interviewing experts and finding unusual facts and information of interest to your readers.

HOW TO EDUCATE YOUR READERS

Educating your reader means adopting a personal and helpful tone. Put your hand around your reader's shoulder and say, "This isn't so hard to achieve. I can help you."

Examples of educational writing include tutorials, step-by-step articles, how-to guides and this book chapter.

You don't have to be an expert to educate your readers either.

Consider the curious case of the teenage maths student struggling with a difficult equation. Instead of asking the teacher for advice, he turns to his friend and asks him how to solve the equation.

In this case, the teenage maths student feels more comfortable asking his friend for advice because he can relate to his friend. This is because the two of them are at similar points along their learning journeys. You can use this principle to relate to your readers even if you're not an expert.

For example, in 2014 I ran the Dublin City marathon. It was my first marathon. I'm not an expert at running or athletics and I would never profess to be.

However, I could draw on the mistakes I made while training for this marathon to write an article like, "Marathon Training Mistakes: 10 Lessons for Beginners".

My beginner's article wouldn't interest serious runners, but a beginner considering their first race might be more interested in what I learnt because we're not so different. If you are going to write an educational article you want people to relate to, use clear and simple instructions the reader can follow.

If you've ever read the instruction manual for an old appliance, you will appreciate how frustrating ambiguous instructions are.

You should also provide practical tips free of jargon or opinion. This way, the reader can learn from your knowledge and decide for themselves what to do next.

Using metaphors the reader relates to will improve your writing too. A metaphor is a clever way of relating a concept to an everyday object or action.

For example, "Running a blog is a lot like servicing a car because..." or "Writing a book is a lot like laying bricks because..."

Finally, encourage the reader to persevere when they feel like giving up. Remind the reader you were a beginner once too, and then show them what success looks like.

HOW TO INSPIRE YOUR READERS

Inspiring readers is a different job. Often, this means drawing on personal stories and passions. You must invoke an emotion or change in your readers. You should persuade them to act and push them over the edge if they don't.

To inspire, consider what they should feel after reading your work or what they should take away from your writing. Play on their fears and hopes.

Paint a version of hell that they should avoid or describe a vision of the future as you see it. Give your readers specific examples of how you both can move towards your version of heaven together.

The most famous example of inspirational writing is Martin Luther King Jr's "I have a Dream speech", within which he paints his dream "that my four little children will one day live in a nation where they will not be judged by the colour of their skin but by the content of their character."

HOW TO ENTERTAIN YOUR READERS

Entertaining the reader means drawing on personal stories only you can tell.

Yes, you can use humour, anecdotes, and clever wordplay, but story is king. We make sense of the world through storytelling and turn to this medium as an escape.

The best way to entertain your readers is to tell a captivating story. There are entire books about effective storytelling, and I recommend reading *Story* by Robert McKee.

If you want to learn about story faster, one of the simplest and best storytelling concepts is this six sentence fill-in-the-blanks template created by Pixar Studios, which they outline on their blog.

Once upon a time there was . . . Every day . . . One day . . . Because of that . . . Because of that . . . Until finally . . .

Here's how this storytelling template works for the popular animated Pixar film *Finding Nemo*:

Once upon a time there was . . . a widowed fish, named Marlin, who was extremely protective of his only son, Nemo. Every day . . . Marlin warned Nemo of the ocean's dangers and implored him not to swim far away. One day . . . in an act of defiance, Nemo ignored his father's warnings and swam into the open water.

Because of that . . . he was captured by a diver and ended up in the fish tank of a dentist in Sydney. Because of that . . . Marlin set off on a journey to recover Nemo, enlisting the help of other sea creatures along the way. Until finally . . . Marlin and Nemo found each other, reunite and learned that love depends on trust.

How about this?

Once upon a time there was a new writer who couldn't finish what he started. Every day, he tried to write but kept getting distracted. One day, his editor boss fired him because he wasn't able to ship his work on time. Because of that the writer almost went broke. Because of that, he taught himself how to find better paying freelance contracts and get more things done. Until finally he made a habit of finishing what he started and got paid for his hard work.

BEGIN WITH YOUR READERS IN MIND

The writer who starts a project without knowing what they want to accomplish will find their work hard, slow and awkward.

Deciding the purpose of your work or beginning with the end in mind before you put words onto the blank page will give confines within which to write. It will give you a goal to write towards and help you finish what you started.

Remember, most readers are hungry for information and for a perspective that only YOU have.

If you want to become a more productive writer, give it to them.

STOP SEARCHING FOR THE PERFECT WRITING TOOL

"Do not wait; the time will never be 'just right'. Start where you stand, and work with whatever tools you may have at your command, and better tools will be found as you go along." – George Herbert

The productive writer knows the perfect writing tool doesn't exist. He or she spends most of their time trying to hit their target word count for the day and improve their craft.

He or she has their quirks too.

Hemingway wrote drafts of his works standing up with a pencil and paper.

Lewis Carroll declined a chair in favour of standing while writing.

Vladimir Nabokov, the Russian-American author of *Lolita,* wrote drafts of his novels on index cards and gave them to his wife to organise.

Every accomplished writer has a routine and idiosyncrasies. Writing while standing up might have worked for Hemingway and using index cards might have worked for Nabokov, but that doesn't mean these tools are suitable for you.

By all means, study how the greats completed their works, but don't let your search for the perfect writing tool (or a novel approach to writing) get in the way of producing more words. Doing the work and mastering your craft is more important than learning how to use the latest writing tool.

For years, I was obsessed with finding the perfect writing tool.

I told myself things like:

"When I get this piece of software, I'll be able to write more often."

"This computer is the one I'm going to finally write a book with."

"I need to learn how to use this piece of software before I write a book."

Just as a bad tradesman blames their tools when they botch a job, a bad writer blames his or her tools when they can't finish what they started.

ON NEW WRITING TOOLS

I'm no Luddite.

Sometimes, the productive writer sets time aside to learn how to use a new writing tool.

Scrivener, for example, is a powerful piece of writing software that's popular with many writers today.

This application has a small learning curve, but it simplifies working on different parts of your book. Scrivener also enables you to manipulate the structure of whatever you're writing and compile different versions for book stores, websites and more.

Similarly, many writers can skyrocket their word count through dictation software. Again, they have to invest some time in mastering dictation and then incorporate this new way of writing into their creative workflow

However, a productive writer sets time aside to master a new tool after they've completed the day's work. Later, he or she masters this new tool by using it.

The procrastinating writer, on the other hand, puts off doing their most important work because they want to learn how to use every feature in their new tool of choice. He or she spends hours setting up this new tool so that everything is perfect when it's finally time to write.

(Please see chapter four in part I of book three to learn more about using Scrivener and dictation software).

ON WRITING WITH A COMPUTER

Computers enable more productive writing. It's quicker to manipulate large blocks of text on screen than on paper, and you stand less chance of losing your work.

That said, computers are far from perfect. The blink of the cursor and the lure of distractions like email, social media and the internet place boundaries around a writer's creativity and productivity.

Some writers find computers confining. Steven Pressfield, author of *The War of Art*, prefers writing on his Smith-Corona typewriter over a computer, for example.

If you're having problems working a piece out, try writing for 30 minutes with pen and paper before returning to your computer. I've found this method forces me to write slower and stay with a thought longer.

It's also a good idea to work on early drafts of your work on pen and paper or with index cards and move to a computer for later drafts.

Find and use what works, and accept it in all its imperfections.

ON THE INTERNET

During a book tour for his 2012 novel *Freedom*, American novelist Jonathan Franzen told a journalist he wanted to write more each day, so he physically removed his Wi-Fi card from his computer and permanently blocked his machine's Ethernet connection with super glue.

I'm not suggesting you wreck your machine or that an internet-free life is the path to becoming a *New York Times* best-selling author.

But disabling your internet access, even for short periods, will help you accomplish more on the page.

Think of your internet-free writing sessions as a respite from the deluge of information you wade through every day.

If you need to use the internet for research, try to wait until after you've hit your target word count for the day.

I've never written anything of consequence while navigating from one site to the next. The internet comes with too many distractions, feeds, unchecked emails, pings and notifications.

The blank page doesn't stand a chance in the face of a digital crowd clamouring for our attention.

Writing off-line can feel liberating and intimate. You won't feel a subconscious tug to log into an account or refresh a feed.

It's just you, your words and your ideas.

ON TIDYING UP

A master craftsman tidies up after themselves and prepares their work for the following day. He knows creativity is a long-term game and to turn up and do the work.

Hemingway, for example, stopped writing in the middle of a sentence so he'd know where to resume the following day.

You don't need to follow his approach. Just have a clear idea of what you're going to write tomorrow.

Perhaps you want to finish your introduction, expand on a chapter in your book, or work on an outline?

Tidy up your work, organise your notes and put your tools away. Tip the waitress in the coffee shop if you need to. Make it easier to find the clear space you need to write again tomorrow and improve your craft.

EMBRACE STRUCTURE

"I fear those big words which make us so unhappy" – James Joyce

Do you want to know how to organise your writing?

If you do, planning and structure are your new best friends.

Finishing a writing project is easier, and readers will enjoy your work more if it's supported by an underlying structure. This is why books have paragraphs, chapters and narrative arcs.

It's why blog posts have subheadings and newspaper articles are broken up with pull quotes, panels and boxes. Even the directors and writers of most successful films break them into three acts.

PLAN AHEAD

Several years ago, I had to write a these longer than 20,000 words about the literary works of Irish author Christy Brown.

For months, I struggled with this thesis. I just couldn't get it to flow, and I couldn't organise my ideas. I told my tutor I was afraid I wouldn't be able to finish my work. She asked, "Why don't you approach your thesis from a different angle? Why don't you outline it?"

I took my tutor's advice and developed an outline of each section and chapter using pen and paper. I wrote down the title of each chapter on almost one hundred 6x4 index cards. (3x5 and 5x8 cards are good too!)

Next, I wrote down points I wanted to cover within each chapter along with quotes, stories and other pieces of factual information. I laid my index cards out on a large glass table and spent several hours reviewing them.

What happened next surprised me.

I was able to shift from one troublesome section or chapter to an easier one without getting lost or stressed. I could see the overall structure of my thesis even if it was unfinished. In effect, I zoomed out from my thesis and moved the chapters and ideas around like the pieces on a chessboard.

I considered where I was repeating myself, what was missing and what I needed to cover. Then, I sorted the index cards into piles to keep, remove or combine. Next I rewrote each of the index cards and repeated this planning process.

I did this until I was left with a structure for my thesis that I could work with. Although the thesis changed during the course of writing and rewriting, this structure served as a light that kept me from getting lost during the creative process.

(Please see chapter eight in part II of book three if you want to learn more about this process.)

REDUCE, REMOVE AND SIMPLIFY

Confession: I hate shopping for clothes. It's time-consuming, draining, and I'm terrible at it.

I never know what to buy, and I always think there's a better choice just around the corner.

One hot summer's day, I had to buy a shirt and tie for a wedding. I spent several hours walking from suit shop to suit shop in Dublin and trying on clothes I didn't like.

I was sweaty, tired and about to give up my search and go home. Then I decided to try an airy and quiet shop near the bus stop.

When I walked inside, the owner took one look at me and pulled out a chair.

"You look like a man who needs a seat," he said. "How can I help you?"

I explained my predicament.

"I just don't know what I want. There's so much out there."

"What do you like? What are you looking for?" he asked.

While I explained, he laid out three shirts and ties on the table.

"Try these three on."

"Why only three?" I asked pointing to all the other suits and ties behind us.

"I never give a customer too much choice," he said. "It makes decisions harder."

He was right. I found selecting from his three choices much easier than considering the hundreds of other choices in the shop.

SIMPLIFY YOUR WRITING

Business writer and online entrepreneur Chris Brogan best sums the benefits of simplification.

He told writer and podcaster James Altucher in a 2014 interview, "The sun can warm an entire field of daisies, or you can focus it such that it can burn through an inch of steel."

Focus on the heart of your writing and cut anything that doesn't add value. If you're struggling to simplify your writing, consider:

- What angles and points can you combine or remove?
- Are you being too technical?
- What should your writing focus on?
- What should it ignore?
- Can you sum up your topic in one sentence?

- If not, what's preventing you from doing so?
- How can you use fewer words?

HOW I SIMPLIFY MY WRITING

When I'm writing feature articles, I reduce the number of interviewees I quote because too many interviewees can become confusing for the reader. This reduction also lends greater weight to the included interviewees, and it gives me room to analyse what they said.

While writing this book, I simplified my work by reducing what I've discovered about productivity into 33 digestible strategies. I did this because 33 strategies was the best way to reduce my idea to the essentials.

When I'm writing a blog post, I pick an idea and consider people who will want to read about it. I ask what new perspective or information I can add to this topic and how I can solve a problem for readers.

I make room for an introduction and conclusion and also for some factual information, personal anecdotes and stories from my commonplace book. Then I write a rough first draft somewhere between 1000 and 1,500 words.

Later, I reread this first draft and consider what I should remove and rework. I check if my sentences are too long and if I can break up paragraphs into a list. Online readers spend more time scanning than reading articles, so I must ensure my writing is easy on the eye.

PLAN TO WRITE, PLAN TO FINISH

Authors like James Joyce and Samuel Beckett wrote without planning or structure, but they still learnt what structure was before abandoning it.

Next time you are faced with an intimidating writing project, break it into chunks that you can tackle one by one. On index cards, jot down words identifying these chunks, and then rearrange these in order of how your writing project unfolds.

This process will give you an early overview of your writing project. This planning will also help you zoom out and see all the pieces on your chessboard. From there, you can create a structure that works for you.

Your writing will evolve during the creative process, but having a plan and using structure can help you get from the blank page to the last page.

WRITE WITH A BEGINNER'S MIND

"When you do something, you should burn yourself completely, like a good bonfire, leaving no trace of yourself." – Shunryu Suzuki

So you're an expert.

You know how to organise your ideas, you've put in your 10,000 hours of dedicated practice, and you know how to write.

But can you still write as if you are considering an idea for the first time?

Shunryu Suzuki was a twentieth-century Japanese Zen monk and teacher who authored *Zen Mind, Beginner's Mind*.

In this book of Zen teachings and talks, Suzuki writes that when we are intentional in our practice, we act, or write, without bias or preconceptions. Instead, when the task at hand consumes us completely.

To take on a task, and know how it will turn out beforehand is to hold something back from the creative fire.

To bring your preconceptions and biases is to forget the perspective of those who know less than you. Instead, put everything you know into the fire of the creative process and let it burn.

- Perhaps the argument you set out to prove isn't as solid as you thought.
- Maybe a character in your story wants to do something that you didn't expect.
- Possibly your research unearths a new angle or story for your work.

If you're an expert, this open-minded approach to writing is hard to take.

When you become practised at a task or skill, your writing voice dulls itself on a groove of repetition. Your arguments establish themselves and opinions solidify before the fire of your hard work takes hold.

You turn to the same haggard metaphors and imagery and drag them out long after their prime.

You fail to see things from the point of view of your less informed readers, and you miss those interesting detours that form part of the creative process.

Remember, a reader will get more from the writer who feels passionate about his or her subject.

USE THE OUTSIDER'S PERSPECTIVE

Consider starting a new job.

For the first few weeks or months, you are an outsider who sees the workplace differently from the rest of the team. Even if you keep your questions to yourself, you wonder why things are done one way and not the other.

In the beginning, you are a unique commodity and sometimes forward-thinking managers will capitalise on your outsider's insight to make informed changes. They know you can see things the rest of the team can't.

When these first few weeks turn into months or years, you will acquire expert knowledge about your company or workplace. You will become the kind of person who does things a certain way because that's how it's always been done.

Your expert knowledge, experiences and insight about a topic or field of study can induce complacency.

How can you write something original when the tinder wood of your creativity is soaked with preconceptions? How many times have you made the same moot point? Have you become an insider?

If the facts change, abandon your arguments. Don't become too attached to any one idea or way of accomplishing things on the blank page.

If you get the chance, leave your old arguments behind and don't look back.

CHANGE YOUR MIND

Writing with a beginner's mind means bringing a renewed sense of curiosity to your project.

Seek out new answers in place of old ones you take for granted.

Evaluate your ideas like you've come across them for the first time.

Throw rocks at your arguments and see if they still hold up.

Accept some of your readers will know things you don't.

Acknowledge your mistakes. But what if you're worried about being inconsistent or what others will think?

You can get away with changing your mind if you take readers on a journey with you. Your loyal readers will forgive you for an about-turn if you explain why you changed your mind. If they don't, at least you had the courage to state what you know is true.

Your readers might thank you for it... later.

QUESTION OLD ASSUMPTIONS

At first, Italian astronomer Galileo Galilei believed the world was the flat centre of the universe like his scientific peers. Then in 1616, after stumbling across new facts with his telescope, he presented his change of mind to an unready Italian audience.

He argued why the world is round.

Although the Church didn't forgive him while he was alive for this "heresy", today we regard Galileo as one of humanity's top polymaths.

Early in life, British author George Orwell believed strongly in the entitlements of the upper class. Later in life, he satirised them in his dystopian novel *1984*. He wrote, "Orthodoxy means not thinking–not needing to think. Orthodoxy is unconsciousness."

Author Leo Tolstoy was a staunch follower of the Russian Orthodox and a man who believed keeping serfs was acceptable.

Later, he explained why he abandoned his old principles in his short book *A Confession*.

> I cannot recall those years without horror, loathing, and heart-rending pain. I killed people in war, challenged men to duels with the purpose of killing them, and lost at cards; I squandered the fruits of the peasants' toil and then had them executed; I was a fornicator and a cheat. Lying, stealing, promiscuity of every kind, drunkenness, violence, murder — there was not a crime I did not commit... Thus I lived for ten years.

You might not have committed a crime, duelled with your fellow man or lost at cards like Tolstoy, but when you look back on the years past, what have you changed your mind about?

Now, write about it.

BURN UP WITH YOUR READER

Hold out your hand to your readers and invite them on a journey that you have never taken together.

Show your reader why your idea warrants his or her attention. Reveal the mistakes you've made, the times you fell down, the lessons you learned and what your world looks like today.

Practice writing from this beginner's mind until you can approach the blank page without any preconceived notions.

Write like you're experiencing something for the first time. Write like it's you and the reader against the world, and together you will burn like a good bonfire.

DON'T STOP EXPERIMENTING

"Every person takes the limits of their own field of vision for the limits of the world." – Arthur Schopenhauer

Roald Dahl found success by experimenting with elements from his life on the blank page.

As a young man, he worked for Shell in Kenya and Tanzania and spent his free time hunting. During World War II, Dahl became a decorated fighter ace and intelligence officer.

He shot down at least two enemy JU-88 planes, took part in the Battle of Athens and was one of the last pilots to withdraw from Greece during the German invasion.

When he became a writer, Dahl wasn't afraid to draw on his old life for his new creative one. He wrote several short stories about his time as a fighter pilot and in his novels and short stories drew extensively on his previous careers.

For example, in *James and the Giant Peach*, the seagulls (or fighter airplanes) attack the airborne giant peach, a talking centipede falls (or parachutes) off the giant peach, and the end of the book references air raids and heroes returning home (from the war).

Even though he first became famous as the author of children's books like *The BFG* and *Charlie and the Chocolate Factory*. Dahl refused to be pigeonholed into one genre or towards catering to a particular audience. He wrote poetry, published screenplays and became a successful adult short story writer.

The embodiment of a productive writer, Dahl wrote more than 17 stories for children, two novels and series of short story collections.

He was a consummate scientist of his craft.

ACCEPT SOME LIMITATIONS

Before you experiment, consider what's possible with the written word. This medium engages only two to three of the five human senses: sight, touch, sound, taste and smell.

The reader can see your words on the page, but when you describe someone's face, the reader must use their imagination to fill in the blanks.

They can feel the weight and texture of the paper in their hands, but when you write about the texture of someone's skin, they bring their biases to your writing.

If you describe the bitter taste of a coffee, the reader's sense of taste and smell are just as likely to be triggered by the environment where they're reading your writing.

There are exceptions.

Poetry read aloud is musical to the ear. You can also use onomatopoeia or words that sound like their meaning – such as cuckoo or sizzle – to engage your reader's senses.

Today many writers read their works aloud at public events or in the form of audio books.

The productive writer sometimes uses picture, video and audio to convey his or her message. He knows alternative media complements fine writing.

He makes lengthy passages destined for the computer screen more digestible by breaking them up with bullet points, headings, pull quotes and the clever use of **bold** and *italics* formatting.

This is particularly true if you're writing for online readers who are just as likely to listen to an audio clip or watch a video as they are to read a blog post.

LEARN TO EXPERIMENT

Have you ever read my erotic fiction?

I'm embarrassed to tell you this, but several years ago I researched what was popular and trending, and I tried to write several different erotic short stories.

My creative experiment blew up in my face.

I discovered erotic fiction is exceptionally difficult to write without coming across as clichéd or sleazy. My stories came across as both.

I never published my stories, and I discovered I don't have the talent or desire to write the next *Fifty Shades of Grey*. Thankfully, my humiliation was a private one, an experiment that helped me find the limitations of my craft.

I realised I preferred writing non-fiction.

The best way to discover the limitations of your craft is to explore what works and what doesn't work for you. Find what excites and bores you.

Take on new creative and writing challenges. Through brave experimentation, you will figure out the rules of writing and discover the ones that are OK to bend and the ones you should snap in half.

If writers didn't take time to experiment with their craft, we wouldn't have books like *Ulysses* or *The Dubliners*. James Joyce is an extreme example, but aspiring writers can learn from the working habits of the greats.

For you, this might mean writing poetry, a novel, a short story or a personal essay. It means getting out of your creative comfort zone.

- If you've written a story in the first person, rewrite it in the third person.
- If you've written a blog post about the benefits of

meditation, turn it into 50 reasons why meditation is better than sex.

- If you opened your article with a statistic, use a quote or a statement that will rile your reader.
- If you've just finished an article, remove the introduction and insert the conclusion in its place.
- If you tried to be impartial, rewrite your work using a strong, personal point of view.

GET RESULTS

Experimenting is time-consuming, and you're going to make mistakes. But nobody has to see them. And the more you make, the better writer you will become.

Dahl said, "A little nonsense now and then, is relished by the wisest men."

So aim for a little nonsense.

Experiment, just like I did by writing awful erotic fiction.

The hard work, the mistakes, failed experiments, and torn-up manuscripts – these activities form 90 percent of what is not seen, like an iceberg under water.

But…

These private little experiments are a great way to develop your writing voice and push your boundaries beyond what you feel most comfortable doing.

At the least, you're less likely to become bored with your craft and more excited about the possibilities of the blank page.

BUILD YOUR PLATFORM

"Compared to the cost of renting eyeballs, buying a platform is cheap." – Seth Godin

David doesn't like marketing his writing. He says his job is to write, not to promote his work. That if he works hard enough on his art, then his readers will come.

But only a few people have come across David's work. And when they do, they don't stay long.

Sound familiar?

Not too long ago, I was David. And if you're a writer struggling to find an audience for your work online, he's you too.

Writing is a hard, demanding craft, and nothing is more disappointing than releasing your work into a vacuum.

You can overcome these problems by building a platform for your work.

BUILD A PLATFORM

The gatekeepers between you and your audience no longer exist. Today, you can create opportunities that were unavailable when writers like John Cheever, Virginia Woolf and Stephen King started out.

You need a platform to tell stories about yourself, showcase your work and find readers.

Your platform should comprise a blog or author website, an email list and a preferred social media channel. The goal of your platform is to provide people with a way to discover you and give you a way to talk to your readers.

Many authors today use social media to connect with readers. Brazilian novelist Paulo Coelho has an astonishing 10 million followers on Twitter (@paulocoelho). Neil Gaiman is also an avid user of Twitter (@neilhimself) and blogs at journal.neilgaiman.com.

However, Facebook and Twitter are outposts that you have little control over. When they change the rules (as they often do), you can't do much about it.

For this reason, you should have full control over your website. It's your home base and the number one place readers can find you. At the least, your website should explain who you are, what you write about and how people can get in touch. You can showcase your books too.

After you've set up your website, create an email list and ask readers to join by offering a free book or some of your best writing.

Having an email list is helpful for communicating directly with readers or customers, particularly if Amazon or Twitter changes the rules. Plus, you'll be less dependent on search engines for traffic and readers. You can ask loyal email subscribers for feedback on early drafts too.

Finally, blogging is a great outlet for non-fiction writers.

You can experiment with different writing styles. Writing blog posts gets you into the habit of presenting your work to more than your spouse, family member or best friend.

WRITE GUEST BLOG POSTS

I used to resent the idea of spending time and energy writing blog posts and then giving them away for free. Surely I was better off publishing posts on my site?

I was dead wrong.

My personal blogging mentor, Jon Morrow, said writing guest posts for large websites is the writer's equivalent of opening for the Rolling Stones when you're an up-and-coming band.

It's the quickest way to grow your audience.

When you write for a large website, a new audience will read your work and potentially visit your site and join your email list.

If you write several successful guest blog posts, ask the site owners to share your writing or promote your book. This is cheaper and more efficient than trying to run an advertising campaign.

Also when an editor reviews your posts, you'll receive feedback that will help you improve at your craft. Many new writers pay for this kind of constructive feedback.

As a productive writer, you can make peace with this marketing strategy because it allows you to write, promote your work and get editorial feedback.

WRITE LIKE CHARLES BUKOWSKI

In his famous collection of poetry *The Pleasures of the Damned*, Charles Bukowski complained about how his heroes (Hemingway, F. Scott Fitzgerald) could find an audience for their work easier in the 1920s than he could in the 1940s and 1950s.

> It was much easier to be a genius in the twenties, there were only 3 or 4 literary magazines.... you could possibly meet Picasso for a glass of wine.

Bukowski then bemoaned the number of publications he had to deal with to build his audience in 1951.

I wonder how Bukowski would have embraced the millions of websites, blogs, and publications today's writers contend with?

Still, if Bukowski found success in the 1950s, you can find it today.

Now let's explore some of the most popular myths about writing guest posts.

Myth: Your Editor Writes the Headline

The headline is the most important part of any article or blog post.

It's the first thing readers see, so it should persuade them to click on a link to your article.

When you're pitching an editor, include a strong headline following the style of the blog you're writing for. This practice is often enough to grab an editor's attention.

You can write a good headline by studying the five most popular blog posts on the site you're pitching.

Alternatively, examine the covers of popular magazines like *Cosmopolitan* or *Esquire* or other magazines in your niche.

Here's how:

1. Type *"Cosmo"* into Google Images search so you can see lots of magazine covers.

2. Pick several headlines from a magazine cover you like, for example "Get-fit secrets for a tight bod"

3. Adapt each headline around your topic, like "7 editing secrets for tight copy".

Myth: One Idea Will Woo Your Editor

If you include one idea, your chances of getting published depend solely on the merits of your single idea.

If you include two ideas, your editor has a dilemma.

If you include three ideas, your editor has options.

You don't need to go into great detail for each idea (and a time-strapped editor with a thousand emails to read won't thank you for a

1,000-word email). You do want to give your editor more than what they're expecting.

Myth: Take Your Time Writing the Post

If your guest post is accepted, either ask your editor for a deadline or submit a completed post within two weeks.

If you're worried, make life easier by writing a rough draft of your article before you pitch the editor in question.

This way you can rework your draft before submitting it.

But what if your post is rejected?

Don't worry.

You can still rework the idea for another website. If that fails, use the post on your blog.

Myth: Style Guidelines Are for Fools

Style or guest-posting guidelines differ from site to site, and woe be the writer who ignores them. Editors might ask writers to do things like:

- Hit a target word count
- Include an image for your post
- Link to other articles or influencers in your post
- Write a linking post on your website
- Email an editor rather than the site owner (more on this in a moment)

One site I pitched hid a password in the middle of their guest-posting guidelines and asked that serious writers (i.e., the ones who read the guidelines) include this password in their initial email.

On most sites, you can typically find the writing guidelines on the About page, the Contact page or another dedicated page on the site.

Myth: Relationships are Unimportant

I sometimes comment on site's popular posts before sending the editor a pitch.

This practice will help you develop a relationship with the site owner or editor.

I also share these posts multiple times using Twitter because it notifies the site owners I shared their posts.

This notification accelerates building a relationship with the site (who doesn't like their writing being shared?) and easier to get a response to my guest-post pitch.

I also recommend linking from posts on your site to the site in question.

This tactic is useful if you're targeting mid-level rather than top-level blogs. The former might not have that many links and will notice yours, whereas the latter will have thousands.

Myth: The Editor's Name Doesn't Matter

In his book *How to Win Friends and Influence People,* Dale Carnegie wrote that "Names are the sweetest and most important sound in any language."

Most larger websites employ a full-time editor who manages content on behalf of the site owner. Whatever you do, don't start your email by saying "Hi" and then moving into your pitch.

Your email pitch will sound cold and impersonal. The guest-posting guidelines of most sites often include the names of the editors. Use them.

Find out the editor's name.

If you're stuck, address the site owner by name.

Myth: Didn't Hear Back Immediately? Move On

The owners and editors of popular websites are busy people with even busier inboxes.

If they don't respond immediately to your initial guest-post pitch, don't take it personally. Instead, seven days after your pitch, send a follow-up email politely asking if they received your inquiry.

A week is long enough to avoid harassing the editor but not so long that they forget about you. In the majority of cases, the editor will respond to the follow-up submission.

Four of my five pitches received a response after I took this approach. If the editor still don't respond, try again in one week or take your idea to another website.

The web is a big place.

Myth: Your Job Is Over Upon Publication

Professional writers are always thinking about the next job. You should too.

When you write a guest post for a popular website, thank everybody who shares or comments on your post and respond to their comments.

If you have time, read the bios of those who share your posts on Twitter.

If these people have a relationship with a site you want to write for, contact them with a new guest post idea.

You will be fresh in their mind, and they will be receptive to your ideas for their site. A few days after your post is published, send the editor a short email thanking them for the opportunity.

This way you can keep the door open for future submissions. Even if you decide not to write for them again, this will leave a positive impression with the editor, which is the hallmark of a professional.

WIN NEW READERS FASTER

Friendship is a long-term game, and so is writing guest posts.

Yes, it takes some time to get started if you haven't written a guest post before.

However, after you've written several guest posts, the editors of larger and more popular websites will become more receptive to your ideas because you can point to a body of work.

Plus, you can use old posts to build your credibility with your audience.

Now go give your best work away for free.

If anyone asks, tell them Charles Bukowski sent you.

BUT I'M A WRITER, NOT A MARKETER!

Can I be blunt?

This is a cop-out, and it's one I spent years making.

I've sat in writing groups and listened to myself and my peers describe how marketing a book or a piece of writing is debasing. At the time, I agreed with the other members of these groups that marketing should be left to the marketers and writing to the writers.

We were wrong.

What's the point in writing if nobody reads your work?

In his book *All Marketers Are Liars*, the oracle of online marketing, Seth Godin, provides numerous examples of companies, brands and business people that tell authentic stories about their products.

He wrote, "When you find a story that works, live that story, make it true, authentic, and subject to scrutiny. All marketers are story-tellers."

Did I mention Godin has published 17 books?

Don't feel bad or sleazy about these kinds of marketing activities.

Instead, you're telling stories about your work. These are stories you know well, but your future readers haven't heard them yet.

As a writer, your most important task for the day is to write. After all, you can't market your work if you haven't produced anything of value. However, your job doesn't end when you press submit or upload your new book to Amazon.

Research what your audience wants, build relationships with thought leaders who can help, and keep searching for ways to get in front of new readers. This is what the productive writer does.

He or she commits to connecting with readers and editors, and writing consistently.

EXERCISE LIKE YOUR CRAFT DEPENDS ON IT

"Exerting yourself to the fullest within your individual limits: that's the essence of running, and a metaphor for life— and for me, for writing as well. I believe many runners would agree." – Haruki Murakami

Physical exercise is a worthy and important pursuit for the productive writer.

Haruki Murakami, the Japanese author of books like *Kafka on the Shore* and *After Dark*, says running and cycling help him become more creative.

When he's working on a novel, and after his work is complete for the day, Murakami swims for 1,500 metres or runs 10 kilometres. He maintains this routine almost every day.

He wrote, "For me, the main goal of exercising is to maintain, and improve, my physical condition in order to keep on writing novels."

Murakami knows what he's talking about.

According to Michael Mumford of the University of Oklahoma, 30 minutes of aerobic exercise will help you become more creative.

Succeeding at intense physical activities takes focus, concentration and discipline, just like writing.

The creative process involves working hard on a single task at length, as do intense physical activities like swimming, cycling, football and so on.

When I'm stuck on a troublesome piece, I sometimes go for a run, a swim or a long walk. I'm not going to lie and say exercising is always easy and enjoyable. Still, this practice helps me cultivate discipline and focus.

There, in the pool or on the road, when I'm not thinking about writing at all, a solution arises, and I see a way through whatever problem I'm facing.

Thirty minutes of exercise a day isn't too much, especially if you're pursuing a craft that requires you to sit down for hours at a time. Exercising will give you more energy, a break and a new perspective on your work.

MEDITATE

Meditation, like exercise, can help you write too. Meditation and writing have a lot in common. They both involve sitting in one place and focusing on one task for extended periods of time.

Meditation is one of the best ways to spark creativity, improve focus and make you smarter. Dozens of high-profile studies demonstrate the links between meditation, creativity and focus.

For example, a 2012 scientific study by the Leiden University in the Netherlands found that "...meditation leads to better performance in a distributed-attention task and reinforces the view that meditation practice can have a lasting and generalizable impact on human cognition."

Sitting quietly on a cushion and focusing on your breath for just 15 minutes each day makes it easier to sit in front of a computer or the blank page and write for extended periods.

Meditation also serves as a necessary and welcome break from a computer screen or troublesome sentence. It won't solve your physical problems directly, but it will help you become more aware of when you need to take a break. And it can help you become more mindful of chronic pain.

The next time you're in a creative rut, put on a pair of runners or meditate on the problem.

VALUE YOUR HEALTH

Writing looks like an easy enough activity.

To the untrained observer, a writer sits on a comfortable chair, plucks words from a dictionary and spins an indulgent yarn.

For most writers, the craft of producing prose is anything but easy or magical.

Writing requires a certain degree of physical and mental endurance and focus. A writer has to sit in one spot for hours every day and sustain concentration for extended periods. And they have to do so alone without the distraction or encouragement of office colleagues or the material world.

A writer must have enough energy to sit and focus without becoming too distracted or tired to write. This kind of work is mentally exhausting. Physically, it can take its toll too.

Some days when I write for an extended period, my back aches, my eyes dry up, my hands cramp and my head spins. Then when I close my eyes, all I can see is floating black and white dots.

In 2014, I spent several weeks attending physiotherapy sessions for sciatica. I experienced this pain up and down my legs because I was spending too much time sitting down.

You can overcome physical complaints like these by taking short but regular breaks from the screen or the blank page and exercising when you're not writing.

The physio prescribed several exercises. He also suggested that when practical I stand, for example while reading my work.

If you are in pain for another reason, say because of an illness, crafting a meaningful sentence is almost impossible.

How can you write while you head throbs?

If you are particularly stressed, angry or emotional, it's difficult to achieve the kind of focus necessary for extended periods of examination and good writing.

Contrary to popular belief, hangovers don't make for effective prose. We might find reading stories about a drunken night out entertaining, but it's almost always impossible to write under the influence or while hungover.

Even Hemingway and F. Scott Fitzgerald attempted to write soberly towards the end of their writing careers because they recognised being wildly intoxicated doesn't always make for wildly intoxicating prose or productive writing.

Fitzgerald famously said, "First you take a drink, then the drink takes a drink, then the drink takes you."

ACCEPT WRITING IS SOMETIMES PAINFUL

I'm talking about the deep introspective writing that real writers put themselves through.

Writing should almost never be physically painful.

If it hurts, get the opinion of an expert like I did.

My physical therapist provided me with an assessment and a series of exercises that worked.

I found paying a professional more productive than diagnosing myself by reading articles online and treating myself by watching YouTube videos.

Don't write while in pain if you can avoid it, and remember your health should come first. Otherwise, you won't accomplish much.

CONSERVE YOUR WILLPOWER

"The life of the professional writer – like that of any freelance, whether she be a plumber or a podiatrist – is predicated on willpower." – Will Self

"I just can't be bothered."

"I'm just too tired."

"I don't have the energy today."

Have you ever made these kinds of excuses when it's time to write?

If you have, don't beat yourself up. This form of procrastination is natural.

In a 2009 study, Roy Baumeister, a psychologist at Florida State University, carried out an experiment where he asked students to sit next to a plate of fresh-baked chocolate chip cookies.

He gave permission to some students to eat the cookies, and he told others to avoid eating any of them. Afterwards, Baumeister gave both groups difficult puzzles to solve.

The students who'd resisted eating the cookies found the puzzles harder to complete, and they abandoned the task. Their mental resources were depleted.

But those students who ate the cookies worked on the puzzles longer. Baumeister found they were able to remain focused because they had more mental resources.

If you're working on a difficult writing project, your productivity will suffer if your willpower is running low. You're also more likely to experience a creative drought.

Have you ever experienced the following issues?

- You plan to write at the end of the day, only to come home exhausted and watch television instead.
- Your word counts are lower when you write while tired?
- You find it difficult to concentrate on writing projects after a stressful event or a busy morning.

If the answer is yes, a dearth of willpower affected your writing. The good news is it's easy to conserve your willpower, avoid a creative drought, have your cookies and eat them too.

HOW TO CONSERVE YOUR WILLPOWER

Anytime I avoid writing because I'm tired, bored or "not feeling it", I remind myself of the importance of self-discipline.

It's not sexy, but almost every writer I've read about sacrificed to pursue their work. They rose early or worked late into the night. And they wrote because they had to, not just when they felt the hand of inspiration.

Virginia Woolf wrote with a pencil and paper every morning until the early afternoon. She described writing and her ordinary moments. "I generally write with heat and ease till 12.30; and thus do my two pages. So it will be done, written over that is, in 3 weeks, I forecast from today."

So set yourself up for success the day before you get to work.

At the end of your day, prepare the next day's writing in advance. Decide what you're going to work on and for how long.

You could go as far as tidying your workspace, arranging your notes, and opening up the writing application on your computer (see chapter 15).

The next morning when you wake and get to your desk, you won't have to make any decisions about your writing, and you won't have to waste time getting your tools or your project ready. All you have to do is sit down and do the work.

Another way to conserve your willpower is to decide on your most important tasks for the following day beforehand.

Productive people use this approach to accomplish more in the workplace. At the end of the day, spend five minutes writing down three to five tasks you want to accomplish the next day.

For example, you could decide to freewrite, edit and then market an article, in that order. You could decide to brainstorm, proofread and research a chapter of your new book. Or you could consider what you're going to do after you finish writing.

BALANCE COMPETING PRIORITIES

Determining your most important tasks each day forces you to review your commitments in advance.

These regular mini-reviews will give you a chance to check in with how your writing is progressing. You'll get into the habit of overcoming the hurdles preventing you from becoming a more productive writer.

The next day when you start work, progress through your most important tasks in order and first thing. The key is to finish these tasks before you check email, make phone calls, arrange meetings or meet with colleagues. Before you attend to things that pop up.

The majority of these other activities are items on someone else's To Do list. Yes, they might be important, but are they as important as your writing?

Remember, every time you say yes to someone else's priorities, you're saying no to your writing. Sometimes, being successful means being a little selfish.

You can also conserve and replenish your willpower by looking after yourself. You can do this by sleeping, eating healthily, exercising, meditating, doing the right thing at the right times, taking naps and listening to music.

Me?

I like writing first thing in the morning because it sets up the entire day. When I succeed, I feel like the entire day is golden because I put some words down onto the page, however ugly.

If a meeting runs over, if there's a last minute appointment or a crisis with a colleague, my day is still a good one.

PROTECT YOUR BEST SELF

Conserve your willpower for the moments when you really need it. For when it's time to write, to create, to live.

If you practice this strategy, you will find writing every day more natural, and you will gain the momentum you need to keep going – even when you want to stop.

When you're done, reward yourself with a cookie.

I won't tell anyone.

START A FIGHT

"After all, the ultimate goal of all research is not objectivity, but truth." – Helene Deutsch

Ditch any notions you have about being an objective writer.

Take a stance.

Objectivity is a falsehood, and objective writing is a style of writing best left to serious journalists and scientists. Even then, the most seasoned journalists and scientific writers bring a natural level of subconscious bias to their writings.

They can write only through the frame of their upbringing, education and years of experience as a journalist or scientific writer. Everything else is second-hand information.

Yes, there are times when a writer should avoid inserting himself or herself directly into the piece they are working on, for example, a journalist writing about a natural disaster.

Yes, sometimes a writer should give information rather than opinion, for example, a scientist writing about a serious medical condition.

Mostly though, this kind of writing is boring and unnecessary. Almost nobody will read it.

When you write, take a stance. Have an opinion and pick a fight. Call out another writer or an expert in your field. Tell readers what you believe.

Argue for or against prevailing thinking. Explain your passion or what you've learnt. If the material you're working with is boring and grey, try and inject some colour.

You can take a stance by writing from the heart, or you can use calculated reasoning. Whatever your approach, nothing is less invigorating to read than an author planted undecidedly in the middle.

If you succeed, you will invoke a reaction in your readers. They might hate what you're saying or disagree with you entirely, but at least they're engaging with you.

Just remember that having a stance doesn't mean being vicious or nasty for the sake of it.

BE MODEST

Some readers will know less than you do; others will know more. Some will be interested in what you have to say, some will think you're wrong, and others just won't care.

Writers who try to impress readers with how much they know or how clever they are almost always fall flat on their faces. Those who hold back on the page for fear of embarrassment or because of foolish pride will produce a mediocre piece of work that will be forgotten.

If you want to avoid these pitfalls, reveal your weaknesses or faults. Let your readers know where you went wrong and how you're trying to improve (if at all).

It's OK to admit you don't know everything and that you made mistakes. These kinds of intimate details help readers relate to you.

Readers love brutal honesty because they've made mistakes too. Readers are not some homogenous group of people who judge your work as one. They're individuals who make mistakes, and they want to hear about yours.

If you're writing a more formal article, such as a step-by-step guide or tutorial, ask readers if they have any questions or suggestions at the end of your article. The best formal articles encourage discussion, debate or feedback.

I've tried to include as many practical writing tips as I could find and think of in this book, but I also accept that some more accomplished writers might have ideas I've yet to consider.

That's OK with me because through writing, I'm seeking to learn more about the craft of writing and share the learnings of my journey with you.

Don't you want to do the same?

PRACTICE HUMAN DECENCY

Somewhere, someone on the internet is wrong.

Is that person you?

Are you hiding behind your computer screen?

Have you ever ranted or told someone that their work is terrible and why they should never create again?

I'm being unfair – you strike me as an honest reader – but if you read the comments on popular YouTube videos, the reviews of books on Amazon or the comments on a popular forum post, you can find hundreds of examples of people who don't demonstrate common human decency.

Some commentators shout in CAPs. Meanwhile, others tell the creator that they've failed and should give up writing.

I've a confession to make.

Years ago, I was a little like that. I reviewed films for a local newspaper. The newspaper didn't have a budget to send reviewers to the films, so I made up my reviews.

I wanted to make a name for myself, so I analysed and criticised the hard work of other creative professionals even though I hadn't watched their accomplishments or failures. It was an awful way to spend my time, and my reviews were terrible.

My editor was OK about it, but I lost my self-respect as a writer.

I learnt it's easier to attack someone's work for its obvious flaws than it is to take the time to leave your comfort zone, create something and put yourself out there by sharing your ugly bastard child with the world.

These days I write about something I like, use or am passionate about.

The act of writing is a gift that writers can use to bring light into dark places. For example, abrasive writers like Charles Bukowski were more concerned with their failings than the failings of others. He said, "If you're losing your soul and you know it, then you've still got a soul left to lose."

Today, I've a lot of respect for established reviewers and critics like American film critic Roger Ebert who died in 2013. The best critics value the creative arts, they're honest, and they engage with their readers.

If you must respond or critique other people's work, look for the higher ground. If the work you're reviewing is badly written, write a *constructive* critique.

Explain the negatives and the positives of someone's work. Or provide a personal context that helps the reader understand if the work in question is worth their time or money.

If work is ill-judged, explain why without humiliating the person on the other end. If this isn't possible, either don't write anything or think of a time when you wrote something that failed.

The productive writer – hell any writer – has failed at some point. All of us should appreciate how difficult creation is.

TELL A LIE

"Fiction is the lie that tells the truth, after all." – Neil Gaiman

Do you enjoy telling lies? Do you have a little something on the side? Are you cheating?

If want your writing to sparkle, you should. New writers sometimes feel paralysed because they are not an expert in their chosen topic or because they just can't think of a good or original idea.

After browsing Amazon or the shelves in a local bookstore, it feels like everything has been said, the best books are already published, and there are no good ideas left.

You've still got time. You can still capture a great idea. You've just got to fake it until you find one.

More experienced writers sometimes say they want to publish more of their work and more frequently, but they often feel hamstrung by deadlines and other professional commitments.

If you're having these kinds of creative problems, you've got to tell yourself a little white lie.

You've got to cheat.

You've got to have a little something on the side.

USE WHITE LIES

When I first started researching *The Savvy Writer's Guide to Productivity*, I lied to myself.

Despite the many great productivity books in publication, I told myself I could find something original to say. I told myself I could offer up fresh insight into the world of productivity.

The sad reality was that when I started this book, I didn't have any good ideas or fresh insights, but then a funny thing happened.

This white lie gave me enough momentum to start writing my book.

When I started writing my book, I began to apply what I discovered about productivity to the art of writing. Through doing this, I discovered a different perspective on both topics. Telling a lie to myself or faking it helped me finish writing my book.

There's a scientific merit to telling yourself white lies.

According to Dr. Paul Seager, a British psychology lecturer, telling a white lie is healthy. He said,

> To keep society running smoothly, we need to tell white lies. If your partner comes home with their latest piece of artwork and says, 'What do you think of this?', it shows they want support. Whether you like it or not, you're going to say it's nice.

Like the supportive partner, why not support your own ideas and work?

Tell yourself you have something original to say even if you don't.

Later on, you'll find you do have something original to say after all. And if you're worried you've deluded yourself, you can always sense-check your ideas with the help of your editor, your writing group and anyone who reads early versions of your work.

FRESHEN UP YOUR WRITING

You can use a white lie to freshen up the way you write about an old topic.

For example, some social media experts claim Facebook is the perfect social media network for business people who want to talk to customers, or in our case writers who want to talk to their readers.

They cite Facebook's two billion users, ease of use and vast data points.

Let's assume these experts are wrong.

Let's tell a white lie to ourselves and say Facebook is the worst social media network for writers who want to talk to customers or readers.

Using this little lie, you write an article that calls on writers to abandon Facebook. Tell them to try Twitter, Instagram or Pinterest and explain how they can get started.

You can do this by writing about what happened when you took this approach. Or you could argue that writers should forget about social media and concentrate on building their email lists instead.

Then you could give your article a headline like:

"Forget Facebook: Your Email List is King"

Or

"What Facebook Isn't Telling You: 7 Shocking Secrets for Smart Writers"

I'm not suggesting you wilfully mislead your reader. Instead, the productive writer sometimes turns a fact on its head and attacks their project from a new and exciting angle.

They look for a way in that their peers haven't thought of. Don't believe me? Writers use this trick all the time.

How often have you clicked on articles with headlines like:

- Everything you know about X is wrong. Here's why
- The Shocking Truth about X
- The Great X Hoax
- 15 Things Your Favourite X Will Never Tell You

- What X Isn't Telling You about Y

These headline writers are using the power of a white lie to grab the attention of their readers. They are suggesting some deception because they know this will arouse curiosity within their readers. They know their readers will want to find out the truth.

HAVE A LITTLE SOMETHING ON THE SIDE

If you're bored with your current writing project, cheat. Walk out on what you're doing and start writing something that fires you up.

Having a writing project on the side can keep you motivated when your book, story or article is losing its lustre. This side project will give you a new chance to turn up in front of the blank page when you want to do anything but.

Many successful writers cheat. They use pseudonyms for their creative side projects.

Stephen King wrote several horror novels under the pen name Richard Bachman because he wanted to publish more than one novel per year. Between 1977 and 2007, King published seven novels using this pen name including *The Running Man* and *Thinner*.

King said he took on this side project because he didn't want to oversaturate his brand. He's not the only high-profile author to take on a side project or use a pen name.

In 2005, Irish literary author John Banville won the prestigious Man Booker prize for his novel *The Sea*. Then in 2006, Banville published the first of his popular series of crime novels under the pen name Benjamin Black.

Several years ago, I attended a talk by Banville in Kerry where he explained why he sometimes uses a pen name.

He told a room of over 100 people he wanted to write something that wasn't so serious and that he could write and publish faster. He wanted a side project he could turn to when he needed a break from writing literary fiction.

J.K. Rowling is another example of a writer with a side project. She has published three crime fiction novels under the pen name Robert Galbraith.

Rowling said,

> I had hoped to keep this secret a little longer, because being Robert Galbraith has been such a liberating experience. It has been wonderful to publish without hype or expectation, and pure pleasure to get feedback under a different name.

Having a side project gives writers opportunities to explore new writing styles and conventions that they typically wouldn't face othewise.

This form of deliberate writing practice will help you become a better writer. It will help you avoid the exhaustion and burnout that comes with focusing solely on a single niche or topic.

TAKE ON SIDE PROJECTS

If your day job involves writing reports, articles or copy for a website, you could write fiction in your free time.

If you spend most of your time writing blog posts, consider expanding one of these posts into a book or a personal essay. And if you've just written a novel, try your hand at a short story in a different genre.

Before you cheat, remember finishing one writing project is usually more productive than attempting two at once.

Now if you're confident you have the time and motivation to write and finish two projects, have a little something on the side.

I won't tell anyone if you won't.

SEEK OUT QUIET SPACES

"Weakness of attitude becomes weakness of character." – Albert Einstein

Are you able to work like Albert Einstein?

He researched and wrote some of his groundbreaking scientific papers while at home, surrounded by his two small children. Einstein could write and think anywhere.

"Even the loudest baby-crying didn't seem to disturb Father," said Hans Albert about his father. "He could go on with his work completely impervious to noise."

Most of us don't have Albert Einstein's genius, talent or focus.

Carving out a quiet space in your house or workplace will help you write and think. Going to this place at the same time every day simplifies sitting in front of the blank page and writing when you want to do anything but.

I have two small children, and it's difficult to write when they are nearby. Instead, I get up early in the morning to write before they rise. I go to a small room near the front of the house and write until they get up.

This quiet time enables me to focus for longer and write more frequently than my failed attempts to write in the evenings when my house is noisier and busier.

Even if you don't have children, eliminate as many distractions as you can from your writing room or office.

This means no televisions, game consoles, mobile devices and, in certain cases, internet connections. A window, heating and air conditioning are nice, but they're not necessary. A good desk, pens, paper and an idea are all you need.

In *On Writing* Stephen King says about having a quiet room in which to work:

> Like your bedroom, your writing room should be private, a place where you go to dream.
>
> Your schedule — in at about the same time every day, out when your thousand words are on paper or disk — exists in order to habituate yourself, to make yourself ready to dream just as you make yourself ready to sleep by going to bed at roughly the same time each night and following the same ritual as you go.

GO SOMEWHERE NEW TO WRITE

I'm contradicting myself, but a productive writer must be able to have two competing ideas in his or her head.

Nobody said our craft is easy.

Writing in a new environment will break your mind free from the shackles of comfortable thinking.

Going to a new location to write can get you out of a creative rut and help you overcome hurdles on the blank page. Sometimes, a new angle of attack will help you finish what you started.

At the end of the first *Star Wars* movie, Luke Skywalker flies into the trench of the Death Star.

At first, Luke follows the same approach as every other fighter pilot and for a few terrible moments it looks like he will be killed by Darth Vadar's minions.

Then Obi-Wan Kenobi tells Luke to "use the Force". So, Luke turns off all his instruments and attacks the Death Star. Using this new approach, Luke succeeds at something no pilot had done before: he destroys the Death Star.

This *Star Wars* example represents storytelling at its finest, and it shows taking a different angle of attack can help you overcome a problem.

In case you're not a Star Wars fan, I've dug up some scientific proof that supports writing in a new environment and coming at your project from an oblique angle.

A 2012 study in the *Journal of Consumer Research* found ambient or background noise positively affects creativity and increases the chances of innovative thinking. The authors Ravi Mehta, Rui Zhu and Amar Cheema wrote:

> Results from five experiments demonstrate that a moderate (70 dB) versus low (50 dB) level of ambient noise enhances performance on creative tasks and increases the buying likelihood of innovative products.

The key takeaway from this report is to find somewhere with a comfortable but not distracting level of background noise. So while a coffee shop might be appropriate, a playground full of children or a noisy bar won't help.

MANAGE YOUR ENVIRONMENT

If you work in an office, you could write at another desk or outside the office. I once worked in an office that had small rooms or booths that could fit only one person at a time.

These booths were designed for making private phones calls away from the noise of the office, but I used them to write website copy and blog posts for the company.

I accomplished more there because I was less likely to be interrupted by the phone, email or a noisy colleague.

Later, when I needed feedback about my copy, I went back to my desk and asked my colleagues for advice.

If your computer is the problem, leave it behind. Take a notepad and pen and go outside. The stimulation of a new environment combined with the openness of pen and paper might help you find your next sentence.

Pen and paper open the mind to new ideas in a way that the screen can't.

You could go to your local library and combine a morning's writing with an afternoon's research.

Several years ago I had to write a 20,000-word thesis. I found it easier to write my thesis in the college library even though I had a perfectly good office at home.

This wasn't just because the library had everything I needed for my research; after all, I could have always rented the books I needed and took them home with me.

It felt liberating to escape from where I normally worked, and I found finishing my work less stressful.

Sometimes writers need a quiet place and a routine to get more done, and sometimes they need to attack their project from a new angle. Or you could just use the Force.

Whatever works.

WRITE IN SHORT BURSTS

"I had to make sure I kept an eye on the real world." – Roddy Doyle

Short writing sessions are the best kind.

If you're struggling to develop a productive and regular writing habit, try writing every day for 15 or 30 minutes.

This is easier to achieve than sitting in front of the blank page for several hours every other Sunday. This goal is achievable as almost every aspiring writer has 15-30 minutes in their day of which they can use more wisely.

If writing isn't your full-time job, short writing sessions are perfect for busy days. You could write between meetings, on the bus or train, before you leave for work or late in the evening.

If you want to write in the evenings, you could skip a television programme, avoid the news or reduce the amount of time you spend on social media.

To get more from your next short writing session try:

- Creating a list of topics to include in your article

- Jotting down key words and ideas instead of full sentences
- Forgetting about perfect grammar, spelling or formatting
- Using pen and paper instead of a computer
- Setting yourself a challenge to produce as many words as possible within five, 10, 20 or 30 minutes
- Focusing on a single angle, section or paragraph
- Writing with the intention that you will fix or flesh out your ideas tomorrow

Short bursts of writing are like small wins. They accumulate over time until one day you look at your work and realise you've written 10,000 words.

LEARN FROM RODDY DOYLE

Irish author Roddy Doyle is famous for writing succinct and punchy sentences.

I attended a workshop about writing that he facilitated several years ago in Dublin. Roddy explained that he wrote his earlier books during pockets of free time in the evenings.

He also said the sentences in earlier books like *The Commitments* and *The Snapper* are short because he wrote them while raising small children.

Roddy just didn't have time for lengthy, three-hour writing sessions, and if he didn't write in short bursts he wouldn't have written at all.

Doyle has even criticised other, more wordy books for being too long and unapproachable. In New York in 2014, he said, "*Ulysses* could have done with a good editor. You know people are always putting *Ulysses* in the top 10 books ever written but I doubt that any of those people were really moved by it."

I have two small children, and I can empathise with writers who must work within short blocks of time. Sometimes, the prospect of several hours' work feels more intimidating than the job of sitting down for just 30 minutes to write.

I also like short writing sessions because I feel like I've accomplished something for the day, and that can be enough to build the momentum needed to continue a troublesome writing project.

T.S. Eliot is another noted writer who wrote around the demands of his day. He worked at Lloyds Bank in London for much of his adult life, and he wrote book reviews and poetry in his free time.

Eliot kept his job in the bank after he became an accomplished poet, as his job provided him with a stabilising routine that he valued as a writer.

More recently, Doyle is quoted as saying that he now spends up to nine hours a day writing. Still, his and Elliot's experiences show a writer can finish what they started, even if they have commitments.

All you need is determination.

ESTABLISH A DAILY WRITING PRACTICE

This time things were supposed to different.

Late last night, you promised yourself you'd write today. Then you woke half an hour late for work. You got stuck in traffic and spent the day dealing with an angry customer/client/boss.

Later that evening at home, your kids needed help with their homework, and you had chores to do around the house.

When things were finally quiet, you didn't have the desire or the energy to sit down and do your most important work. Or maybe you forgot about your promise altogether.

To write every day is a simple ambition, and it's one many new writers struggle to achieve.

If you're having trouble, don't give up.

I don't doubt your commitment or your talent; the only reason you don't write every day is because you haven't cultivated a daily writing practice.

In his book *The Power of Habit*, author and journalist Charles Duhigg provides a simple but effective framework for creating habits. He said that, "Habits are a three-step loop— the cue, the routine, and the reward."

SET UP YOUR CUES FOR WRITING

A habitual cue is something you see or do before you start writing. If you want to develop a writing practice, consider these cues.

Location: Know in advance where you're going to write. This could be your office, a quiet room in your house or a coffee shop.

Time: Commit to writing at the same time every morning or evening. Don't make any plans that break this commitment

Emotional state: If you're stressed after a difficult day in the office, you'll find it harder to write. Figure out when you're calm and use this time for your best work.

Other people: Writing is mostly a solitary activity, but the support or critique of other writers is useful too. You could join a local writing group to hold yourself to account.

Immediately preceding action: Whatever you do before you write should encourage your writing practice. If you're exhausted from spending the night at a party, you're not going to have much luck filling a blank page.

If you want to write every day, kill the cues for other habits that have nothing to do with your writing practice.

Do WHATEVER IT TAKES to keep your promise to protect your writing time and complete your most important work (see chapter 10).

STICK TO YOUR WRITING ROUTINE

Routines are powerful because we don't have to think about them. If you spend your day wondering how and where you're going to write, these questions will drain your mental willpower and make you more likely to say, "I'll do it tomorrow."

A good writing routine will help you overcome procrastination, become more productive and shape your creative life.

If you want to spend less time thinking about your routine:

Gather what you need in advance. If you spend precious writing time searching for a laptop charger, your notes or for a file on your computer, you're already behind.

Use the same tools each time. I use Scrivener for almost all of my writing projects; whatever you use, the tool should never get in the way your writing.

Make a choice to trigger your cue. If you want to write in the morning, set your alarm clock for an hour earlier. If you want to write at night, turn off your phone and television and disconnect from the grid.

When you're starting out, it helps to decide in advance what you're going to write about.

Are you writing a blog post, short story or a chapter for your novel? What topic are you going to address today?

This decision will help you avoid the horrible moment when you sit down in front of the blank page and wonder, "What now?"

PICK YOUR REWARD FOR WRITING

Writing is tough and even more so when you're starting out.

Go easier on yourself.

If you succeed in writing for 20 minutes, reward yourself with a treat like a cookie.

If you can chain three or four 20-minute sessions together, go for a walk, sleep or watch a favourite television programme. If you succeed in finishing an important writing project, buy something for yourself.

When I completed my thesis, I bought an expensive a entertainment system that I otherwise couldn't have justified. This reward system will trick your brain into associating pleasant activities with your writing practice.

Obviously it's not practical to eat a cookie (or to spend several hundred dollars) for every page. However, as you become more confident, you can extend the length and quality of your writing practice sessions and gradually remove these rewards.

If you succeed in cultivating a habit of writing every day, filling the blank page with your words and making small but determined progress towards a personal or professional goal will become a reward in itself.

MAKE A PLAN AND STICK TO IT

Once you've figured out your cue, routine and reward for writing, have a plan for putting this into action. Duhigg suggests people can make a plan for habit change by keeping a diary.

Here's an entry in my writing diary:

Where am I? At home
What time is it? 07.00
What's your emotional state? Tired but calm
Who else is around? Wife and two children (asleep)
What action preceded the urge to write? My alarm clock went off.

I also sometimes record what I wrote about during writing practice and what I'd like to focus on next. I don't write entries like this all the time, but they help me when I'm stuck.

Seeking out this kind of self-knowledge will help you identify your cue, routine and reward for writing.

WRITE EVERY DAY

Creating a habit of daily writing practice isn't as difficult as it first seems. It takes determination and self-knowledge, and these are all traits every writer should cultivate.

Commit to this craft, and you will naturally become more determined as you progress. Learn to enjoy seeing your work improve, and you will come to value writing practice.

Take Duhigg's tips for cultivating a habit, and you will gain the self-knowledge you need to write every day.

If you're about to apply this plan, I envy you.

One day, you'll stop typing, realise you've written 3,000 words in one session, and you'll wonder, "How the hell did I get here?"

Now, go write something.

TRACK YOUR PROGRESS

"After a few days you'll have a chain. Just keep at it and the chain will grow longer every day. You'll like seeing that chain, especially when you get a few weeks under your belt. Your only job next is to not break the chain." – Jerry Seinfeld

How many words did you write today? Did you accomplish more than yesterday? And while I'm asking questions, did you write more this week or last week?

Almost every personal productivity strategy involves tracking your progress on some level because what gets tracked gets managed and what gets managed gets done.

Let me explain.

Professional athletes track themselves or use self-quantification techniques to record their diet, how much they lifted, how far they ran and how many lengths they swam and so on.

They use this information to train harder and smarter and to perform better in events. Writers can use this approach to become more productive too.

You can track your time (which I'll cover in the next chapter) or your output.

KNOW THY WORD COUNT

Writers talk in terms of word counts rather than pages. They care less about page counts because the number of pages a piece takes depends on how the fonts, spacing and images are set and laid out. A page count is fluid, whereas a word count is less so.

I've met writers who use daily word counts for personal competitions; they make a point of breaking their personal bests just like the runner in search of a faster time.

I respect word counts because they can break a writer out of a creative funk and help you find something worthwhile to say. Knowing their average daily word counts can help writers achieve more.

For example, if your word count rises when you write in the morning and drops when you write at night, use this new information to cultivate an early morning writing habit.

Obsessing about word counts comes with a caveat. They are no indication of quality, as a particular type of writing demonstrates.

FLASH FICTION

Flash fiction is a special form of fiction writing for those who want to tell a story using as few words as possible. One of the most famous flash fiction stories (which might have been attributed to Hemingway) is just six words long.

For sale: baby shoes, never worn.

Behold the power of brevity.

This is why I also track how long I spend writing each week. While working on this book, I set myself the goal of writing 10,000 words a week or 10 hours a week.

I used a spreadsheet to do this.

Each Friday, I totalled up how long I spent writing and how many words I produced. This way, I could see how my book was progressing in terms of a word count and hours spent writing.

This self-quantification helped me during the editing process too because although I cared less about reaching a specific word count, I still needed a goal to write towards.

USE SMALL DAILY WINS

Getting the most from small daily wins means working on something a little every day and accomplishing your goals over time rather than trying to finish everything at the last minute.

Consider putting a euro or a dollar in a jar every day to save; it'll take you some time, but you'll get there in the end.

Now if you want to harness the power of small daily wins, I recommend a simple trick invented by a famous (and rich) comedian.

DON'T BREAK THE CHAIN

Comedian Jerry Seinfeld invented this popular productivity trick to motivate himself to write one new joke every day. It's built on the principle of increasing your creative output through small, daily wins.

I've used "Don't Break the Chain" to write feature articles, news stories, a thesis, academic papers, blog posts and this book.

If you procrastinate about sitting down in the front of the blank page regularly, this technique can help you get your ass into the chair. Here's how you do it:

1. Get a large calendar and pin it on the wall next to where you write.
2. Write for 5, 10, 20 or 30 minutes.
3. Using a felt pen, mark an X on your wall calendar through today's date.

4. As the week progresses, write each day and build up a series or a chain of Xs.
5. Now you have one job: Don't Break the Chain.

Don't Break the Chain makes you feel guilty about ruining a productive writing streak.

After all, nobody wants to a see a chain of Xs for every day spent writing, only to break this row because of procrastination.

I'm speaking from personal experience when I say it's encouraging and reassuring to see the black Xs line up one after the other as a project processes. Each little X feels like a small victory in the war against procrastination.

This strategy is useful at the beginning of larger, more difficult writing projects. It gets you into the habit of turning up each day and slowly progressing your project.

It will help you accept that, even if today's writing session doesn't go well, there is always tomorrow's session and the one after that. What's more important is that you turn up and put the work in.

There's just one problem with Seinfeld's technique. It's an unforgiving method because there's no allowances for going on holidays, falling sick or other personal commitments.

Hey, maybe Seinfeld doesn't get sick or take holidays?

Don't Break The Chain

Mon Tue Wed Thu Fri Sat Sun

BECOME A *Writer* TODAY

A sample Don't Break the Chain chart

EMPOWER YOURSELF

The productive writer knows how much she can accomplish on the blank page each day.

She uses the power of small daily wins to write consistently rather than leaving everything till the last minute. Sometimes, she uses little tricks to write more frequently, like *Don't Break the Chain*.

She knows it's better to turn up and do the work than to do nothing altogether.

MANAGE YOUR TIME

"It's really clear that the most precious resource we all have is time." – Steve Jobs

Do you know how to manage your time?

The productive writer does. He understands how long his writing projects will take, he takes charge of his other commitments so they don't impact his work, and he gets the most out of the time he has for writing each day.

This is something I learnt the hard way.

For several years, I worked as a technology freelance journalist, and I made money through writing commissions for magazines in Ireland.

Although some commissions paid by the hour, editors still expected me to complete them by a deadline. For others, I was paid only for getting the job done.

This kind of freelance work meant I earned less for my time if I spent twenty hours on a commission that should have taken only ten hours. I learned the hard way that earning a living from writing means finishing freelance projects on time.

USE YOUR CALENDAR

Some professional writers book periods for writing each morning and/or evening in their calendars.

They avoid making personal or professional commitments during these times because they consider themselves "committed" to their writing. They treat their craft like a job with professional obligations that must be honoured.

The calendar is the productive freelancer's best friend. It should be yours too. Get deadlines and appointments out of your head and into Google calendar, Outlook or some other tool you trust.

Then check your calendar each morning or evening. At the end of every working week, spend 20 minutes reviewing the entries in your calendar too.

Check what's coming up for the next seven days and how you spent your time over the previous seven days. While reviewing your calendar, ask questions like:

- What took up the most of my time last week?
- Are these activities likely to reoccur?
- What resources do I need to complete these activities faster?
- What do I need to prioritise next week?
- Am I likely to meet or miss my imminent deadlines?
- What's my most important task next week?

MANAGE AN EDITORIAL CALENDAR

Editorial calendars are another great way of managing your time, particularly if you work with other writers or if you are a blogger.

The editors of professional media organisations use editorial calendars to plan writing projects in advance and to allow teams to juggle projects.

You can use an editorial calendar to map articles, stories, blog posts or chapters that you'd like to write over the next few months.

This will help you gauge if you're progressing towards your writing goals.

You can keep an editorial calendar in a notebook, spreadsheet, file on your computer or on a digital calendar. Whatever your tool of choice, an editorial calendar should identify some or all of the below issues:

- The topic
- The deadline
- The resources required
- The state of the project i.e., first draft, second draft, etc.
- The publication date
- The priority of the writing project
- The media outlet or platform e.g., blog post, newsletter, social media

MAKE FRIENDS WITH DEADLINES

Deadlines are the productive writer's best friend; don't let anyone tell you otherwise.

Several years ago, I attended a workshop by Irish short story writer Claire Keegan. She explained that when she was starting off as a fiction writer, she used submission deadlines for short story competitions as something to work towards.

"Deadlines are not to be feared," she said. "They add a sense of urgency to our work."

Claire's point struck a chord with me, perhaps because I wasn't long out of college. Some writers (or students) leave writing projects till the last minute.

When the deadline looms, they stay up late the night before smoking, drinking coffee and working hard on their projects. If you went to college, you're probably familiar with this last-minute approach.

Professional writers like Keegan use deadlines to write more often. Amateur writers skip right past deadlines and tell editors their articles or stories will be ready when they're finished.

If you're good, you can get away with telling your editor to wait. For the rest of us mere mortals, staying up late the night before a deadline might accomplish the task, but it's not a great way to work or write.

In the past, I missed deadlines because I was overworked, sick, unfocused and disorganised.

My editors made allowances when I was overworked, understood when I sick, chastised me when I was unfocused and gave their next commission to someone else when I was disorganised.

If you're going to write for someone else, accept deadlines as part of your life. Respect them. Put them in your calendar and be honest about your ability to hit them.

Deadlines give productive writers a goal or endpoint to write towards. They force us to make decisions and *commit*. A looming deadline can cause stress and anxiety, but this kind of tension is natural when it comes to hard work.

MEET YOUR WRITING DEADLINES

If you're having trouble meeting deadlines try the following tactics:

- Keep a list of your projects, assign a deadline to each project and review this list each week
- Break projects into mini-projects with supporting deadlines
- Focus on the first or next action you need to take to advance a project
- Make more time for projects that are causing stress
- Diary your deadlines in a trusted system
- Communicate your deadlines to colleagues
- Abandon projects that won't help you achieve your goals in favour of higher-value projects
- Examine why you missed deadlines in the past
- Use existing deadlines as a reason for saying no to new projects

These days, I set myself artificial or soft deadlines for my writing projects. This helps me focus on what I'm writing, and it also gives me time to review and polish my work before publishing it.

Even if this approach doesn't work for you, ask yourself why you missed deadlines in the past and how you're going to solve this problem.

As a productive professional writer, you must finish your writing projects on time.

Almost every writer will tell you that finishing one project before a deadline makes it easier to finish the next one on time.

CONTROL SOCIAL MEDIA

To some people this is sacrilege, but unless social media is your business, it's a side attraction.

You can use social media to promote your work, engage with readers and research your market. However, if you're doing this at the expense of writing and finishing what you are working on, then you are wasting valuable time.

Spend your time writing, and afterwards approach social media as a way of amplifying existing content and a free market research tool.

GET PAID

Freelance journalists learn how to write fast. They need to eat, sleep and work on their next commission.

When I received my first 3,000-word commission from a national newspaper, I spent an entire week working on it. I carried out multiple long interviews and spent hours researching the topic online and offline.

I probably shouldn't be telling you this, but much of my research and interviews were unnecessary. I had to cut this extra work from the piece, and I still struggled to finish the article on time.

Later that month I was paid for the article itself and not how long I spent on it, which meant I'd put in a lot of unnecessary extra work.

I wasn't always paid per commission when I worked as a journalist. Several editors paid me in terms of hours spent on a writing project and not for how many words I wrote. These editors provided me with guidelines about how long a commission should take. In other words, I couldn't bill an editor for 20 hours of work for a 300-word article.

Getting paid by the hour meant I had to complete writing projects within a set time period. If I spent too long on a commission, I was effectively paid less per hour.

If I completed a project too quickly, it was either of poor quality (in which case my editor was quick to let me know) or I was paid less money.

So I started tracking how long I spent on each commission using a timer on my computer and a spreadsheet. This information simplified invoicing clients too.

It also helped me figure out which kinds of commissions were easy to complete, which were more difficult and how I could become a more productive writer. I also used this information to set prices for other clients and to decide which commissions to accept and reject.

Figuring out how long to spend on a commission is a difficult balancing act. Give yourself some breathing room before you tell your editor how long you need. If you think a commission will take six hours to complete, tell your editor it will take seven or eight hours.

This way, if there's an unforeseen circumstance, such as an interviewee cancelling at last minute, you will have extra time to complete your project. And if the commission takes only six hours, you can please your editor by under-promising and over-delivering.

Tracking your writing might seem tedious at first, but it will help you figure out which projects are taking longer than others, how you can complete these projects quicker and if you should accept or reject certain projects in the future.

This process will also save you time submitting invoices at the end of the month, and it will give you confidence to negotiate a better rate from an editor or client.

SPEND YOUR REWARD

If you're having trouble managing how you spend your time on projects, review your calendar and commitments, do your most important work when you're productive, and track what's working and what's causing you problems.

Succeed, and you will become a productive writer who has time to find new commissions or take a break.

Fail to manage your time effectively and your work will either spill into your personal life or dry up.

Remember, the productive writer who manages her time effectively also gives herself permission to take a break. The productive writer knows when she needs to eat, sleep and recharge.

Most importantly, she knows when to stop.

FOCUS ON YOUR WORK

"I t does not matter how slowly you go as long as you do not stop."
– Confucius

Flow is a productive mental state whereby you are entirely focused on the task at hand. If you've ever exercised intensively or lost yourself to a piece of music, you've experienced flow.

If you've ever started writing and lost track of the passage of time, you've experienced flow. It's a mental state you must seek if you want to become a more productive and accomplished writer.

An ability to focus on the task at hand is an important skill to cultivate.

The problem is technology wants us to do anything but. Phones, emails, notifications, feeds, applications and updates all pull on our attention throughout the day.

According to a report by Carnegie Mellon University published in the *New York Times*, a typical office worker is interrupted every 11 minutes. The researchers found it can take 21 minutes to refocus on a task, once interrupted.

This finding suggests it's almost impossible for the average office worker to experience flow because of these day-to-day interruptions.

Writing is not meant to be multi-tasked with answering email, checking social media and attending to the 1,001 other demands.

If you approach your craft with a start-stop-start mind-set, you will never achieve the kind of flow writers need to reach the end.

The belief that multi-tasking helps people get more done faster is another pernicious myth. It taxes your brain and complicates finishing your writing project.

MIT neuroscientist Earl Miller told NPR in 2008, "Switching from task to task, you think that you're actually paying attention to everything around you at the same time. But you're not."

A true writer can't pay attention to everything around them at the same time.

How can you write one true sentence when you're checking your friend's holiday photos on Facebook?

How can you craft a perfect call-to-action for your copy when you're on the phone with a colleague?

How can you massage a paragraph into something readable when you're clicking from one blog post or website to another searching for something, *anything* that backs up your argument?

Commit yourself entirely to writing, and then when you're finished for the day, commit to whatever else is important.

HOW TO MAINTAIN FOCUS AND FLOW

Did you ever sit down to write and almost immediately think of something you forgot to look up?

When was the last time you put down your writing so you could research a new angle for your work?

Do you sometimes stop typing and pick up a book to check a fact or a quote?

I get it.

Research forms the backbone of many successful writing projects.

Academic writers, journalists, bloggers and writers interview experts, read books, search for topics online and go through the archives of their libraries.

Many writers enjoy research because they get to spend time talking to people and learning about topics in their area of interest. They enjoy it because writers like reading and finding out new things.

Research is an altogether different skill from writing. It involves moving from one question to the next, following a thread or searching for a specific piece of information.

Writing, on the other hand, means working deliberately on one sentence or idea for an extended period without giving up.

These two activities are almost impossible to undertake simultaneously. You can't jump from one topic to the next and concentrate entirely on a sentence or an idea.

Next time you're working and you want to check an important fact or how a word is spelt, DON'T STOP WRITING.

If you do, you will break your flow of concentration and possibly disappear down a rabbit hole of meaningless Google searches and needless research.

Instead, **annotate** the section of the document you are writing with an asterisk, an X or with your writing programme's annotation tool. When you've hit your target word count for the day, address these annotations.

Commit yourself entirely to writing and entirely to research, just not at the same time. When I work this way, I'm always amazed by how a seemingly important question didn't need to be answered after all.

Similarly, **keeping a notepad and pen at your desk** will help you concentrate on what you're writing.

Use this notepad to record ideas or thoughts that come to mind. Record things you want to look up on the internet, people you want to call and food you have to buy. If a colleague drops by your desk with a request, record their request and then keep writing.

Unless the task or request is urgent, like a hungry child or an iron still plugged in, don't get up and do it. Later, when you're finished writing, you can spend time attending to the tasks on your notepad.

The purpose of annotating your work and using a notepad is to help you maintain a sense of flow.

This way, you can concentrate on your work. Later, you can concentrate on whatever else you want to do.

TIPS FOR FOCUSING ON YOUR WRITING

- Don a pair of noise-cancelling headphones and listen to white noise on repeat (look for albums of rainfall by Joe Baker on Spotify).
- Use a timer and work on one thing until the buzzer sounds.
- Disconnect from the internet while you write.
- Remove all distractions from where you write e.g. a television, games on your computer etc.
- Set aside time after your writing for doing something unproductive guilt-free like checking your Facebook feed.
- Leave your phone in a different room on silent.

MAINTAIN FOCUS

The productive writer knows it's difficult to get into the mindset needed to finish a project. He knows multitasking is a dangerous myth that stands in the way of his word count or writing milestone.

He knows his research, editing, writing, reading and so on are all different activities, and he doesn't try to do them all at once. Instead, he brings a single-minded focus to the blank page, and this is how he finishes writing what he started.

LET YOUR WRITING FERMENT

"The truth will set you free. But not until it is finished with you." – David Foster Wallace

Do you enjoy the taste of wine?

The best-tasting vintages are left to ferment for weeks, months or years in a cool, dark place before being decanted into bottles.

Winemakers and drinkers know the product becomes better with age. Writing is a little like making fine wine.

You must gather ingredients, equipment and materials. Both professions demand artistry, hard-work and craft.

Inevitably, it pays to wait for something good.

When you've worked on a difficult writing project at length, it's hard to know what to remove and what to keep.

When you're writing with flavour, should you cut a chapter or expand a key point? Should you insert more research or write a personal story?

These creative problems can become so exhausting you just want your writing project to end.

These kinds of creative problems are also natural. The more you write, the more comfortable you'll become with such challenges.

DON'T PRESS PUBLISH IMMEDIATELY

Don't publish a piece of writing immediately after you've reached the end.

It'll be too raw and bitter for public consumption. Every writer needs a dark place for their work to ferment.

Leave your early drafts in a drawer and rest, write something else, and forget about what's fermenting. Later, take this writing out into daylight and taste it. Approach it with an editing pen and a set of fresh eyes.

Thanks to this time away from your work, you will discover flaws and gaps you overlooked. You'll be able to address your problems with renewed vigour. You'll be able to write with flavour.

Unlike before, this rewrite will feel more natural. The solutions you searched for last time round will be within your reach.

When you finally publish your writing, your readers will enjoy the taste more, because you gave the flavour time to develop.

DECIDE HOW LONG TO WAIT

The time a piece of writing belongs in a drawer depends on how long it is, who it's for and your other professional commitments.

I let blog posts rest a day or two before publishing them. It's easier and faster to edit or change a blog post. If it's a longer article, I wait a week or more before sending it to an editor.

This is because I've professional relationships with editors who expect a certain standard of work.

I've also put my short stories and book chapters in a drawer for several months until I've almost forgotten what they're about.

This gives me time to cast a fresh eye over my work, remove clichés (there's one), ttypos (there's another) and fix other structural problems.

These different fermentation periods give me the distance I need to improve my writing.

I embrace this time away, because when I finally take my writing from the drawer, I'm fresh enough to expand, clarify or condense my points and sentences. I have the energy to back up my arguments with additional research.

Thanks to the drawer, I can face that much needed, and often dreaded rewrite with a thirst to fix what's broken. The drawer is a good place to let your writing ferment, but as a professional writer, you won't always be able to rely on this luxury.

LEARN FROM PROFESSIONAL WRITERS

Professional writers can't always put a piece of writing into a drawer and let it sit for weeks at a time. They have to work to deadlines imposed by editors, contracts, publications and even their readers. This is why professional writers don't work alone.

They invariably have the support of editors, who can catch these errors and mistakes. Supportive editors will show the writer how to avoid these kinds of errors in future.

Becoming a professional writer means enlisting an editor who serves as your ally in the war against perfectionism.

BEHOLD THE MYTH OF PERFECTIONISM

Writing with flavour doesn't mean waiting for the day when it's finally perfect. Even wine becomes undrinkable if it's left to ferment too long.

Remember, the perfect creative work doesn't exist.

A vast chasm exists between your ideas and how your words gather on the page. This chasm makes many writers and creative people feel squeamish. The philosopher, Nietzsche said, "And if thou gaze long into an abyss, the abyss will also gaze into thee."

When I see my words arranged on the page, I remember everything has already been said and in more ways than I can ever imagine.

The gaze of all those more talented and creative writers from times past gazes back at me. And I want to jump.

So I turn away.

And I press publish.

BEWARE OF PERFECTIONISM

If you insist on endlessly polishing and rewriting your work, you will delay your writing projects indefinitely.

This procrastination will frustrate colleagues, clients and readers (yes, your readers!), who are waiting for you to finish your work.

I hate to break it to you, but perfectionism is an excuse for putting off publishing your work. These kinds of excuses are indulgent.

Eventually, they turn the productive writer into a miserable, procrastinating failure.

The good news is, you can overcome perfectionism today.

CONQUER YOUR DEMONS

In a 1996 interview with radio station WYNC, American essayist and author David Foster Wallace explained the dangers of perfectionism:

> You know, the whole thing about perfectionism. The perfectionism is very dangerous, because of course if your fidelity to perfectionism is too high, you never do anything.
>
> Because doing anything results in– It's actually kind of tragic because it means you sacrifice how gorgeous and perfect it is in your head for what it really is.

I try to remember Wallace's advice when I approach the end of a writing project. I set publication dates for my writing, do my best to stick to them and occasionally have a little fun with the written word.

All I can do is keep practicing, falling forwards and using these painful writing lessons to improve my work.

If you're struggling to expose the myth of perfectionism in your writing, don't endlessly work and rework your writing alone.

So, whom can you ask for help?

An editor, trusted friend, member of your writing group or an honest family member all can help. The only caveat is this person must be able to offer you candid feedback you will act on.

Don't wait years to publish your writing.

Accept doubt as part of the process and understand you must share your writing with the world. Put it in the drawer and let your writing develop. Then take it out and release your work into the world.

Let them love it or hate it and all its ugly imperfections.

ASK FOR HELP

"We are all here on earth to help others; what on earth the others are here for I don't know." – W.H. Auden

There's no shame in it.

Writing might be a solitary craft, but if you're going to succeed with your writing, help is key.

You could look for a more experienced writer to act as your mentor or join a local writing critique group.

You might need to hire a designer to create a cover for your ebook or images for your website. Or you could hire someone to market and publicise your work or your business.

You can learn how to do all of these things yourself, but consider where your time is better spent: learning a skill secondary to your craft or writing?

Don't be all things when one is enough. The secret to becoming a more productive writer is to leverage your strengths and offset your weaknesses.

- Can you find an assistant for your research?

- Can an editor help you organise your work?
- Should you a hire a designer to create your book cover so you can concentrate on writing?
- Do you need a developer to manage the technical parts of your website?

I paid a designer to create a cover for this book. I could have designed the cover myself, but the results wouldn't have been as professional, and my time is better spent writing.

Similarly, I know a successful blogger who writes outlines for his posts. He gives these outlines to an editor to complete and format in WordPress. The blogger says writing like this enables him to finish up to eight blog posts per week.

The longer you work on a piece, the harder it is to see your mistakes and figure out if you have gone astray. What's interesting to you might not be interesting to the reader.

If you haven't talked to any readers, then how can you know?

Friends and family, if they will be honest with you, are a good start. They can help proofread your work and offer advice on how to improve. Or you could ask colleagues to check if your copy is getting the job done.

If your friends or colleagues are any good, they'll come back with suggestions for words and ideas you can remove, include or rework. They'll probably pick up a few typos that you missed too.

Don't expose your unedited writing in all its ugliness to the world. Get help now before it's too late.

VALUE FEEDBACK

If you write, you must seek out feedback.

I was a member of a creative writing and non-fiction writing group in Dublin for several years.

They hated almost everything I wrote.

These more accomplished writers told me how I could improve my work. So I listened.

Other more accomplished writers expose you to new kinds of writing and new ways of looking at your work. They encourage and push you to write beyond anything you've attempted before.

You could join a writing group in your community or a critique group online. Non-fiction writers can join numerous professional online writing courses and communities too.

Not every writer needs to join a writing critique group, however.

I interviewed famous Irish novelist Jennifer Johnston several years ago. Since 1972, she has published more than 20 books and numerous plays. Johnston told me she has little time for creative writing groups.

"They take you away from your work," she said. "I didn't need them."

Johnston didn't need a writing group, but she is an exception. Her father Denis was a famous playwright. He provided his daughter with the feedback she needed to improve.

Unless you're Johnston or you've someone like Denis who can review your work, joining a writing group is beneficial. Your participation encourages accountability, and it opens you up to criticism. You also get to spend time in the company of other writers and learn from their experiences.

Not everything these people have to say will be correct or of value, just like not everything you write will succeed or have merit.

Finding this out is half the fun.

FIND YOUR MENTOR

Do you have a mentor for your writing?

Finding a mentor who knows more about writing than you do is a shortcut to better prose. I've met several people who helped me improve my writing.

A tutor in university explained how to write for an academic audience. The instructor of a creative writing showed the students and me how to improve our prose and kill our darlings.

An English teacher taught me how to bend any topic towards an idea that I wanted to write about. And an editor I didn't get along with demonstrated how to write clearly and without obvious bias.

Some of these people knew they were mentoring me; some of them didn't.

I never met one of my mentors. His name was John Cheever, and he died in 1982, one year after I was born.

So, how can John Cheever be my mentor?

Several years ago, I considered abandoning writing altogether. My freelance contracts had dried up, I'd received multiple rejection letters from various competitions and editors, and my writing was rotting in my drawer.

Then I discovered *The Journals of John Cheever*. I'd read some of Cheever's short stories before, but his journals are a different beast entirely.

In his journals, Cheever wrote about his personal demons and his journey towards becoming an accomplished writer. Through reading his works, I rediscovered my passion for writing, and I found a reason to keep going.

Even today, when I become disillusioned with writing, I think of Cheever's mantra that a "good page of prose remains invincible".

I think of him writing day after day through a difficult marriage, alcoholism, depression, being a parent, happiness and success.

No matter what, Cheever wrote.

MODEL YOUR MENTORS

Another great way to get the most from your mentor or an expert you admire deeply is to apply as many of their practices as possible. This process is called **modelling**, and it will help you achieve mastery faster.

In his book *Mastery*, Robert Greene explains how this process works:

> The key then to attaining this higher level of intelligence is to make our years of study qualitatively rich. We don't simply absorb

information - we internalise it and make it our own by finding some way to put this knowledge to practical use.

By modelling your creative betters, you can avoid many of the mistakes your mentors made on their way to success and save time because they will have done the hard work of sifting through good and bad information for you.

No, I'm not advocating you steal your mentor's work. Instead, figure out a way to get close to your creative hero and learn from them ethically.

Today, many creators and writers offer online courses and coaching classes. When you sign up, they will teach you what they know. If this isn't possible, read as much of their work as you can get your hands on.

Whatever your approach, absorb and implement as many lessons as you can from your mentor(s).

To avoid becoming overwhelmed, focus on learning only from one or two mentors at a time. Then when you've learnt or applied as many of their lessons as you can, find your next mentor.

HANDLE CRITICISM LIKE A PRO

The first time I wrote an article for a newspaper my editor hated it. He told me he wasn't going to publish my work.

"If you don't improve your writing, I'm going to fire you," he said.

I went into the bathroom and thought about quitting. What kind of person was I? Was I lazy and incompetent? Did I deserve to be fired?

Until this point, everybody had told me I could write. My identity was intimately connected with the idea of being a writer and if an accomplished writer like my editor hated my work, then who was I?

The first time I submitted a short story to a creative writing group, the instructor of the group announced to the class that my story reminded him of a hammy B-movie.

"You need to spend more time writing something we can believe in," he said.

I went home and tore up the next short story I was working on. What was the point in wasting so much time working on a story only for another person to hate it?

Perhaps my nights were better spent watching television.

It took time, but I accepted their criticisms. They were right. My article was terrible and my short stories were stuffed with clichés. I vowed to try harder. I promised myself I'd improve.

Now I seek criticisms out. Praise is useful but negative feedback is more valuable. It gives the productive writer a chance to expose a fault in their craft and fix it.

Some criticism might be constructive, and some of it won't help at all. But your fiercest critics could become your biggest enablers for better writing.

My favourite story of a writer embracing criticism involves social media guru and business author Gary Vaynerchuk. He read each of the one-star and two-star reviews of his book *Crush It* on Amazon – always a disconcerting experience for an author – and replied to them.

One of Vaynerchuk's comments said,

Frank. I am so so sorry I under delivered for you, I hope to meet u and spend 15 minutes apologizing and answering any questions u may have, I guess I needed more details in there for u, I am so sorry.

A critical reviewer Vaynerchuk replied too was impressed. He wrote,

Gary, I still don't agree with you, but I so appreciate the time you took to reach out to me and understand where I was coming from.

The next time you finish what you're working on, seek out criticism. Ask your friends, your family and your enemies to tell you what they love and hate about your work. Like Vaynerchuk, don't let the bad reviews get you down.

Use feedback to become a better, stronger, more accomplished writer.

LEARN WHEN TO EDIT

"If it sounds like writing, I rewrite it." – Elmore Leonard

You spent hours working on your article or book chapter.

You gathered up fresh ideas, researched your arguments meticulously, and put hours in in the chair. The work paid off, too.

You got the words out of your head and onto the blank page and now, finally, you've finished writing your first draft.

Or have you?

When you read through your draft, something terrible happens.

You know deep down it's not very good. Those ideas you thought were great don't quite hold up, there are gaps in the research and the writing.

Ugh.

Now, you're unsure what to do, and a deadline is looming like a guillotine.

How are you going to take this messy first draft and turn it into something you can serve up to your readers?

If you've ever struggled with these types of problems, you are not alone.

SEPARATE WRITING AND EDITING

Writing is the process of getting ideas out of your head and onto the blank page, telling stories and communicating through the written word.

Editing is the process of reviewing, arranging and polishing your writing, so readers understand and enjoy what you're saying.

Whether you write fiction or non-fiction, they are two distinct activities demanding different skillsets.

The secret to productive writing is editing your work after you finish writing a messy first draft. To do both at once is to indulge in the myth of multitasking (see chapter 28).

To edit productively, you must be able to zoom out from your writing and consider it as a whole.

This just isn't possible if you're still trying to hit a word count or produce an early draft.

So when you finish a draft, let it in your computer or on your desk for a day or two, or at least long enough so the writing doesn't feel so fresh (see chapter 29).

For this reason, many successful authors write early drafts during the morning and edit later drafts during the afternoon, taking care to space out both activities. Or they hire an editor to prepare their work for publication.

FOCUS ON EDITING

Editing your first draft is more important than obsessing about finding the right tools.

So, by all means use the "Track Changes" feature in Word or Google Docs if they work for you.

Your editing tool of choice should enable you to restore earlier drafts of your article in case your changes don't work.

That said, while employed as a print journalist, I learned several self-editing tricks.

My colleagues often printed out at least one draft of their articles.

Then, they turned their computer screens off and read through this draft, marking up the pages with a red pen.

I asked my editor, "Why?" and he said:

"Paper is less distracting than a computer, and it forces you to concentrate on the flow of your ideas."

Now, before you print out your draft, change the font of your writing to a monospace font like Courier and the line spacing to double. This way, your eye will spot issues easily.

This will give you space to write your edits with red pen in between sentences and along the margins.

Then, all you need is some paper and a quiet place to work.

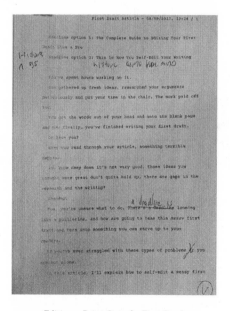

Editing a Print Out of a First Draft

KEEP YOUR CUTOFFS

Where do your unpublished blog posts and articles, leftover research and abandoned chapters go?

The productive writer keeps them in a digital or paper file where he or she can refer to them. These abandoned ideas might not belong in the writer's current writing project, but he or she will find a future opportunity to turn cutoffs into rounded, usable ideas.

Relying on your cutoffs isn't a shortcut, and it's not cheating. Let no one tell you otherwise.

If a cook can reuse ingredients for another meal and a technician can reuse computer parts, why can't a writer return to his or her abandoned ideas?

Writers shouldn't have to reinvent themselves every time they are presented with a new writing project. If we did that, we wouldn't have time to finish anything.

Not everything you discard will be of merit, but why take the chance of letting a semi-formed idea disappear into the ether?

If you researched a topic only to find you couldn't use what you found, you could always draw on this research for your next project.

Or if you've argued a point only to edit it out entirely, you can use parts of your argument in a future article, blog post or chapter.

Keeping your cuttings is one way to overcome writer's block and advance troublesome projects because instead of staring at a blank page, you can peruse your old musings.

Sometimes I take an abandoned idea and use it as a jumping-off point, or a writing prompt, for something new (see chapter 3).

I've written dozens of blog posts that were never published, and I've interviewed many people only to set aside large portions of what they had to say.

In both cases, I've used extracts from my abandoned blog posts and interview transcripts for new writing projects.

Even if you never use your cutoffs, they don't represent wasted time or energy.

Instead, consider them markers on the path towards a more polished and coherent work. For a productive writer, nothing is ever lost or wasted.

EDIT AND THEN EDIT SOME MORE

So what should you do if you've spent hours editing a second or third draft, but it's not quite right?

There's a good chance you've reached the point of diminishing returns.

At this stage, getting help is the only way you'll improve your draft.

Consider the curious case of author and entrepreneur James Altucher.

He presented a version of a near-final manuscript of his 2013 book *Choose Yourself* to marketer, editor and writer Ryan Holiday.

Holiday wanted Ryan to help him with an aggressive marketing plan to promote *Choose Yourself*.

Instead, Ryan insisted on sixteen more rounds of edits over the following six months including a restructuring of the book, the removal of four chapters, and the addition of two more.

In the end, *Choose Yourself* sold over 600,000 copies and USA Today called it one of the twelve best business books of all time.

GET HELP

Books require more rounds of editing than articles. So if you want your writing to succeed, it pays to enlist the help of your peers.

In his 2017 book *Perennial Seller: The Art of Making and Marketing Work that Lasts,* Ryan Holiday explained,

> "Nobody creates flawless first drafts. And nobody creates better second drafts without the intervention of someone else. Nobody."

Send your later drafts to your editor for critical feedback and explain where you're stuck.

He or she may be able to give you a fresh angle or point out what to remove or expand on.

You can also use professional editorial services to improve your work. At the back of this book, I've included some resources for finding an editor.

Alternatively, give the draft to an early reader or close family member and ask them to be honest about what works and doesn't work.

Learning how and when to edit, like cooking, takes practice. So put your time in, and your readers will keep coming back for more.

GET OVER YOUR FAILURES

"Whenever a thing is done for the first time, it releases a little demon." – Emily Dickinson

If you want to become a more productive writer, accept you're going to fail time and again.

I've written dozens of blog posts and articles nobody read. Editors rejected ideas I pitched. I've published articles only to find they contained typos or even factual errors. I've also spent hours preparing stories and articles for competitions only to find they weren't even long-listed.

Each one of these failures hurt and, at times, questioned what I was doing.

However, my collection of failures gave me the opportunity to improve my writing. On the occasions when I passed up these opportunities, I met with the same failures weeks or months later.

Failing is part of the writing process. This little demon is a sign that you turned up and tried. Just ask Cheever, Melville or Dickinson.

LEARN FROM OTHERS

Some writers and artists say they can't bear to look at their old work, and once they're done with something, they never want to see it again.

Before he died, Cheever told the *Paris Review* he felt a "sense of clinical fatigue" after finishing a novel.

Despite the success of his short stories, he described having little time for many of them after they were published.

"I love them, but I can't read them; in many cases, I wouldn't love them any longer if I did," he said in 1969.

Hundreds of writers became successful only after their death.

For example, many critics cite *Moby-Dick* as one of the greatest works of all time, but Herman Melville didn't live to enjoy the book's acclaim.

Emily Dickinson struggled for much of her life to find anyone who would print her work. She famously received this rejection letter from a publisher:

> Your poems are quite as remarkable for defects as for beauties and are generally devoid of true poetical qualities.

Rejection and failure hurt, but they didn't stop these writers and they shouldn't stop you.

LEAVE YOUR DEMONS BEHIND

As I progressed from one media organisation to the next, I built a portfolio of articles, news stories and clippings that I was proud of. I cut out these clippings out and stored them carefully in an expensive leather case.

I told myself this portfolio was for potential employers. It was my insurance policy against future unemployment, and I believed that every accomplished journalist kept these kinds of portfolios.

Witness my exercise in vanity.

By keeping this portfolio, I was holding onto past successes. I was telling myself I didn't need to move forward as a writer because "Look! I've already been published in a national newspaper. Surely I'm good enough."

I wasn't good enough. Many of my articles were badly written or poorly researched. Part of me knew this, but in keeping my portfolio I was holding onto failures.

My clippings reminded me of missed opportunities. I thought of promising jobs that came to an abrupt end and of stories that felt important at the time but meant nothing weeks or months later. I couldn't live like that. Something had to change.

One Saturday morning, I gathered old boxes, broken appliances, empty paint cans and my portfolio. I put them in the car, and I drove to the dump. I threw everything into the skips.

Keeping this portfolio was holding me back from seeing new opportunities, such as a college course I wanted to take and later a blog that I wanted to start.

After throwing away my old clippings and articles, I felt empty, but like an empty vessel, I was ready for something new.

I was able to go home and consider how I was going to make a living from writing without trying to become a successful journalist. I was able to fall forwards.

REFRAME YOUR SETBACKS

Like the runner who falls down while training, a writer must get back up again after failing.

The only other option is stopping altogether, and that's not a realistic choice for anyone who is passionate about the written word.

So write about your failures and how they've shaped who you are. Explain how your setbacks helped you become the person you are today. Describe how you overcame some failures and learnt to live with others.

I'm not advocating wallowing in failure. Instead, reframe your setbacks as learning experiences.

Ask yourself:

- Do your older articles (the ones you're proud of) add value to your writing career today?
- Are you holding onto the past?
- Can you explore writing in a new genre?
- Could a writing teacher or coach help you get over this plateau?
- What does success look like in a month, a year or five years?
- Who has already accomplished what you want to do?

Perhaps you lack the skills to achieve what you want with your writing. Or maybe you need to spend more time building relationships with your readers or editors. Or you could simply need to put more time into improving the quality of your work.

For the first problem, improve by taking a class, online or otherwise. For the second, study marketing and spend time getting to know who you're writing for (you could speak to a reader over Skype for 30-minutes). For final, commit to spending twice as long on your next piece of writing.

Remember, you're better off trying and failing, falling forwards and learning what you can from painful experiences than sitting on the couch and doing nothing.

FINISH WHAT YOU STARTED

"Most people have dozens of things that they need to do to make progress on many fronts, but they don't yet know what they are." – David Allen

When was the last time you took 30 minutes out from your week to review how your writing is going?

Would you like to see how your writing is progressing?

How can you figure out what you need to write next and what you should stop working on?

A simple strategy can help you answer these questions and gain some control over your writing – the weekly review.

I learnt about the weekly review several years ago from David Allen, author of *Getting Things Done*.

It's a strategy for business people and professionals to take charge of their lives. This strategy is also useful for writers who want to accomplish more faster.

Since putting this strategy into practice, I've found it to be a great way of taking charge of my writing and other areas of my life.

The weekly review gives me confidence that I'm working on the right things at the right time, and it helps me shine a light on neglected parts of my creative or writing life.

The good news is implementing a weekly review, and this final strategy doesn't take a lot of time or extra work.

HOLD A WEEKLY REVIEW

At the end of the week, put aside 30 to 60 minutes for your review. If it's helpful, book this time in your calendar as a recurring appointment and make a commitment to keep it.

Use this time to stop writing, zoom out and gain some perspective on your work.

The goal of your weekly review is to figure out what you accomplished over the past few days, what you overlooked and what you need to do or write next.

During your review, be honest with yourself. Ask and answer questions like:

- What did I accomplish or write this week?
- What went well/didn't go well?
- What are my most important task(s) for next week?
- What was my word count for the week?
- How many hours did I spend writing?
- How many ideas did I generate?
- How did I market my writing or my work?
- What events or deadlines are in my calendar for the previous/next seven days that I need to act on?
- What have I been putting off?
- What should I stop doing or say no to?

Remember, this review is not the time for working on your projects or writing.

Use your weekly review to clarify your priorities and make plans for future writing projects. This might mean adding missing activities or upcoming deadlines to your calendar or deciding if you need to renegotiate commitments with your editor or clients.

If you use a To Do list, this is the time to update it with new items and remove old items you have no intention of completing.

You can ask and answer these questions in a journal if you like. When you've answered these questions and you're clear about what you need to do next, you'll be able to hit the blank page feeling better about yourself and your work.

During the weekly review, I file my research, organise my notes and quickly read through the ideas I came up with during the week. This helps me evaluate if there's anything I've overlooked or if there's an idea I can use over the coming days in my work.

I also write down or mark minor accomplishments during the week such as hitting a target word count or completing a book chapter. These minor creative accomplishments are important to mark and a great way to boost your motivation.

Think of it this way: Paragraphs make up book chapters, and finished chapters will fill a book. In other words, the accumulation of minor achievements contributes to a major accomplishment.

The weekly review is a powerful productive strategy, which if used correctly, will help you plan for future writing projects secure in the knowledge that you have the resources and time to finish what you started.

DISCOVER WHAT LIES AHEAD

Finishing what you started writing isn't so tough now that you know how to manage your time and commitments. Once you get into the habit of finishing, the rewards are immense. You'll get:

Your hands dirty: Studying the work habits and creative strategies of writers like Hemingway and the ad copywriter Caples is fun, but writing isn't a spectator sport. You'll learn more of this craft by wading in up to your neck.

Learning opportunities: If you ship your work and it's badly received, you can use this feedback to become a better writer. If you don't ship, you won't get feedback, and you'll never get a chance to improve.

Smarter: Finishing a piece trains your brain to make new connections and come up with better ideas for your next writing project.

Answers: Are you a non-fiction writer, a copywriter, a story-teller or a non-fiction writer? Finishing your work will help you answer these questions because you'll know more of what you enjoy and what you're good at.

Over blindspots: Do you have trouble writing strong introductions? What can you do to write better headlines? How can you deepen your research? Treasure the difficult moments; they are the foundations of your writing practice.

Faster: You're an athlete and writing is a race. It might be a sprint, a 10-mile event or a marathon. Whatever the length of your work, get through it and you'll finish the next one faster.

More confident: When your article appears in print, your short story in a magazine or your blog post on a popular site, you'll feel lighter than you have in months. Then when you sit down to write again, you'll be hungry for more success.

A free education: If you guest post for a popular website, you'll have the chance to talk to another editor who can help you improve your work and (if the relationship goes well) provide you with opportunities for future work. Some writers pay money for this kind of feedback.

Paid: Professional writers turn up, they do the work, and they move on. They get paid. You deserve to get paid too.

BECOME THE PRODUCTIVE WRITER

Now that you've digested the 33 productivity strategies in this book, you know writing will always feel like a messy and sometimes disjointed pursuit. It doesn't fit neatly into any box or to do list.

That doesn't mean you can get away with missing deadlines and permanently unfinished projects. These are the hallmarks of amateurs who don't know where they're going or what they're doing. If you made it this far, you're not an amateur.

Several years ago, I was an amateur (albeit one who had convinced some people otherwise).

I worked as a journalist for a local newspaper in Ireland. I had to write news stories each week, cover council meetings, political speeches and business stories in the area.

This was my first real job since graduating college, and I saw it as my big break into the big, bad, wide world of print journalism.

For a man with such ambitions for his career, I had one big problem.

I spent more time talking to people in the office, reading the news online and doing anything but my job. Eventually, my procrastination caught up with me.

One sunny Wednesday morning, after I'd missed a big deadline the night before, my editor called me into the office. He told me to close the door and take a seat. You know it's not good when they tell you to take a seat.

"I'm not happy with your progress here Bryan, you're letting things slip," he said leaning back in his chair. "The reality is if you can't finish the damn thing, you're not doing your job, and if you're not doing your job, this newspaper will have to let you go."

"I can do better, I can explain," I said. "Give me another chance."

I didn't deserve another chance, and I had no genuine excuses. My editor was right. I wasn't doing my job. Luckily, he didn't fire me (at least not that day).

Since then, I've made every possible mistake writing fiction and non-fiction. I've learnt the hard way that finishing something, anything, gives a writer the confidence to write again.

If you can't finish the damn thing, you're not doing your job. You're not fulfilling the challenge productive writers like Stephen King laid down for the rest of us.

Ask yourself:

- What's the last writing project you abandoned?
- When was the last time you published or submitted a writing project for publication?
- Are you constantly seeking new ways to get feedback about your writing?
- When will you finish what you're writing?
- Why are you procrastinating?

If you finish what you are working on, you will feel a sense of accomplishment alien to the writer who gave up altogether. Creating, writing and finishing your work will teach you far more than polishing pages of prose for months on end.

Whether you're writing fiction or non-fiction, shipping is more important than perfection. Instead of abandoning a writing project or slaving away indefinitely, set a target for submission or publication.

Stick to this target, and if you miss it, finish, publish or submit your work as soon as you can.

Don't ship mediocrity or publish a writing project for the sake of it. Conversely, don't let your writing stagnate in a drawer.

Confidence comes when you reach the end.

When you finish your next writing project, some people might criticise or reject your work. They could be right, but you still gain a victory.

Even if your writing project is a failure, at least you will be free to write something else, something better.

I've finished a lot of awful articles in my time, but finishing gave me the confidence to see the writing process through.

Afterwards, I was able to show people my work (warts and all) and learn from their feedback, which is invaluable. It's your chance to learn how to become a better writer for free.

If you get into the habit of finishing your work, you can become a writer who thinks of an idea, fleshes it out, edits, rewrites, polishes and then rewrites some more, before finishing the damn thing.

None of this is possible if you get hung up on creating the perfect piece of writing.

My editor and I long since fell out, but I'm still writing.

Are you?

WHAT ARE YOU WAITING FOR?

Y ou must know that words are all you need to succeed.

In the wrong hands, they can become weapons to tear down others. In the right hands, they are a salve for the boredom, frustration and pain around you.

If you are lonely or depressed, if your wife or husband has left you, if you are broke or greedy, if you are hungry for success or sick of your ambitions, if you are on a creative high or stuck in rut, if you know who you are or if you've outgrown your ambitions, whoever you want to be, *you must write.*

Writing is hard. Every writer will tell you a battle wages between us and a finished work.

Pressfield, author of *The War of Art*, explains we writers have to slay our dragons on the page:

> We're facing dragons too. Fire-breathing griffins of the soul, whom we must outfight and outwit to reach the treasure of our self-in-potential to release the maiden who is God's plan and destiny for ourselves and the answer to why we were put on this planet.

Go now from this book and sit in a quiet room and face your dragons. Put one word after another on the blank page. Your sentences will make you feel sick. The awfulness of their construction will wound you.

Your head will spin, and you will look outside and wonder how else to spend your time. Then when you're ready to quit, a great thing will happen.

You will write one true sentence.

You will create something meaningful and reinvent yourself.

This is how you will leave a mark on your world, however small.

I apologise because I deceived you.

This book isn't a guide for more creative or productive writing. This book is my *Manifesto for Writing*.

What's yours?

REFERENCES

Books

Altucher, James. *Choose Yourself*. 2013.

Allen, David. *Getting Things Done*. 2011.

Austen, Jane. *Pride and Prejudice*. 1992.

Babauta, Leo. *The Power of Less*. 2009.

Brown, Christy. *Down All the Days*. 1990.

Brown, Christy. *My Left Foot*. 1990.

Carnegie, Dale. *How to Win Friends and Influence People*. 1998.

Cheever, John. *The Journals*. 2011.

Covey, Stephen R. *The Seven Habits of Highly Effective People*. 2013.

Currey, Mason. *Daily Rituals: How Artists Work*. 2013.

Dickens, Charles. *A Tale of Two Cities*. 2011.

Doyle, Roddy. *The Commitments*. 2010

Doyle, Roddy. *The Snapper*. 2008.

Fitzgerald, F. Scott. *The Great Gatsby*. 2013.

Franzen, Jonathan. *The Corrections*. 2010.

Gelb, Michael J. *How to Think Like Leonardo da Vinci*. 2000.

Holiday, Ryan. *Perennial Seller: The Art of Making and Marketing Work that Lasts*. Profile Books. Kindle Edition. 2017.

Isaacson, Walter. *Einstein: His Life and Universe*. 2008.

Isaacson, Walter. *Steve Jobs: The Exclusive Biography*. 2011.

Joyce, James. *Ulysses*. 2012.

Kafka, Franz. *Metamorphosis*. 2009.

Kennedy, Dan S. *The Ultimate Sales Letter: Attract New Customers and Boost Your Sales* (4th Ed). 2011.

King, Stephen. *On Writing: A Memoir of the Craft*. 2010.

Murakami, Haruki. *What I Talk About When I Talk About Running*. 2011.

Kleon, Austin. *Steal Like An Artist: 10 Things Nobody Told You About Being Creative*. 2012.

McKeown, Greg. *Essentialism: The Disciplined Pursuit of Less. 2014.*

Levy, Mark. *Accidental Genius: Using Writing to Generate Your Best Ideas, Insight and Content* (2nd Ed). 2009.

Nabokov, Vladimir. *Lolita*. 2012.

Pressfield, Steven and Coyne, Sean. *The War of Art*. 2011.

Plath, Sylvia. *The Bell Jar*. 2005.

McKee, Robert. *Story: Substance, Structure Style and The Principles of Screenwriting*. 1997.

Melville, Herman. *Moby-Dick*. 2014.

Orwell, George. *1984*. 2013.

Platt, Sean. Truant, Johnny B. Wright. *Write. Publish. Repeat. The No-Luck Required Guide to Self-Publishing Success*. 2013.

Salinger, J.D. *The Catcher in the Rye*. 2014.

Suzuki, Shunryu. *Zen Mind, Beginner's Mind*. 2011.

Tolstoy, Leo. *Anna Karenina*. 2012.

Vaynerchuk, Gary. *The Thank You Economy*. 2011.

Vaynerchuk, Gary. *Crushing It!: How Great Entrepreneurs Build Their Business and Influence & and How You Can, Too*. HarperCollins. Kindle Edition. 2018.

Woolf, Virginia. *A Writer's Diary (1918-1941)*. 2013.

Zinsser, William. *On Writing Well*. 2006.

Articles and Online Resources

80Pct Solutions. Freedom. 2014. https://macfreedom.com/

Altucher, James. The James Altucher Podcast: Episode 17: "Chris Brogan: Are You a Freak?". 2014.

Björk, Johanna. "Benjamin Franklin's Routine: Do Good Each Day". 2013. Taken from http://www.goodlifer.com/2013/02/benjamin-franklins-routine-do-good-each-day/ on July 4, 2014.

Burrell, Diana. "Renegade Writer Q&A David Allen". Taken from http://www.therenegadewriter.com/2007/03/19/renegade-writer-qa-david-allen/ on June 24, 2014. Renegade Writer.

Chrisafis, Angelique. "Overlong, overrated and unmoving: Roddy Doyle's verdict on James Joyce's Ulysses". 2004. Take from http://www.theguardian.com/uk/2004/feb/10/booksnews.ireland on June 21, 2014. The Guardian.

Colzato, Lorenza S. Ayca, Ozturk. Hommel, Bernhard. "Meditate to create: the impact of focused-attention and open-monitoring training on convergent and divergent thinking". 2012. Taken from http://journal.frontiersin.org/Journal/10.3389/fpsyg.2012.00116/full on July 2, 2014. Leiden University.

Conradt, Stacy. "Vladamir Nabokov Talks Synesthesia". 2013. Taken from http://mentalfloss.com/article/49442/vladimir-nabokov-talks-synesthesia on June 21, 2014. Mental Floss.

Blank on Blank. "David Foster Wallace on Ambition". 2013. Interview by Leonard Lopate, WNYC. 1996. Taken from https://www.youtube.com/watch?v=w5R8gduPZw4 on June 24, 2014.

Devey, Joseph. "Francis Bacon. The Advancement of Learning". 2014. Taken from http://oll.libertyfund.org/titles/1433 on June 21, 2014. Online Library of Liberty.

Godin, Seth. "The platform vs. the eyeballs". 2009. Taken from http://sethgodin.typepad.com/seths_blog/2009/09/the-platform-vs-the-eyeballs.html on June 21, 2014.

Gudgel, Andrew. "Commonplace Books – Old Wine in New Bottles". 2010. Taken from http://www.andrewgudgel.com/commonplace.htm on June 21, 2014.

Guildhall, Olivia. "The Science of Why We Live". Daily Telegraph. 2014.

Gilbert, Elizabeth, TED. "Your Elusive Creative Genius". 2009.

Taken from http://www.ted.com/talks/elizabeth_gilbert_on_genius on June 21, 2014. TED.

Gray Matter. "Brain, Interrupted". 2013. Taken from http://www.nytimes.com/2013/05/05/opinion/sunday/a-focus-on-distraction.html?_r=1& on June 24, 2014. New York Times.

Hamilton, Jon. "Think You're Multitasking? Think Again". 2008. Taken from http://www.npr.org/templates/story/story.php?storyId=95256794 on June 24, 2014. NPR.

Holiday, Ryan. "How and Why To Keep a Commonplace Book". 2014. Taken from www.ryanholiday.net on June 21, 2014.

Isaac, Brad. "Jerry Seinfeld's Productivity Secret". 2007. Taken from http://lifehacker.com/281626/jerry-seinfelds-productivity-secret on June 21, 2014. Lifehacker.

Lavinsky, Dane. "Pareto Principle: How To Use It to Dramatically Grow Your Business". Forbes. 2014. Taken from http://www.forbes.com/sites/davelavinsky/2014/01/20/pareto-principle-how-to-use-it-to-dramatically-grow-your-business/ on June 21, 2014. Forbes.

Lev Grossman. "Jonathan Franzen: Great American Novelist". Time Magazine. 2010. Taken from http://content.time.com/time/magazine/article/0,9171,2010185,00.html on June 21, 2014. Time Magazine.

Mehta, Ravi. Zhu, Rui (Juliet) Zhu. Cheema, Amar. "Is Noise Always Bad? Exploring the Effects of Ambient Noise on Creative Cognition". 2012. Taken from http://www.jstor.org/stable/10.1086/665048 on June 21, 2014. Chicago Journals.

Nielsen, Jakob. "How long do web users stay on webpages". 2011. Taken from http://www.nngroup.com/articles/how-long-do-users-stay-on-web-pages/ on June 21, 2014.

Plimpton, George. "Ernest Hemingway: The Art of Fiction No. 20. 1954". Taken from http://www.theparisreview.org/interviews/4825/the-art-of-fiction-no-21-ernest-hemingway on June 21, 2014. The Paris Review.

No name. "Side Dish What Was Benjamin Franklin's Daily Routine?". 2013. Take from http://www.sidedishmag.com/2013/07/me-and-benjamin.html on August 14, 2014. Side Dish.

The Air Force Departmental Publishing Office. "The Inverted Pyramid". Taken from http://commons.wikimedia.org/wiki/File:Inverted_pyramid_2.svg#mediaviewer/File:Inverted_pyramid_2.svg on June 21, 2014.

Watts, Robert. "J.K. Rowling Unmasked As Author of Acclaimed Detective Novel". 2013. Taken from http://www.telegraph.co.uk/culture/books/10178344/JK-Rowling-unmasked-as-author-of-acclaimed-detective-novel.html on June 21, 2014. The Telegraph.

Viatour, Luc. "Vitruvian man". 2014. Taken from www.Lucnix.be on June 21, 2014.

Writer's Relief Staff. "Famous Author Rejection Letters: True Stories Of Unbelievable Rejections". 2011. Taken from http://writersrelief.com/blog/2011/07/famous-author-rejection-letters/ on July 3, 2014. Writer's Relief.

THE ART OF WRITING A NON-FICTION BOOK

AN EASY GUIDE TO RESEARCHING, CREATING, EDITING, AND SELF-PUBLISHING YOUR FIRST BOOK

THE ART OF Writing* A NON-FICTION BOOK

An Easy Guide to Researching, Creating, Editing and Self-Publishing Your First Book

BOOK 3 IN THE BECOME A WRITER TODAY SERIES

BRYAN COLLINS

PAGE ONE

It's in your hands.

You lift the pages up to your nose and can almost smell the ink. This is a victory. It's the culmination of months of editing, writing, research, revisions and sacrifices.

You've done something most aspiring creative people put off. You've stopped talking about having a book inside you that you'll write *one day*, got the words out of your head and onto the blank page. You've shaped, edited and revised your book and then had the guts to release it into the world.

Flicking through page after page, you're amazed you possessed the mental discipline to write it and proud you saw the idea through. You should be too.

But what if you're not there yet?

What if you've spent months or even years writing your non-fiction book, but it's still languishing inside your computer or drawer.

It's unfinished, unpublished and a painful reminder of how far you still must go.

When you sit down to write, you wonder: *Is this a waste of time? Why can't I write my book? Am I ever going to become an author?*

It's enough to make you want to give up writing altogether.

I'll let you in on a secret: you're not alone.

Like you, I'd been dreaming about writing a book for years. But every day, I woke up and something got in the way: kids, a job, the front doorbell ringing and more.

My friends would ask me, "Is your book finished yet?" And I'd reply, "It's coming along."

I spent years talking about writing this mythical book, but I didn't know how to finish it. I felt tired and embarrassed by my lack of progress.

I knew I could have written the book inside of me had I taken a different approach. So I studied what successful non-fiction authors do, and I changed how I wrote. Now, I want to share what I learnt about writing a non-fiction book with you.

WHAT THIS BOOK WILL TEACH YOU

This book offers practical, real-world advice for new writers and aspiring non-fiction authors. It's suitable for you if you have an idea you want to turn into a book and if you've never written a book before.

In the **first part of this book**, you'll discover what it takes to become a non-fiction author. I tackle how to find ideas if you don't have any, how to organise them and express yourself.

Then, I'll cover how to get your messy first draft out of your head and onto the blank page. I'll also go cover the one thing you shouldn't do while researching and writing your first draft.

If writing non-fiction books is already your thing, there are still a few technical and a few craft-related skills you must acquire.

Don't let this put you off.

In the **second part** of this book, I'll explain how to gain the skills you need to write your book. You'll learn how to master research, your tools and what to do about that messy first draft.

Does writing a book sound like it will take up a lot of time?

I get it. I wrote my first two non-fiction books around the margins of the day while balancing a full-time job, two small children, a wife, friends and so on.

As an aspiring author, you may lack the time and freedom to work on your book full-time. I'll explain how to master your free hours for writing and set up your environment for success.

I'll also tackle how to cultivate the mental discipline it takes to write a book by mastering the one thing you have complete control over: yourself.

Because hey, creating a book is tough. Once you finish writing your first or second draft, it's time to edit and revise your manuscript.

Many new writers have trouble with editing and revisions. Their editor sends them back the manuscript covered in annotations, and the writer wonders...

How will I ever finish this?

How will I ever write something readers will want, let alone pay for?

I won't lie, critical feedback is hard to swallow.

In the **third part** of this book, I'll tackle the ins and outs of self-editing and the art of revising your drafts. I will also explain what to expect when working with a professional editor.

Of course, if you want to sell copies of your book – what writer doesn't want to sell their book? - you'll need to publish something your readers want. So it's best to involve them early and often, and I'll explain how.

Editorial and real-world feedback are nice, but, there's no point getting stuck in a cycle of revising, editing and reworking your non-fiction book.

Don't let the siren's call of perfectionism seduce you.

You need to have a plan for finishing, shipping or self-publishing your book. Today that's easier than ever to achieve. Once you publish your book, you're free to decide what to do next.

Should you focus on earning a living from your writing, try to make an impact with your ideas, or write something new?

With a finished book in your hands, you'll have the answers you need.

You'll be an author.

THE 7 MOST COMMON MISTAKES OF ASPIRING NON-FICTION AUTHORS

It's exciting, isn't it?

Writing your first book and then sending the final version to your editor and later having it available (and SELLING!) on stores like Amazon, iTunes and Kobo.

The months (or even years) of hard work are over, and now you can watch with pride as your book goes out into the world.

Now, you can sit back as your ideas and stories make an impact on readers and earn you a side income.

You can finally call yourself an author.

But what if you're not there yet? What if you're still struggling to finish writing your first book?

Then I think you'll agree with me that trying to write a non-fiction book is tough work.

So I'm going to be honest with you and reveal seven of the most common writing mistakes aspiring non-fiction authors must avoid.

These are the writing mistakes that tripped me up before I published my first book.

If you want to become a non-fiction author, don't let them hoodwink you.

BOOK WRITING MISTAKE #1: I SHOULD WRITE DIFFERENT THINGS AT ONCE

A blog post.

An article for a magazine.

A book.

Perhaps the great American novel.

There are so many tantalising and exciting new ideas to explore.

Often new writers work on different writing projects at once, and then they struggle to make real progress.

Writing lots of things at once is fine if you're John McPhee, Malcolm Gladwell or a professional author who has been at this for years.

If you're just starting out, it's a common writing mistake.

Here's why:

According to a 2012 article in *Psychology Today*, people who jump from one task to the next are up to 40% less productive. What's more, when you multi-task or switch tasks, you incur a cognitive penalty. You perform worse than the person who brings a single-minded focus to his or her work.

Writers are no exception.

It gets worse too.

When you are working on lots of projects, you'll find it harder to create a writing routine that sticks.

What's more, you'll delay finishing your drafts and postpone the feeling of accomplishment that comes when you finally press publish.

This state is an essential reward if you're serious about your writing.

So one book at a time, please.

BOOK WRITING MISTAKE #2: I DON'T NEED TO ORGANISE IDEAS FOR MY BOOK

Did you ever think of an idea for your book and feel excited about using it?

You can't wait to put this idea into practice and start writing.

But you wonder...

What if I did a little bit more research?

So you pick up the phone, open a book or a web browser, and you look into your first idea. And the next one. And the one after that.

You spend hours clicking and browsing from one blog post to the next or reading books you love. There are too many ideas to choose from.

When you have time, you scribble your notes on Post-Its, on the back of notepads and in the margins of various books. More often than not, you don't write anything down, thinking you'll remember these golden nuggets later on.

After all, isn't the human brain a magnificent organ?

Later, when it's time to write, it's a struggle to produce even 300 words because you don't know how to make sense of your research. It's in too many different places, and that great hook for a chapter you thought about in the gym... it's gone.

Successful non-fiction writers don't risk losing their best ideas. Like a doctor, lawyer or academic, they treat research seriously. They keep their ideas in one place, and they review what they find.

To write your book, you need a system (digital or otherwise) for capturing, sorting and evaluating your ideas. You shouldn't have to spend time trying to think of a scientific study you read months ago.

Instead it should sit next to anecdotes, interviews, quotes, reader surveys...and the rest of your research.

When you do this, you'll be able to write your non-fiction book, all the while knowing your best ideas are there, when you need them.

BOOK WRITING MISTAKE #3: I SHOULD WRITE MY BOOK WHEN I FEEL PASSIONATE OR INSPIRED

I'm all for feeling passionate about your creative work, but let's be logical about this...

Imagine you're training to run a marathon.

(I picked a marathon because writing a book can feel like a long, intensive slog.)

So if you want to run 26.2 miles for the first time, you can't turn up on the day of the marathon and expect to finish the race.

You've got to train when you don't want to, practice when you're tired and squeeze your sessions into your otherwise busy week.

Now, you might feel passionate about training when it's sunny outside, but what about on a cold, wet Tuesday evening?

You're going to have to do the work anyway.

The same applies to writing.

When you turn up in front of a blank page, it takes a precious amount of creative time to warm up and figure out what you're trying to say. And if you haven't practiced writing in days or weeks, it'll take even longer.

Look, inspiration and passion are nice.

There's nothing better than sitting down in front of the blank page with a hot idea and an urge to write your book.

But if you wait around all day to come up with an idea and for inspiration to strike, what will you do if nothing comes?

Will you wait until tomorrow, next week or next month for inspiration to tap you on the shoulder and say, "Hey, it's time to write chapter five of your book"?

Because that's a sure-fire way never to finish writing your book.

Believe me, I've been there.

BOOK WRITING MISTAKE #4: I SHOULD WRITE MY NON-FICTION BOOK ON THE WEEKENDS

Between your job, family and personal life, finding time to write your book is difficult.

Now, I don't want to upset you, but...

....deciding it's okay to write a chapter in your book only on the weekends is a sure-fire way to finish nothing at all.

Sure, there'll be an occasional productive Saturday morning. You'll write for two or even three hours and produce 1,000 great words.

You'll say, "That was a morning well-spent."

But what happens if you don't find time to write on a Saturday or Sunday and you miss a weekend?

Or what happens if the weekend's writing session is a flop?

It'll be an entire week before you put your butt in the chair, your hands on the keyboard and turn up in front of the blank page. And if you miss a weekend?

You're putting seven, fourteen or even twenty-one days between writing sessions.

You'll never get into the rhythm and momentum of writing your book.

I don't know about you, but I can't wait that long to finish what I started, which is why I changed how and when I write.

Getting a writing schedule in place or even finding time to write is a real struggle when you're new at this.

A writing routine you stick to will help, as will one you follow before the demands of the day take over.

Now, this brings me to...

BOOK WRITING MISTAKE #5: I WILL FINISH WRITING MY NON-FICTION BOOK IF I JUST WORK HARDER

When you're working on a book for the first time, telling yourself to 'work harder' or 'don't be lazy' is TERRIBLE advice.

Here's why:

Self-talk might get your ass in the chair on day one, but when you miss a day, you'll feel bad.

And if you miss two days, you'll feel even worse.

Then, your book becomes this BIG THING you've got to do.

Like any hard and difficult task, you'll procrastinate about it, put it off and even forget about it.

Again, this is a common writing mistake.

I once stuffed a manuscript in my drawer and 'forgot' about it for three months because I felt guilty about my lack of progress.

Yes, writing a book is tough when you're starting out (remember my marathon analogy?), but don't make it harder than it needs to be.

I discovered telling myself to 'work harder' wasn't helping me write a book and would never help me publish one. Then, I found a solution that helped me get better results.

And my secret?

Well, you need a way of breaking down your book into milestones that you can reach one by one.

You need a way of tracking your progress until you reach The End.

(God, I love getting to The End.)

More on that later.

BOOK WRITING MISTAKE #6: IT'S OKAY TO EDIT AND WRITE MY BOOK AT THE SAME TIME

Have you ever written a paragraph, rewrote it, written another paragraph and then went back and rewrote that too?

And on and on and on...

An hour goes by.

You realise you have written nothing. All you've done is rewrite the same part of your book.

Ouch!

I used to write like this all the time. I spent hours tinkering with my sentences, and I often went back to perfect them.

Again. And again.

This is a terrible way to write your book.

Here's why:

When you try to write and edit at the same time, you're doing TWO different activities.

The part of your brain that must write to get ideas out of your head and organise them – your internal writer – shies away from your internal editor.

The part of your brain that turns your first draft into writing that shines – your internal editor – does his or her best work with a complete first draft.

BOOK WRITING MISTAKE #7: I SHOULD ONLY PUBLISH MY BOOK WHEN IT'S PERFECT

When I was in my mid-twenties, I wanted to write literary non-fiction.

So I enrolled in an intensive creative writing class in Dublin.

Our tutor was a balding American in his early thirties from Texas.

"Jeff," I said. "I'm struggling to finish this idea I have for a story... what do I need to do to write something great?"

"Bryan, your writing is full of clichés," he said. "You write like a 1920s pulp fiction novelist."

"I can work on that," I said. "Tell me how I can get better."

"Trying to write one true great sentence is like throwing a type-writer at the moon?"

"What do you mean?"

"It's impossible."

We laughed.

He laughed harder.

And I spent my weekends editing and rewriting the same sentences until I felt they were just right.

I threw typewriters at the moon for four years, and in that time, I finished just six short stories. Sure, they had pretty sentences, but here's the painful truth:

They were lousy.

My quest for the perfect sentence consumed me. I forgot great stories succeed because of the tale and the characters within in them.

That wasn't the worst part either.

Because I'd failed to finish a lot of my stories, it was impossible for me to get candid, real-world editorial feedback about the quality of my writing.

Much later, I learned from my painful writing mistakes, and I discovered I wasn't a fiction writer after all.

Like you, my passion was – is – writing non-fiction.

Sometimes, I make embarrassing and common writing mistakes.

Recently, I spent two months rewriting an old book when I should have concentrated on publishing my new book, but that's okay.

I still fall, but I read as much as I can about writing and our craft. I use what I discover to fall forwards, instead of falling down.

Now, I'll reveal what I've discovered about non-fiction book writing. I'll help you avoid these mistakes and learn from the masters of our craft.

The blank page awaits.

PART I
BECOMING A NON-FICTION AUTHOR

SO YOU WANT TO WRITE YOUR FIRST BOOK?

"The more beautifully you shape your work around one clear idea, the more meanings your audiences will discover... as they take your idea and follow its implications into every aspect of their lives." – Robert McKee

You've got competition.

According to the UK Office for National Statistics, there are over 70,000 authors, writers and translators in the UK. Meanwhile, according to the US Bureau of Labor Statistics, there are over 43,380 writers and authors in the United States

These are professional writers who publish books or get paid for their work in some form. Both figures above say nothing for the many thousands more who take creative writing classes and tell their friends over a drink that they have this great idea for a book, and how they'll write it... one day.

Like many authors, I wanted to write a book ever since I was 12 years old. When I was a teenager, I was playing football in a field near my house. After the match, one of my friends produced a marijuana cigarette (a joint) and asked if I wanted a drag.

I told him, "Words get me high!"

I first tried to write a book when I was 19, but I couldn't get past page five. I didn't understand how to keep a story moving or even how to sit in a chair for more than 30 minutes and write about one thing.

That didn't stop me from boring friends to death in the pub about my ideas for short stories, novellas and non-fiction books.

It was a lot easier to talk about becoming an author than it was to actually write a book.

I always liked the idea of writers up against the blank page and waiting for their muse or divine inspiration to strike, but those moments never came. So I spent most of my twenties figuring out successful non-fiction authors do a lot of work upfront *before they* start writing a book.

It's not enough to want to write a book. If you wish to join the ranks of professional, successful authors, start by considering why you want to write a book. Then determine what your non-fiction book is about.

WHY ARE YOU WRITING A BOOK?

Many authors don't talk about the loneliness of their craft. You spend hours researching your book, writing and rewriting it, and sit in a room with only your words and ideas for company.

In the middle of every creative project, there's a moment when your initial enthusiasm drains away. You wonder if you should continue writing your book.

Hey, it's easier to sit down in front of the television with a bowl of Häagen-Dazs and watch old shows on Netflix.

If you've never written a book, these moments of self-doubt can feel overwhelming. But they'll pass if you press forwards, one sentence at a time.

You'll face other challenges too. If the people close to you aren't writers, they won't understand what you're doing. For instance, while

I was writing this chapter, a new writer struggling to finish his book emailed me to say:

> One of the reasons I have not gone farther with writing is because my family sees me working at a computer, or like today with a cell phone, and thinks I'm goofing off.

Even the most supportive wife/husband/friend/cat/dog isn't going to be able to carry your book over the finish line. Still, there's a reason lots of authors dedicate their books to family members and friends. It takes a single-minded focus, and even a dash of selfishness, to finish writing a book.

You'll be able to recommit to writing your book and explain to others what you're doing, if you figure out *your why* in advance. To do it, ask yourself:

- Am I writing this book to improve my craft?
- Is my book a passion project?
- Is a book the best medium for me to express my ideas?
- What do I want to achieve with my book: money, recognition or to make an impact?
- Will this book help me advance my dream of writing full-time?
- Will this book help me advance my career or become an expert in my field?
- Do I want to generate a side income from my book, and if so, how much?
- How will I serve existing and/or new readers with my book?

Establish at least five to ten reasons why you're writing your non-fiction book. Over the coming months, understanding your why will help you conquer self-doubt. It will also help you answer difficult questions from others and keep writing.

WHY I WROTE THE POWER OF CREATIVITY

During 2015 and early 2016, I researched and wrote a non-fiction book for writers and artists called *The Power of Creativity*. I knew the book would be tough work. So before setting out on page one, I created *my list of whys*.

On more than one occasion, I re-read my list to overcome problems like self-doubt and not feeling motivated to write.

Here's the list:

1. I want to serve my readers with more than productivity advice. (Up until this point, I wrote articles mostly about how to get things done.)
2. Writing a book about creativity will help me become a better writer.
3. This book will give me credibility about the subject of creativity.
4. I've researched the market, and there's a demand for books about creativity.
5. I want to master the art of non-fiction storytelling.
6. Writing and shipping this book will help me clarify if I should spend my time writing fiction or non-fiction. (A question I've struggled with for years.)
7. I want to increase my side income from writing and self-publishing books.

DISCOVERING YOUR BOOK'S OBLIGATORY CONVENTIONS

When I buy a ticket to see the latest superhero film, I expect to feel awed by a hero possessing strange and unusual powers. I want him or her to get into a ridiculous costume and fight a bizarre-looking nemesis before the credits roll.

If this doesn't happen, I'll feel short-changed. The hero's origin story and their confrontation with a nemesis are two of the obligatory conventions of the superhero genre.

Every good director includes them.

Writers who exclude the obligatory conventions of their genre are short-changing their readers. But you can avoid this problem by becoming a student of the market.

Spend at least an hour browsing the Amazon categories relevant to your book, and find ones with a sales ranking below 30,000. Typically, these sell at least five copies a day, meaning they earn income for their authors.

Study the good and bad book reviews so you can see what readers like and dislike and how you can do better. I'm drawn to the three-star reviews because they're mostly written by people who aren't all-out fanboys/girls or haters.

At the end of your research, you'll know whether you're writing about a topic with few writers or wading into a genre with serious competition.

Now, perhaps your genre is underserved.

Think carefully about why nobody is writing about this topic and whether you're going to be able to sell your book.

Find would-be readers and ask them if they'll open their wallets or purses to pay for what you're about to write.

If they say yes, that's good news!

There's a demand for the book you're about to write, and these other books will help you figure out what to include and exclude.

Next, read at least five popular books in your genre. During your first read-through, enjoy the book in question. Later, go through the books again, studying the front matter, chapter titles and their lengths, the index, the conclusion and so on.

Then ask yourself:

- What's the most important idea or concept in each book?
- How does each author present information to their readers?
- How can I summarise each book?

- What are the typical word counts of the chapters and books within my niche?
- What types of research, stories and exercises (if any) do my chosen authors include?
- What's the tone of voice within each book?
- What ideas do I agree/disagree with?
- What does this book and other books include?

I answer these questions and summarise the books using a mind map (I'll address how to do this later on). As you evaluate each book, consider if you can combine these ideas with your perspective.

ESTABLISHING WHAT YOUR BOOK IS ABOUT

Writing your first non-fiction book without knowing what it's about and who it's for is like trying to cut a tree trunk in half with a rusty, old saw. If you're determined enough, you'll get there in the end, but why complicate things for yourself?

There are easier ways to write a good non-fiction book that people will pay for.

Like many new non-fiction writers, you may have a topic in mind for your book. You may want to write about a sports or diet regime, tell a personal life story or offer a guide to a complex topic like teaching science to kids.

Your job will be a hell of a lot easier if you get yourself a chainsaw.

For authors, that chainsaw is the controlling idea behind a book.

The American creative writing instructor Robert McKee introduced this concept, explaining:

The controlling idea shapes the writer's choices. It's yet another Creative Discipline to guide your aesthetic choices toward what is appropriate or inappropriate in your story, toward what is expressive of your controlling idea and may be kept versus what is irrelevant to it and must be cut.

According to McKee, the controlling idea of the *Dirty Harry* series of films is: "Justice triumphs because the protagonist is more violent than the criminals."

Although McKee concerns himself with screenwriting (and fiction to a degree), the controlling idea applies to non-fiction writing too.

I read Joan Didion's memoir *The Year of Magical Thinking* on New Year's Eve in 2015. My wife went out with friends to the pub, and we didn't have a babysitter.

So I stayed up late at home and read about how Joan Didion's husband John Gregory Dunne died unexpectedly of a heart attack at their kitchen table in 2003.

It was a depressing way to bring in the New Year, but I couldn't put Didion's non-fiction book down. She explores the impact of grief and the nature of death by telling stories about her life before and after Dunne's death.

Didion weaves in psychological and medical research. She contrasts the story of John's death against her daughter's health problems and hospitalisation. She writes:

A single person is missing for you, and the whole world is empty.

I've no idea if Didion overtly established a controlling idea. Yet, it's clear to any reader: "No one is ready for death and it can arrive at any time with devastating consequences."

You can figure out your book's controlling idea by spending an hour asking and answering some simple questions:

- Who is my book for?
- What am I trying to say?
- Who or what is the subject of my book?
- What is the point of view of my book?
- What is the core value underpinning my book?
- How is my book different to everything else that's out there?

Your answers are for you alone, so be as honest as you can. Then, distil them into a single sentence, and pin this next to where you write. You could start your book without doing this extra work. But your controlling idea will help you avoid spending hours writing about the wrong things.

Here's the controlling idea for this very book:

> With the right ideas, skills and hard work, you can become a successful non-fiction author today.

During the editing process, your controlling idea will help you assess whether each chapter achieves its purpose. It will help you prop your book on a firm foundation.

Don't worry if you don't get your controlling idea right at the start. You can update your idea *while* writing your book.

THE PAGES AHEAD

Lots of aspiring writers sit around bars, telling their friends they have a great idea for a book. Then they order another beer, coffee or glass of wine and carry on talking without any real intention to start writing.

Then there are the would-be writers who complain they *could write a book*, but they don't have the time, they're not committed to doing it, or they don't know what their book is about... yet.

You are a different kind of writer. You know what your book is about and who it's for and you've even got a controlling idea.

Now, you're about to put together a plan for writing and publishing your non-fiction book, and that's more intoxicating than anything you can order in a bar.

YOUR WRITING EXERCISES

- Clarify why you want to write your non-fiction book and what you'd like to achieve with it.
- Spend 30-60 minutes establishing the controlling idea for your non-fiction book. Rather than trying to perfect this idea and procrastinating for weeks, adjust your controlling idea while you write.

FINDING OUT WHAT YOUR READERS EXPECT (AND WHO THEY ARE)

"Everyone wants to climb the mountain, but the big difference between those at the top and those still on the bottom is simply a matter of showing up tomorrow to give it just one more shot." – Gary Halbert

The American writer Gary Halbert (1938-2007) was a master of writing to just one person - his ideal customer. Halbert built a career and earned millions of dollars for his clients working as a copywriter and direct response marketer.

He wrote about and sold the benefits of his clients' products and services, but it was never the quiet life for Halbert. He once said:

I have been robbed, tied up, gagged blindfolded, threatened. I've made and lost millions. I have been eulogized, ostracized, and plagiarized. I've also... been both a prison guard and a prison inmate.

Halbert's father died when he was 57 years of age, and Halbert was always afraid of facing the same fate. So at the age of 46, Halbert decided to teach his son, Bond, all he knew about earning a living and getting by.

At the time, Halbert was serving a ten-month prison sentence in a federal prison camp in California. Prison isn't the most conducive environment for a father-son relationships. So Halbert used the single most powerful tool at his disposal to teach Bond what he knew – the written word.

During his stretch inside, Halbert sent Bond over 25 letters – each several hundred words long.

In the letters, Halbert tackled topics like "How to keep going when the going is hard!", "The surest way to become a big money writer!" and "How to get flowing again when you are stuck!"

The ultimate salesman, Halbert even offered his son "an emotional 'tool kit' which can save your life!"

Much later, Bond gathered his father's writings and published them as *The Boron Letters*.

When I first read this book, Halbert struck me as a copywriter focused on adding to his bottom line, but then I dug a little deeper into his letters. The letters are less about earning a living than they are about learning **how to live**.

In one letter, Halbert describes losing himself to a song on the radio. A roommate shattered his brief mental respite from prison, screamed at Halbert to turn off the radio and threatened him.

Gary, a big and physical man, wasn't the kind of inmate "to get sand kicked in his face", and he considered fighting his roommate.

He knew one or both of them would get hurt and that this would complicate things for himself and Bond in the long term. So Halbert kept silent, turned off the radio and "ate humble pie".

Halbert wrote to his son about this ugly confrontation. He told Bond to avoid emotional decisions when feeling hungry, angry, lonely or tired.

"What should you do?" he asks his son. "What I did. Write, run, walk, talk, jog etc."

In a reply, Bond thanks his father for this advice and says he now waits 72 hours before making big decisions.

"This little rule has saved me a ton of grief," says Bond.

It's saved thousands of other readers a lot of grief too, but Halbert didn't write his letters for thousands of readers: he wrote them for his son.

Today, *The Boron Letters* is a cult-classic for copywriters and marketers seeking to discover more than just how to earn a fast buck. The letters are an instruction manual for living, and they succeed because Halbert wrote for his ideal reader first.

Halbert begins almost every letter with "Dear Bond" and ends with "I love you and good luck! Dad."

He knew exactly who he was writing to, and unless you're into the cliché of the penniless artist, you should write for your ideal reader too.

DETERMINING WHO YOUR IDEAL READER IS (AND WHAT THEY WANT)

If you're writing a book about fitness, it's not enough to write for men and women aged 18-65. That's too broad and open, and your book will get pneumonia.

For example, I typically write for men and women with a college education. They are aged between 30-50, and they live in the United States, Ireland, Canada and the United Kingdom. They are primarily new writers too.

And if I'm honest, that's a little broad.

My audience is new writers, and solving their problems informs many of the chapters in this book.

Remember, narrow and deep is better than wide and shallow. Halbert went so narrow and deep that he only wrote to one person – his son.

Don't gaze out the window and wait for a divine insight. Go to where your readers hang out. And no, I'm not talking about skulking around your local library.

If you have readers, ask them what they need help with.

Check your blog or website analytics, and figure out what posts are most popular. Then use this information to determine what you should write more or less of.

Send your readers an email or a short survey. For example, I ask readers who subscribe to my email list this question: "What are you struggling with right now?"

Over the past twelve months, I have received answers like:

- "My biggest struggle as a time-strapped blogger is finding the right balance between editing to perfection and publishing as is."
- "When I'm writing, the biggest frustration is distraction."
- "I feel like I'm at the stage where I need someone to keep me accountable, someone who is a writer and understands."
- "For me, writing is easy. The ideas, dialogue, scenes are all in my head waiting to pour out through my fingers. The frustrating part is finding the time to make this happen."

If you don't have readers, you'll need to find and interview three potential readers of a book like yours. Ask yourself:

- What kind of person would read my book?
- Who do I know that represents my ideal reader?
- Who can introduce me to my ideal reader?

Reach out to people on relevant Facebook groups, to your LinkedIn connections and to your personal network.

The question and answer site Quora is also a great source of reader information. There, you can see the real-world problems of your target audience and what they respond to. While researching this book on Quora, I came across questions like:

- "Do writers ever run out of ideas about what to write about? And what do they do to overcome this?"
- "What makes a writer great?"

- "As a writer, how does it feel to be suffering from writer's block?"

It's always best to ask real people about your idea before writing a non-fiction book. You can conduct these reader interviews over Skype, the phone or face-to-face.

Explain that you're writing a book about [insert topic] and that you need their help and value real-world feedback. Remember, you're not trying to sell your book – you're only looking to validate your ideas.

While speaking to your ideal reader, open up with a minute or two of light conversation to put the interviewee at ease. Buy them a drink or coffee if it's a face-to-face meeting. Then, ask them open questions related to your subject matter like:

- What are you struggling with right now?
- What would your life be like if...?
- What have you tried so far that worked/didn't work?
- What would it mean to you if...?
- Can you tell me about a time you...?

Be respectful of your interviewee's time too, and send a thank-you email or message when you're done.

I keep my reader research in a single document in Evernote. Through interviews and online research, you should be able to establish a sense of the following for your ideal reader:

- Age
- Sex
- Job
- Income
- Education
- Hopes
- Dreams
- Fears

- Frustrations

Then, while writing your book, hold in mind your ideal reader. Write to them alone. Empathise with their pains, and solve their problems. Use their language in your book. Let other authors worry about everyone else.

CRAFTING YOUR BOOK'S POSITIONING STATEMENT

By now, you should have an idea of who your ideal reader is, what they worry about and dream of. Now you're going to craft a positioning statement.

It's a succinct description of what your book is about and who it's for. A positioning statement will help you and your readers understand why your book is different from the competition and what's valuable about it. In short:

Controlling Idea + Ideal Reader = Positioning Statement

Here are three typical positioning statement templates for most popular self-help books:

- My book helps _____ who
  _____ get _____.
- My book teaches _____ how to
  _____.
- My book helps _____ who
  _____ achieve _____.

Now, here's my positioning statement for this book:

My book helps new writers write and sell copies of their first non-fiction book.

Writing a positioning statement for your book will help you with your book's title, sales copy, book cover and more. For example, consider the book *The 7 Habits of Highly Effective People: Powerful Lessons in Personal Change.*

It's clear from the title that this book helps people who want to overcome a personal or professional challenge. Readers should expect proven, real-world advice.

Not every author works their positioning statement directly into the title. And that's okay – but once you understand what your book is about and who it's for, you're far more likely to be able to sell it later on.

What's more, if you're self-publishing your book, you'll be able to market it in a way that attracts the attention of would-be readers. It's easier to explain who should and shouldn't buy your book if you can distill thousands of words into a single sentence.

THE SWEET SPOT

What if you don't care about your ideal reader or what's selling today on Amazon? By all means, write for yourself. Earning a living from writing doesn't equate to every writers' idea of success.

After the success of *The Catcher in the Rye*, the novelist J.D. Salinger turned away from the gaze of the public and his fans. Instead, he wrote for himself without publishing his work.

Rumour has it, upon his death, he left over two dozen completed and unpublished manuscripts in a safe in his house in New Hampshire.

You've got to admire Salinger for turning away from the public gaze. And yet, this luxury was only possible *after* the critical and commercial success of *The Catcher in the Rye*.

But what if you're not a Salinger in the making and only write what your readers want without caring if it fires you up?

Well, you'll probably get by for a while, but there are easier ways to earn a living than writing books. You'll eventually burn out.

Instead, there's a place between passion and pragmatism where you can earn a living from your craft *and* feel excited about what you're creating.

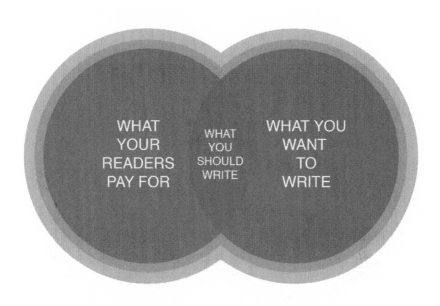

The best books appeal to their readers and the authors who write them

So position your book's ideas so they appeal to the marketplace and your creative muse.

Remember, you don't have to dominate the market or obliterate the competition to earn a decent living from your non-fiction book. Instead, find out what's keeping your ideal reader up at night and write to them with an answer that fires you up.

THE PAGES BETWEEN PASSION AND PRAGMATISM

Halbert died in his sleep in his apartment in Miami just shy of his 69th birthday. Although he wrote these letters for his son Bond, you too can apply them to write better non-fiction books

Like Halbert, find a place between passion and pragmatism. You must give your readers what they want and still feel good about sitting down to write.

Once you're there, you'll be able to make a real impact with your words and ideas... and get paid for doing it.

I believe in you and your book, good luck!

Bryan

YOUR WRITING EXERCISES

- Find three potential readers of your book and interview them for at least twenty minutes. Listen to their hopes, fears, dreams and frustrations.
- Using your research and your work from the previous chapter, craft a positioning statement for your book. Explain what it does, who it's for and why people should buy your book.

LEARNING TO EXPRESS YOURSELF FASTER

"Everything great in the world is done by neurotics; they alone founded our religions and created our masterpieces." – Marcel Proust

You dreamt of crafting pages of immaculate prose and publishing books that get more five-star reviews than you know what do to with.

You imagined your peers telling each other, "Now there's talent!" and all the while your bank balance is getting larger and larger.

And the reality?

On a good day, you sit down in Starbucks, sip your Mocha Frappuccino, nibble on a blueberry muffin, fire up Word, check your phone, email, Facebook, Twitter and Instagram... and do anything but write.

Every moment you spend with your work feels like a struggle, and what you write takes hours longer than you planned.

Even worse, when you read it, you've no idea if your work sounds reasonable or even if an alien from Mars could understand it.

Well, I've drunk the same Mocha Frappuccinos. I know many non-fiction book writers struggle to express themselves when they first try to write a book.

I CAN'T FIND MY VOICE

Before J.K. Rowling had her way, the Philosopher's Stone was a long sought-after artefact from the Middle Ages. According to legend, it could turn base metals into gold.

When they write the history of this craft, the writer's voice will stand as our Philosopher's Stone. It's an elusive entity you can spend your whole life chasing, yet never find.

I don't have it, your editor doesn't have it, and your readers certainly don't have it.

You don't set out in search of your writing voice *because you already have one*. Instead, you must develop your voice through continued and disciplined practice.

When I started writing non-fiction, I spent a lot of time trying to find my voice. I worried about writing in the first person, third person and even the second person (don't ask).

I tried to figure out how much of myself I should inject into my work and how much I should hold back. I even mimicked the style of other writers I admired.

I spent way too much time fussing about what my writing sounded like when I should have been, you know, *writing*!

HOW MARCEL PROUST CRAFTED HIS LITERARY SIX-PACK

Frenchman Marcel Proust (1871-1922) was determined to become a famous fiction writer.

His first novel, *Pleasures and Days*, was a commercial success, but Proust's critics dismissed it as all form and no substance.

They said his portrait of French society was the effort of a man who wanted to impress.

Ouch!

An unhappy Proust set out to write a more honest non-fiction work. He decided to base his work on the many stories, character sketches and lessons about psychology and life he'd collected over the years.

Proust regarded almost every setback as challenges he had to overcome. He knew what he wanted to achieve. So he committed to his idea of writing the ultimate portrait of 19th and early 20th century French society.

It took Proust more than 18 years to finish the eighteen volumes of *In Search of Lost Time*, and that's to say nothing of the research beforehand.

Today, that book is one the 20th century's most respected non-fiction books.

Proust overcame failure, he stopped trying to impress, and he developed his writing voice.

He said:

> When you work to please others you can't succeed, but the things you do to satisfy yourself stand a chance of catching someone's interest.

Proust developed his writing through consistent practice, and he crafted the writer's equivalent of a six-pack.

DEVELOPING YOUR WRITER'S SIX-PACK

Let's say you spent six months eating Häagen-Dazs and watching re-runs of *Keeping Up with the Kardashians*.

Then one day, you get up, go to the gym and try to bench-press your bodyweight.

What would happen next?

A small coronary event perhaps.

Even if you're not inclined towards reality television or chocolate ice cream, any gym coach worth their protein shakes will say:

You must gradually increase the amount of weights you lift each session.

While in my early twenties, my career as a journalist came to a depressing halt. To pay the mounting bills, I found a job as a care-worker for people with intellectual disabilities.

I struggled to find some time outside of work to write every day.

I told myself the blank page would keep until tomorrow and that I could write at the weekend. I even tried looking at myself in the mirror and telling myself, *Don't be lazy, just work harder*.

When I finally had the guts to sit down in front of the blank page and write, I could barely remember where I left off or what I wanted to say.

It took me so long to find the right words that each time I wrote, I felt like a beginner. I only learnt to write by showing up consistently and increasing how long I spent writing gradually.

You must progress towards your goal of writing a book day-by-day. You must develop your literary chops.

'But I'm a writer, not a weight lifter.'

I get it... but you'll learn to express yourself through measured progress.

For today, write just 300 words. Tomorrow, write 350 words. The day after that, write 400 words. Keep going until you can write 1,000 or even 2,000 words in a single session.

What if word counts aren't your thing?

Practice sitting down and writing for 15 minutes today, 20 minutes tomorrow and so on. Do this until writing for an hour or two each day becomes a habit.

Showing up consistently each day will help you express yourself. It's the secret to developing your writing voice. From there, you can capture the attention of new readers.

USE EVERYTHING

Proust spent much of his young life reading books, going on long walks and writing letters He loved frolicking at aristocratic French parties, and he didn't care for accomplishments. His friends and even Proust himself bemoaned the time he was wasting.

How wrong they were.

Proust applied or used almost every lesson he learnt from these activities, and he included these lessons in *In Search of Lost Time*.

Proust used everything for his greatest work. When Proust wanted to write about plants and flowers, he drove into the countryside and studied them for hours.

When Proust wanted to create a character like a wealthy debutante for his work, he found her equivalent in French society.

Then, he got himself invited to the same events she attended. He even went as far as gathering his friends for a dinner party where he studied them intensely and recorded what they said.

Yes, Proust's approach was extreme, but you should try and use everything too.

Consider the topics you're passionate about and always ask yourself if what you're writing fires you up. Dive deeper into your genre. Dive beyond superficial reading online or a simple Google search.

Read often and outside of your comfort zone. Mine your personal life for relevant stories and anecdotes. Consider the last thing you learnt and what you can say that no one else can. Be outrageous. Take a bloody stance.

Put it all in.

(Later on, you can edit your writing and take out the bits that don't work or where you've said too much).

PLOTTERS VS. PANTSERS

Okay, so you're ready to take a stance and do the work – what now?

Well, most people think there are two types of writers: rich ones... and the rest of us. Dig a little deeper, and you'll find out there are also pantsers and plotters.

Pantsers are writers who sit down in front of the blank page with only a vague idea of where they are going or what they want to write a book about.

They write from the seat of their pants, inventing things as they go along, and they are happy to see where their ideas and research take them.

They write with a connection to God, their muse or their subconscious. More often than not, *they write fiction or literary non-fiction.*

Proust's writing is exploratory, and it has all the hallmarks of a pantser. The American essayist Henry Miller was probably a pantser too, as he approached his literary essays like a "voyage of discover".

Plotters, on the other hand, spend weeks or months organising their ideas and deciding what they want to write about in advance.

When plotters sit down to work, they have a strong idea of what they're going to say, and they have the research to back it up.

Robert Greene, the author of *Mastery, The Art of Seduction* and *The 48 Laws of Power*, is a plotter.

Those non-fiction books are a curious blend of psychology, history and self-help. They've also sold millions of copies, and *The 48 Laws of Power* is particularly popular in US prisons.

Greene says he typically reads an eye-watering 300 to 400 books about a particular topic before he starts "typing up" his books.

He spends hundreds of hours reading and researching, taking care to organise his ideas on a series of annotated 4x6-inch index cards.

Greene colour-codes these cards based on categories or themes and files them in a box. He sorts through his research regularly, finding great value in bumping up against old ideas while working on new ones.

In a Reddit AMA, Greene says about this trusted system:

> I read a book, very carefully, writing on the margins with all kinds of notes. A few weeks later I return to the book, and transfer my scribbles on to note cards, each card representing an important theme in the book.

Malcolm Gladwell combines elements of both approaches.

He interviews subjects extensively for his books before he starts writing. However, he cautions against making up one's mind until the research is complete:

> I would say that probably half of the interviews I do end up on the

cutting room floor–or, at least, are used in later articles. The purpose of research is to cast as wide a net as possible. I tend to start researching something with only the vaguest idea in mind of where I want to end up. It's a mistake to make up your mind too soon.

FINDING OUT WHAT KIND OF WRITER YOU ARE

I've tried plotting and writing from the seat of my pants. After years of painful rewrites, unfinished manuscripts and pulling my hair out, I found out I'm a plotter.

I need to know what I'm writing about in advance. Being a plotter enables struggling non-fiction writers to finish their books faster.

Being a pantser is more useful for fiction writers and literary non-fiction writers.

That said, there are no hard-and-fast rules. You'll discover what kind of writer you are if you put down the Häagen-Dazs and turn up in front of the blank page.

GET READY TO CRUSH IT LIKE MARCEL PROUST

Proust saw expressing himself through writing as a lifelong pursuit. He finished his 18-volume memoir just two days before he died, and he never saw the final version of his masterpiece in print.

I'm not suggesting you write on your deathbed, but doing the work often means going at it longer and harder than what feels like normal. It means practising expressing yourself day after day – every day.

If you're struggling, find a great book that you enjoy reading. Then pick a paragraph, page or chapter from this book and write it out by hand.

No, don't type it!

Handwriting a piece you like will help you draw upon the author's style and approach. I know it may feel inefficient, but sometimes new writers need to slow down.

This practice will enable you to figure out how successful writers

277

tell stories and organise their ideas. Besides, there's plenty of time for efficient and productive writing later on.

Like the weight lifter who finally crushes it in the gym, you'll improve your craft through consistent practice.

Anything else is just Häagen-Dazs.

YOUR WRITING EXERCISES

- Are you a plotter or a pantser? The only way to find out is to start writing and test both approaches.
- Lift your literary weights by writing for 30 minutes or by producing 300 words today. Then increase your output gradually, because today's pain is tomorrow's gain.

TAKING CHARGE OF YOUR TOOLS
BEFORE THEY TAKE CHARGE OF YOU

"The big artist keeps an eye on nature and steals her tools."–
Thomas Eakins

Should you write your book on a computer, by hand or with that gold
Montblanc pen that you break out for special occasions?

What killer writing application do six-figure authors use?

And *just when* is your pencil sharp enough?

Of course, many aspiring authors wonder if they should write
their book with pen and paper or if they need the perfect writing app
to get going.

Well, there's a time and place for both types of tools.

GOING ANALOGUE

Marcel Proust, Leo Tolstoy and W. B. Yeats did just fine without a
computer or access to the internet.

There's something refreshing about a good notebook. You don't
have to upgrade, refresh or recharge it. You don't have to worry about
index cards freezing or not syncing properly.

A whiteboard will never prompt you for your password, need to be reset or have trouble connecting to your WiFi.

Science is on the side of analogue tools too.

Here's what top psychologists Pam A. Mueller of Princeton and Daniel M. Oppenheimer of the University of California found:

They discovered that students learn better when they take notes by hand rather than when typing on a keyboard. They wrote:

> ...whereas taking more notes can be beneficial, laptop note takers' tendency to transcribe lectures verbatim rather than processing information and reframing it in their own words is detrimental to learning.

Now you may not be studying for an exam, but writing by hand could help you produce a better book.

So file your notes, wipe down your desk, pair your pencils and fill your pens. Or if you're editing your book, print out early drafts, and read through your manuscript and mark it up with a red pen while standing up.

If it pains you to sit at a desk, take a pen and a notebook and go to your local coffee shop or into nature.

I love the writing practice of copying out other people's works by hand. I take a chapter from a book I like or a piece of writing by an author I admire, and I write it out.

Longhand writing is slower and more meditative than anything I achieve with a digital tool. And yet, this practice helps me to learn more of other authors' writing styles. It's also useful if you feel blocked or uninspired by your book.

If you get distracted while using analogue tools, take a note from William Faulkner.

He removed the doorknob from his door and brought it into his study to prevent people from intruding and distracting him while he wrote. (At the very least, you could unplug your modem and turn off your phone.)

When I'm blocked, I turn off my computer, disconnect from the grid and write a rough draft (or an outline) in a notebook or A4 or letter paper pad. There's nothing to update, backup, search or check. All I can do is write.

When to Use Analogue Writing Tools

- For capturing ideas on the go
- When you keep getting distracted
- For getting a messy first draft out of your head
- When you're blocked or uninspired
- For practising your craft
- When you want to create a rough outline of your book

GOING DIGITAL

Although I use analogue writing tools, I always find my way back to a digital writing tool once I'm unstuck. I break out in cold sweats when I think about losing a paper copy of a first draft (or even an outline).

Besides, publishing the contents of a tattered Moleskine notebook is unpractical.

I capture ideas on the go and store them in Evernote. Later, I write book chapters like this one using Scrivener. The latter is ideal for managing complicated and even multiple writing projects.

Yes, there's a small learning curve, but you'll save hours of time editing your book. For example, you can organise the chapters or sections of any book using a drag-and-drop interface. That's a lot faster than manipulating large blocks of text in Word or playing around with multiple files on your machine.

The Scrivener Binder: Here you can drag and drop individual book chapters

Scrivener also features several powerful in-built editing tools. My favourites include:

- Digital index cards (more on those later)
- Target word counts for individual chapters
- A custom status option for each chapter
- The ability to work on chapters side-by-side
- A progress bar for individual chapters

For example, I use the custom status in Scrivener to mark chapters as "Done", "Not done", "Ready for an editor" and so on. This helps me track what I need to write next.

Notice the custom status for each chapter

When I finish a manuscript, I export it from Scrivener, and I lay it out using the self-publishing tool Vellum.

This tool helps me prepare the book file for uploading to stores like Amazon. Before using Vellum, I paid designers to do this for me. Later, I'll cover self-publishing a non-fiction book in detail.

When to Use Digital Writing Tools

- For organising your ideas and research
- When you're ready to write a more polished draft of your book
- For editing your book
- For preparing your book for publication
- For marketing and selling your work

283

MASTERING DICTATION

Several years ago, I struggled with repetitive strain injury, or RSI. Spending hours hunched over a keyboard for a day job and then again at night wasn't good for my fingers.

One day, I spent two hours transcribing an interview by hand. When I got home, I filled a sink with ice-cold water and plunged my aching hands into it for relief.

I overcame RSI by buying a special mouse and also by using a mouse mat and keyboard with wrist guards.

That eased my RSI for a time, but mastering dictation helped too.

Dictation software, like Dragon Dictate and Dragon Naturally Speaking, is easier to learn and more accurate than ever.

If you suffer from RSI or get pain in your fingers from typing, dictation is ideal. You can dictate your book while standing, walking around the room or even without using your hands.

I can type about a five hundred to thousand words in 30 minutes if I know what I'm writing about. On the other hand, I can dictate up to 3,000 to 4,000 words in 30 minutes.

Dictation is also ideal for writing first drafts. Matthew Weiner, the showrunner of *Mad Men*, recently revealed he hired a transcriber to record his thoughts for early drafts of his hit show:

> I paid people to do research, inundated myself with material, and even hired a writer's assistant to dictate to because I was too tired to type. (It also freed my imagination).

The job of any first draft is to exist. With dictation, it's harder to edit and write at the same time. You're more likely to hit your daily target word count and get a messy first draft out of your head and onto the blank page.

Dictation helps you focus too. It's harder to stop dictating because you want to check your email, browse Facebook or do something that has nothing to do with writing.

It also encourages conversational types of writing. Because I'm speaking and not typing, I'm less likely to use bigger words or turn to complicated language and turns of phrase.

Arguably, dictation holds less value for literary non-fiction writers. It's not ideal for experimenting with your sentences or playing around with words either.

HOW TO DICTATE YOUR BOOK

The poet, teacher and non-fiction author Natalie Goldberg tells new writers to "keep your hand moving."

When it comes to dictation, keep your mouth moving!

You'll need to dictate in a quiet room with the right equipment. The quality of your microphone and environment directs the accuracy of your software.

I first tried using the inbuilt microphone on my computer for dictation, but my accuracy was below 50%. Then I tried using a cheap headset I had in my wardrobe. That didn't improve the quality much either.

So I spent around $100 on a professional dictation headset and that dramatically improved my accuracy.

If you haven't dictated a book before, it'll take time to learn this new skill so don't expect a dramatic increase in your word count... at least at first.

As with acquiring any new writing skill, allow time for a learning curve. It took me some trial and error to figure out how to build dictation into my writing workflow.

For example, you will have to learn how to speak punctuation commands. So when I want a full stop, I have to say the words "full stop." When I want to start a new paragraph, I have to say "new paragraph."

And so on.

You'll also have to avoid using filler words like "you know."

Don't expect 100% accuracy.

This will improve as the software adapts to your voice. However, it won't recognise every word you say, particularly technical terms and words affected by your accent.

For instance, my daughter has a traditional Irish name. No matter how many times I tried, I couldn't train the dictation software I use to recognise her name. I tried spelling the name and using various other tips and tricks, but the software still insisted on mangling it.

So now whenever I'm dictating a journal entry and I want to use her name, I speak a placeholder word Dragon Dictate recognises.

In this case, I'll use the name "Sarah", or I call her "my daughter." Then when I'm editing the journal entry, I search for the word 'Sarah' and replace it with my daughter's name.

Tips for Dictating Your Book

- Before investing in expensive software or a microphone, experiment with the dictation software built into Windows/OSX or Google Docs.
- When you're ready, use a microphone purpose-built for dictation.

- If you're using Dragon Dictate or Dragon Naturally Speaking, teach the software using your writing, rather than completing the built-in training. This approach will improve your accuracy.
- Speak in complete sentences, and speak your punctuation.
- Keep your chapter outline next to where you dictate, so you know what you're about to say next.
- Use filler words for complicated terms dictation software gets wrong.
- Write early drafts using dictation software; edit later drafts using your keyboard.

OWNING YOUR TOOLS

Today's digital writing tools may be powerful, but (if you're like me) you can spend more time looking for the perfect setup than writing. Only use as many digital tools as you need. Your time is better spent improving your craft and building relationships with readers.

Your writing tools of choice should support your writing, and you should own them rather than letting them own you.

How?

Turn off all the notifications on your computer so you're not dragged into another application while writing. Then close everything except your writing application of choice.

If you're getting distracted by viral cat videos, disconnect from the grid. I know one writer who even plugs out her modem while working on her book and stashes it in the attic.

Do whatever it takes, write with whatever you want, wherever you want, as long as you can finish your drafts.

GETTING THE JOB DONE

Many writers use analogue tools at some point. American non-fiction author Robert Greene, for example, uses index cards to outline his books before writing them. Digital tools, too, can save you a lot of time and help you connect with readers.

Knowing when to go analogue and digital is a useful writing skill to build. That said, always remember, your craft and readers come before any new tool.

In his book *Tribes*, Seth Godin writes:

> The tactics are irrelevant, and the technology will always be changing. The essential lesson is that every day it gets easier to tighten the relationships you have with the people who choose to follow you.

So spend most of your time working on your drafts. Concentrate on improving your craft. And then build relationships with your readers.

YOUR WRITING EXERCISES

- After you've finished the day's writing, set aside a little time for learning a new tool. Sure, there's a small learning curve to mastering Scrivener and even dictation, but you could save hours later on.
- The next time you feel blocked or when your word count plummets, take out a notepad and write out a passage by your favourite writer.

KNOWING WHEN IT'S TIME TO WRITE (AND FINDING SPACE TO DO IT)

"Tell me, what is it you plan to do with your one wild and precious life?" – Mary Oliver

I spent a year working as a copywriter in a large, air-conditioned office half an hour outside Dublin. I wrote alongside 100 other people, almost none of whom were writers.

One Monday, my boss asked me to produce a 3,000-word guide about the advantages of using cloud-based software, and he gave me a deadline to sweat over.

It didn't help that the topic was drier than a gin and tonic. I trudged through the first 200 words of an early draft, hoping I'd submit the piece on time.

While writing, I didn't pay much attention to the dull sound of my co-worker Jackie's voice or to what she was saying... at first.

While I clacked away on my keyboard, she stood:

"But you told me our deposit for the house was good and that we'd have the keys by the summer. I can't wait until September."

"Jackie, you must be patient," the estate agency said.

"I've been patient for months," Jackie shouted into her phone. "This isn't good enough. You're full of it."

Jackie berated her estate agent for five minutes before walking out of the office and slamming the door behind her.

I tried to focus on what I was writing, but all I could think about was the time I bought a house with my wife and how I hated the entire process. We'd argued for weeks about which one to buy. I didn't envy what Jackie was going through or her estate agent.

What did Jackie's real estate agent think of her? And what did any of this have to do with cloud-based software?

Ten minutes later, Jackie sat down at her desk, looked at me and said, "Don't ask."

She produced a Granny Smith apple, a bottle of Coca-Cola and packet of salt and vinegar crisps from the recesses of her brown leather handbag.

I put my fingers on the keyboard and tried to type, but then Jackie began to bite into her apple and crisps.

Crunch. Crunch. Crunch.

Jackie only stopped eating to sigh, swear under her breath and tap out a message on her phone.

I'd type and then... *Crunch. Crunch. Crunch.*

When five o'clock rolled around, I'd only written 150 words.

The next morning, my manager asked about the guide.

"It's going well," I said, thinking of the 2,850 words I still had to wade though.

"When can I expect a draft to review?" he said.

"It'll be on time," I said. "Don't worry."

I didn't want to tell him how behind I was. I needed this job to work out, and Jackie's real estate problems weren't helping.

So I took my laptop and notes and locked myself alone into a small room at the back of the office, a room devoid of apples, crisps and Jackie. I forced myself to sit in the chair, and I wrote for three hours until I finished a workable draft.

After lunch, I sat back at my desk and emailed a draft to my boss.

"Where were you Bryan?" Jackie asked.

"I was in a meeting," I said. "And it lasted all morning. How's your house coming on?"

ASSOCIATE ONE PLACE WITH WRITING

If you're having trouble finding time or space for your book, don't give up. I don't doubt your commitment, and you're not alone. Before writing this chapter, I read an email from one new writer who said:

> What I get from my wife is lip service (which would be OK if she'd let me kiss her once in a while). She knows my desire to be an author. She tells others how much time I spend writing in a way that makes me believe she's behind me. Then, like the other day...she tells me...she has something more important for me to do.

Now, instead of paying lip service to your book, take a note from Virginia Woolf. She wrote:

> A woman must have money and a room of her own if she is to write fiction.

Woolf was referring to a woman's ability to support herself and her writing financially. And yet, even today, male and female writers need a warm and quiet place with a desk, a chair and a computer or a pen and notepad.

It's up to you to seek out the quietness and space you need to write your book. Going to a room to work alone may look strange to others, but take heart: you're putting your book first.

These days, I write in a small room at the top of my house. I have a sunlight lamp, a mic for dictation and a set of noise-cancelling headphones. This setup enables me to enter a bubble. I can concentrate on writing that first draft without worrying about the logistics of writing.

When I'm feeling blocked, I go for a long walk and dictate to my phone, or I go to a coffee shop and bang out the first draft over an Americano.

You could carve out a quiet space in your house, in a coffee shop, the local library or your car. The 'where' doesn't matter as much as having that space, where you write consistently.

When the short story writer and poet Raymond Carver was starting off, he often wrote his drafts alone in his car. He told the *Paris Review*:

> I used to go out and sit in the car and try to write something on a pad on my knee.

Associate a place with writing and little else, and you'll slip into your creative groove more easily.

If it's somewhere public, just remember to leave a tip.

YOUR BULLET-PROOF GUIDE TO CREATING AN EARLY MORNING WRITING ROUTINE

For years, I wrote late at night, after the kids went to bed.

Then I'd struggle to get up the following day, go to work and spend time with the kids. It was all I could do not to pry my eyelids open with matchsticks.

Inevitably, I wrote less.

Putting writing last meant it was least likely to happen.

Then I discovered science is on the side of early morning writing. The American philosopher and psychologist William James said:

> The great thing, then, in all education, is to make automatic and habitual, as early as possible, as many useful actions as we can, and to guard against the growing into ways that are likely to be disadvantageous to us, as we should guard against the plague.

Famous early morning artists include the composer Ludwig van

Beethoven, the Danish philosopher Søren Kierkegaard and American author Ernest Hemingway.

My writing routine starts with climbing out of my pit sometime between 5.30 and 6.15 a.m.

I wash my face with cold water, meditate for 20 minutes and brew a strong coffee sweetened with honey.

Then I record five to ten ideas on paper or in Evernote. This act helps me warm up before writing for 60 to 90 minutes. My morning routine ends around 8 a.m. when it's time to get the kids up for school. Now, my writing routine works for me, but yours will look different.

Ask yourself what your ideal morning routine looks like, and write it down on paper. Thinking it through will help you find more time for working on your non-fiction book.

DECIDE WHEN TO GET UP

Pick your target time for getting up, and work slowly towards this time. Don't be a hero. If you set your alarm clock for 4 a.m. tomorrow morning, you may get up, but you'll feel exhausted. You're also unlikely to repeat this heroic feat of endurance.

Instead, set your alarm clock for half an hour earlier than your regular rising time. On the following day, set your alarm for 45 minutes earlier.

And so on.

If I rise any earlier than 5.30 a.m., I'm too exhausted to function during the day. If I rise any later than 6.15 a.m., I don't have enough time to write before life arrives. My target rising time gives me a 45-minute window between 5.30 a.m. and 6.15 a.m.

If you want to create an early morning writing routine, find enough time to write without interruption before the day begins. But don't get up so early that you risk falling asleep on your keyboard.

... AND WHEN TO SLEEP

Before you go to bed, write a note to yourself about what chapter you're going to work on. Then open up your writing application and arrange your notes.

These small acts prime your subconscious to wrestle with your book even while you're sleeping.

Each night, I prepare the following day's writing. I tidy up where I work, and I leave a short note to myself.

It says things like "fix the damn conclusion" or "work viral cat videos into chapter nine."

Setting an alarm clock for going to bed helps too. This act may sound bizarre, but you probably set one for getting up, so consider it a mindset shift.

When it rings, stop checking your emails, using your computer, playing with your phone or doing anything else that keeps you up.

Before you go to bed, put your alarm in a different room from where you sleep.

When it rings, you'll have to get out of bed and go into the other room to turn it off. The act of moving complicates pressing the snooze button or rolling over and going back to sleep.

Finally, if your partner goes to bed later than you, consider using earplugs or an eye mask.

WHAT YOU GET FOR RISING EARLY

One evening over a beer, I explained my early morning writing habit to a friend.

"When you get up before everyone else, you give the best of yourself to yourself," I said.

My friend almost choked on his beer.

"You're crazy," he said, laughing. "Where do you get this stuff from?"

My friend isn't a writer, and I couldn't expect him to understand it's the job of a writer to sit alone in a quiet room and work for hours at a time.

If the demands of your job leave you physically or mentally exhausted, you're less likely to sit down and write. What's more, when you do, the quality of your writing will suffer.

Like a lot of writers, I doubled my weekly word count by rising early to work on my book.

When you get up early in the morning, you're at your peak. No matter what happens during the day, you'll already be ahead because you've worked on your book.

BUT I REALLY AM A NIGHT PERSON!

I don't get up early every day. I sleep late at least one day on the weekend, and some days it's not possible or practical to get up early because of the demands of the previous day.

I accept these days as times to rest instead of seeing them as setbacks that prevent me from finishing a book.

I'm not going to lie and say I find time to write 365 days a year either, but when I write, I feel lighter. When I write first thing, even if it's just a journal entry, I don't come home after an exhausting day and think:

Oh no, I still have to sit down in front of the computer and fill a blank page.

If the demands of daily life aren't intruding, by all means, work on your book during the afternoon or at night. Every writer is different.

The most important thing is turning up in front of the blank page consistently and being able to work without interruption.

KEEPING UP WITH THE PROFESSIONALS

These days, I rarely have to deal with unreliable estate agents, crunchy apples and noisy packets of crisps. And yet, working alone presents a different set of challenges.

No matter where I write, I'm still free to put things off, procrastinate and say it will keep till later. I've often woken up, checked email, phoned the cable company about my bill, cleaned up after the dog and done everything else but write 500 to 1,000 words.

It took me years to learn writing is one of the most important things I need to do each day, and it's my job to minimise interruptions.

Before email.

Before social media.

Before the news.

And sometimes even before breakfast.

Remember, a doctor doesn't look at their scalpel and wonder if they'll operate now or when *Keeping Up with the Kardashians* is over.

They do their work because they are professionals.

So pick a time for working on your book every day, block-book it in your calendar and keep your appointment. Like pennies filling a jar, these writing sessions will accumulate in value over time.

One day, you'll stop typing, see you finished a 2,000 word chapter in one session and wonder, "How did I get here?"

YOUR WRITING EXERCISES

- Dedicate one place in your house, apartment or where you live to working on your book, and go there each day.
- Expect life to get in the way. When it does, pour it a glass of wine, listen to its problems and, when it passes out on the couch, get back to work.

PART II
WRITING YOUR NON-FICTION BOOK

FINDING MORE IDEAS THAN YOU
KNOW WHAT TO DO WITH

"I think like a genius, I write like a distinguished author, and I speak like a child." – Vladimir Nabokov

The Stradivarius violin has an unparalleled reputation for tone and clarity, and a single instrument is worth up to $16 million. Now, that's a lot of money to pay for a violin, so why is it so lust-worthy?

Italian craftsman Antonio Stradivari created these violins from wood affected by a mini-Ice Age during the 1700s.

Only 600 of these Italian violins exist today... and it's impossible to replicate them. Recently, a team of Dutch scientists led by Dr. Berend Stoel scanned five of these instruments and compared them to modern violins.

Dr. Stoel said:

It could be a difference in climate when the trees were harvested, or it could also be that the masters used some secret treatment on the wood, or it could be that over the course of three hundred years the violins just get better in tone.

What does this talk about violins have to do with finding ideas for your non-fiction book? Well, you need great materials if you want to create your masterpiece.

Hell, you need good materials if you're going to write something that sells.

By materials, I don't mean a pot of ink and a golden pen with a twelve-inch pink feather dangling off the end. I'm talking about the kinds of ideas that are everywhere and that you can use to write a great book... if you know where to look.

I WROTE WITH LOUSY MATERIALS... AND THIS IS WHAT HAPPENED

Confession: when I was a fresh-faced freelance journalist in my early twenties, I didn't care for research or finding ideas.

I spent days sitting on my ass waiting for my editor to send me a commission when I should have been on the lookout for ideas and news stories.

I'm a writer... I don't have time for research.

I thought writing meant pressing my fingers against the keyboard. I believed 'doing the work' meant filling the screen with random musings about what it's like to have a quarter-life crisis.

Picking up the phone and talking to living, breathing people felt like a distraction from putting one word after another on the blank page. I should have listened to Truman Capote, who said, "That's not writing, that's typing."

If I sound like I was a hard-working (if misguided) freelance journalist, don't let me fool you.

I had enough time to sit in front of the computer screen in my underwear, pick at half-eaten chocolate bars, drink cold tea and play *World of Warcraft* until 3.23 a.m.

Who has time to interview people or read through old books when you could be going on a four-hour dungeon raid?

I didn't bother looking for materials and ideas for my writing, and suffice to say, my editors didn't call with new commissions.

So, classmates from college landed jobs with national newspapers and with radio stations, while I languished on the sidelines, wondering what I'd done wrong.

After a stint on the unemployment line, I quit on journalism, but I didn't quit on writing. I looked at successful authors and wondered: *Where do they find their ideas?*

Here's what I discovered:

PROFESSIONAL AUTHORS ARE ALWAYS LOOKING FOR IDEAS

I know a smart freelance writer who keeps a **future file** of news stories and other articles that she has worked on or read. She returns to these articles every few months to write an updated version. Her editors love it.

Who plans that far ahead?

Freelance writers who earn six figures a year, that's who, and it's a strategy I wish I'd known about before I handed back my press pass.

Even Thomas Jefferson jotted down notes about everything from the growth of plants and flowers to observations about daily life.

But I'm a storyteller, why should I care about future files and swipe files?

Well, if you wait for inspiration to arrive, you'll be stood up.

From the age of 19, Mark Twain carried a personal pocket notebook with him and recorded his observations. The novelist John Cheever kept a journal throughout his life, and he often left entries about stories he was writing or wanted to write.

George Lucas also keeps a notebook with him when he's shooting a film.

Perhaps he should have carried around that notebook a little longer while writing the prequels, but you can't deny his creativity.

WHATEVER YOU WRITE, YOU'RE A COLLECTOR OF IDEAS.

Perhaps you collect stories from your personal life in a journal?

Here's one I found:

One time, my two-year-old daughter jammed a pink crayon up her nose, and I had to buy a pair of tweezers to take it out.

Perhaps you collect small details from your day?

And another:

One time, I was waiting outside a gym to collect my wife from her class. A shaven-headed bodybuilder walked outside, opened a pack of cooked chicken fillets and ate them one by one.

Or perhaps you collect random information from magazines you read?

And one more:

There's a funny type of violin from years past. It's made of whiskey water and a special wood, and it costs millions of dollars.

You may know what to do with these stories today or even tomorrow, but it's all material.

FINDING CREATIVE IDEAS THROUGH READING

I've always loved to read, but when I was a budding journalist, I preferred reading fiction I enjoyed. I didn't spend much time reading non-fiction books outside my comfort zone.

Now, that might be okay for somebody whose career doesn't involve words and ideas, but it's poison for an ASPIRING PROFESSIONAL AUTHOR.

If you're writing a non-fiction book, then reading is part of your job. You must read outside of your comfort zone. You must include the work of writers you admire and writers you detest, all while taking notes and writing ideas and your opinions down.

If you fail to feed your mind, don't expect it to serve you quality ideas when you sit down in front of the blank page.

THE ART OF WRITING A NON-FICTION BOOK

YOU NEED MORE BUTTERFLIES IN YOUR LIFE

Lots of writers use their curious side-interests and hobbies for their works.

The British author Virginia Woolf chronicled her long walks around her neighbourhood in her journals and essays.

Henry David Thoreau moved to the woodlands near Walden Pond in Massachusetts for two years, where he wrote about his self-imposed exile.

The American essayist and novelist John Cheever wrote about swimming, cycling and his extracurricular activities:

> I do have trouble with the dead hours of the afternoon without skating, skiing, bicycling, swimming, or sexual discharges or drink.

Now, Cheever liked to fill a glass or take off his pants to pass the time, but if you're struggling to find ideas, put your book and pen (or your partner) down.

Go for a short walk, work out in the gym or do something strenuous. The flow of blood and change of environment will kickstart your brain in intriguing directions.

Think of yourself as like the Danish philosopher Søren Kierkegaard. He wrote early in the morning before setting off for an afternoon walk around Copenhagen. Then he returned to write in the evening.

Charles Dickens was another prolific walker you could aspire to. On a given day, Dickens walked 12 or more miles around Kent or through the streets of Victorian London.

He used many moments from these walks as inspiration for his novels. In *Charles Dickens: A Critical Study*, critic G.K. Chesterton writes:

> There are details in Dickens' descriptions – a window, or a railing, or the keyhole of a door – which he endows with demoniac life. The things seem more actual than things really are.

303

Even if you don't think of an idea while exercising, you will have more energy for tackling your creative problem.

The ever-humble Russian writer Vladimir Nabokov fed his writing with one of the stranger hobbies I've come across. He had little time for eating, socialising or drinking coffee with friends.

Instead he loved to solve chess problems and study butterflies. Both interests informed his work; his novel *Zashchita Luzhina* (*The Luzhin Defense*), features an insane chess player.

Nabokov writes in his memoir:

And the highest enjoyment of timelessness...is when I stand among rare butterflies and their food plants. This is ecstasy, and behind the ecstasy is something else, which is hard to explain. It is like a momentary vacuum into which rushes all that I love.

THE CASE FOR TAKING A BREAK

One Sunday afternoon last July, I spent two hours trying to write a chapter for my last book. Getting nowhere and being all out of ideas, I put on a pair of trainers and went for a run.

I was ten km in and half-way around the local park when I thought of a breakthrough.

Covered in mud, I stopped running, pulled out my phone and opened the voice memo app.

I was standing in a puddle with water up to my ankles, soaked in sweat and roaring into my phone about 'needing more butterflies' in my life, when a 72-year-old lady and her manicured white poodle walked around the corner.

She mouthed 'morning' and hurried along with her dog.

When I got home that evening, I wrote for two hours without interruption; that woman and her judgmental poodle be damned.

So the next time you feel stuck or uninspired, read, pick up the phone, interview someone, go for a walk with your poodle or chase rare butterflies... no matter what kind of writer you are, your side-interests will help you reignite your creative spark.

Every time you do this, you'll learn more about how your creative process works and where the best ideas for your book come from.

HOW TO CAPTURE YOUR CREATIVE IDEAS

Keep a **swipe file** where you store facts, figures, headlines and ads relating to your area of interest or book.

You could swipe headlines and first lines, inspiring videos and pictures and compelling emails. Your file is a repository of information that, if it's not relevant to your book, will be of use at some point. Pinterest, for example, is a social swipe file.

Copywriters and advertisers keep ideas and research in their swipe files.

Famous copywriter Gary Halbert wrote a letter from prison telling his son to keep a swipe file up to date with "hot new ideas, good layouts, unusual propositions and so on."

You can also take notes using digital tools, like an app on your smartphone, or by using a small notebook that fits in your pocket.

I like using the tool Evernote. It acts as my digital brain and enables me to tag each idea. I save interesting articles, research, quotes, thoughts about books, anecdotes and more into this software. I also categorise the notes by project and type.

When I was researching my last book, *The Power of Creativity*, for example, I used the tag 'creativity' for relevant notes and ideas I wanted to find later on.

You don't have to use Evernote or worry about painful categorisation methods. Use the note-taking app on your phone, record audio files with a memo app or turn to a simple plain text editor.

Don't obsess about going digital.

Halbert got by without his digital brain. Write your ideas down on the back of your hand if you must. When I do this in public, people look at me funny.

There's that weird guy who looks off into the distance and then scribbles on the back of his hand.

If this happens to you, pay no attention to these misguided fools!

You don't want to sit down in front of the computer and realise "Baby, I've got nothing."

WHAT TO DO WITH GREAT MATERIALS

I can't promise your book will sell for $16 million in three hundred years' time. I also don't have any ancient water from a church to offer unless you count whisky.

Even if I could offer you a secret ingredient for finding amazing ideas, there's no guarantee you'll produce a masterpiece. Dr. Stoel and his team offer this caveat:

> If you are a lousy violin maker and use the best wood, you will still end up with a very bad violin.

The same applies to writing a non-fiction book.

If you're a lousy writer, all the best ideas in the world aren't much use to you. You have to take time to organise your ideas, gain the writing skills you need and then express yourself.

Then, you'll stand a better chance of finding readers and earning a living from your writing. And that's what we'll cover throughout this book.

YOUR WRITING EXERCISES

- If you're feeling blocked or devoid of ideas, fill up with someone else's ideas.
- Go for a walk/run/swim or climb your personal Everest, because exercise is fuel for finding inspiration.

RESEARCHING YOUR BOOK: THE NOBEL PRIZE APPROACH

"Study hard what interests you the most in the most undisciplined, irreverent and original manner possible." – Richard Feynman

Richard Feynman (1918-1988) was a top US scientist (and a renowned bongo player). After WWII, he spent almost a year teaching science in Rio de Janeiro. He went to Brazil as part of a programme sponsored by the US government to instruct would-be teachers.

During WWII, Feynman helped his country build the atomic bomb, but he faced a different set of problems in Brazil.

The Brazilian elementary students' habit of buying and reading physics books impressed Feynman. And yet he couldn't understand why the country produced so few physicists.

His college students perplexed him too. When he asked them specific questions, they answered correctly almost immediately.

When Feynman asked a follow-up question or asked the same question while teaching a related topic, his students looked at him like he was speaking Swahili. After some digging, Feynman discovered his students had memorised their textbooks line by line.

They were able to recite basic physics laws like, "Light is reflected from a medium with an index," but they had no idea as to *the why* behind these laws.

One day in an engineering lecture, Feynman watched students write down what the lecturer said, verbatim.

He asked one student what he was doing.

And the student replied: "Oh, we study them. We'll have an exam."

To this student and many others, mastery of a topic meant memorisation.

Feynman gave a lecture at the end of his trip and told students and faculty, "No science is being taught in Brazil."

He picked a page at random from a physics book and read out a definition of triboluminescence. This concept describes the emission of light from a substance caused by rubbing and so on.

Feynman explained anyone could read this definition aloud, but that wasn't enough. He told the perplexed group of attendees:

> And there, have you got science? No! You have only told about what a word means in terms of other words. You haven't told anything about nature—what crystals produce light when you crush them, why they produce light. Did any students go home and *try it?* He can't.

Feynman argued the Brazilian system was denying his students a useful college education. He claimed students were passing exams and teaching others how to pass exams, without understanding what they'd memorised.

When it comes to what you're teaching or writing about, I wouldn't want you to deny yourself or your readers a useful experience. So ask yourself, *'Do I understand what I'm writing about?'*

It's not enough to simply plop down what you found on the blank page like a toddler does his dinner and tell the reader, "Here, look!"

It's your job to immerse yourself in a topic through deep reading and then bring back what you find for your readers.

THE PLEASURES OF DEEP READING

Researching a non-fiction book is like diving to the bottom of the ocean and looking for treasure. You often don't know what you're going to find or even where to look.

Some days, you'll return to the surface with valuable pearls. Other days, you'll come back with nothing more than yellow plastic bottles, rusty cans and a chewed-up plastic Barbie doll to show for your trouble.

You can increase your chances of bringing back treasure through deep, active reading.

If you're reading a paperback or hardback book, annotate it with a pen or write in the margins. Affix Post-it notes or jot down your thoughts on index cards.

If you're reading a digital book, on a Kindle for example, highlight key sentences. Whatever your medium of choice, look for:

- Key statistics
- Interesting findings and insights
- Sentences that sum up the book's controlling idea
- Common concepts running throughout the book
- Sections you agree/disagree with
- Compelling turns of phrase
- Unique stories and insights

Once you finish reading a book, go back and review your notes, annotations and so on. If you're using a Kindle or e-reader, export your notes to your computer.

I also like looking on sites like Goodreads to see what other readers thought about the book. I enjoy reviewing their highlighted quotes, key takeaways and more.

Once you're finished reading and marking up a book, get ready to arrange your research.

MIND MAPPING YOUR RESEARCH

Mind mapping is a great way of arranging your research (and even your book; see next chapter) into different topics. This creative technique will help you connect different ideas and offers a means of reviewing a topic without having to re-read a book later.

It shouldn't take more than ten or 15 minutes to mind map a topic or even a book you've read. You'll need:

- A blank piece of paper (A4 size or larger)
- Some multi-coloured pens or markers
- Your book notes, highlights and annotations

Now, turn the paper on its side and write down your topic in the centre of your mind map. While reviewing your notes, draw out each of the connecting ideas using different colour pens. Thicken your branches at the root and thin them out as they move away from the central idea.

Using red, blue, black and green pens or markers will help you create a more memorable mind map. Sketch images representing concepts you came across while reading, and reorder your branches or draw another mind map if you need to.

You should be able to see the central idea and the overall structure of a book, as well as how different concepts relate to each other.

You don't have to become a Picasso of mind maps or obsess about the structure either. They're for you and you alone.

My mind map of Richard Feynman's autobiography

HOW TO TEACH YOUR READERS ABOUT A CONCEPT (LIKE RICHARD FEYNMAN)

One time while working as a journalist, I had to write a feature article about the best computer keyboards. I spent seven hours reading reviews on Amazon and watching videos on YouTube.

Was I doing the work?

God, no.

The article was about keyboards, not the atom bomb. You can only spend so much time reading before it turns into procrastination. So start using your research as part of your writing.

Do it sometime before they excavate your remains from beneath a stack of books, index cards and half-drunk cups of coffee.

As for the how?

Feynman offers four steps for understanding and teaching complicated topics.

Step One: Choose Your Concept or Topic

Think back to the work you completed earlier. You've picked a controlling idea for your non-fiction book, and each one of your chapters should have a central topic.

Now, read up on each of these topics. Arrange your research and take care to put into practice (or least interrogate) as much as you can. Do this before you start writing.

Later, you'll be able to tell stories about what you did and what happened next.

If you offer your perspective, you'll avoid the problems Feynman's Brazilian students faced. Your book will become more than regurgitated information.

Step Two: Teach Your Topic

Did you ever think, *But, I need to carry out more research.*

Well, when you're up to your eyeballs in mind maps, dog-eared books and tattered index cards, it's time to open up the blank page and get going.

Write down what you know, what you did, what you experienced and what your readers should do.

Use simple language that a small child would understand. This will force you to take apart complicated concepts and put them back together for your readers.

Be concrete. Provide practical examples. Give your readers exercises and takeaways they can use immediately.

For example, while I was training to run a marathon, I read a popular training book, full of day-by-day training plans for athletes of all levels. Suffice to say, this book sold a lot of copies.

Step Three: Go Back And Fill In Gaps in Your Knowledge

Non-fiction writing often feels like painting. You'll spend time going back over your work. Softening an introduction. Adding colour to a conclusion. Touching up a chapter here. Smoothing out a chapter there, and so on – until your chapter and your book achieves a distinctive look.

As you write about concepts in your book, you will naturally come across gaps in your knowledge. For example, you may need to look up someone's date of birth. Or you may need to go back to your research and pull out another idea to strengthen your arguments.

When this happens, *don't stop*. Mark up your manuscript or highlight the section and keep going.

During your rewrites, fill in the gaps in your book (and by extension, your knowledge about the topic).

Step Four: Review and Simplify Your Work

One of Feynman's famous principles about science is that you "must not fool yourself – and you are the easiest person to fool." This principle applies to non-fiction book writing too.

Don't presume you understand a topic if you've relied on complicated language, jargon and the original author's turns of phrase.

Despite what some authors think, you're not doing your job if you bamboozle your readers with technical concepts and lots of facts. Challenge yourself to refine your work until it's as clear as possible. During each rewrite, ask questions like:

- Do I understand what I'm writing about?
- Have I made assumptions about myself or my readers?
- Have I said this in the easiest way possible for my readers?
- Have I explained technical terms, jargon and so on?
- What can I take out?
- *What else* can I take out?
- Is this clear?
- Is this concise?

- Would Richard Feynman approve?

Surely You're Reading, Mr. Feynman!

Don't be afraid by the name(s) on the front of a book or if you're reading something by an 'expert'. Once you get deep into research and have shattered the ice protecting a topic, you'll find many conflicting – and even lousy – ideas.

Several years after his Brazilian escapade, the US Board of Education asked Feynman to serve on a curriculum commission. They wanted him to choose textbooks for the state of California.

Against his better judgment, Feynman agreed, and he looked over the proposed schoolbooks based on the merits of their advice.

He set up a special shelf in his study downstairs and stacked the books 17 feet high, and he began to read through them. Feynman said his wife likened the experience to living over a volcano.

He described her experience living with him, saying:

> It would be quiet for a while, but then all of a sudden, 'BLLLLLOOOOOOWWWWW!!!!'–there would be a big explosion from the 'volcano' below.

Feynman blew up loudly and frequently.

Many of the textbooks were lousy, false and hurried. He didn't like the examples within them and couldn't see how they would help elementary students learn scientific topics.

Feynman became increasingly frustrated with the "useless, mixed-up, ambiguous and confusing books." He complained:

> Everything was written by somebody who didn't know what the hell they were talking about, so it was a little bit wrong, always!

While on the commission, Feynman read a math book that 65 engineers approved. Feynman knew there were some good engineers at the company. But he argued taking the opinions of 65 engineers to write a book will produce an average one at best:

It was once again the problem of averaging the length of the emperor's nose... It would have been far better to have the company decide who their better engineers were and to have them look at the book.

When Feynman found out other people on the commission didn't even read the books, he resigned and wrote the experience off as wasted effort.

If you want to avoid producing an average book, or one no-one reads, don't water down your opinions. Avoid writing for the masses or deferring to 'so-called experts'.

Be honest about your opinions. Have the courage of your convictions. Hold your research and topic to account.

THE CURRENTS OF GREAT RESEARCH

Theoretical physicist. Nobel Prize winner. Renowned bongo player.

Richard Feynman had a lot of credits to his name. He was also the kind of reader and non-fiction writer who could tell the difference between a good book and a lousy book. Between memorising an idea and understanding it. Between interrogating a concept and regurgitating it.

He understood it's not enough to know an idea. You must understand the thinking behind it...and this is particularly true if you're going to write about it.

The best non-fiction books contain more than the author's experiences. A current of research flows beneath each chapter, giving the book a life of its own.

Like Feynman, it's your job as an author to break through the frozen ice protecting many books and research sources. Figure out what you agree or disagree with and how concepts and ideas relate to each other.

Commit to reading books, to understanding the thinking behind them and to putting into practice what you find. Just remember to point readers to your sources at the back of *your book*.

If you master the research process, you'll be able to connect abstract ideas to your experiences and your readers' problems.

They'll thank you for it.

YOUR WRITING EXERCISES

- Consider the last book that you read: What were the key topics within this book? How do these topics relate to each other, and can you connect them to ideas in other books?
- Create a simple mind map of the last book you read, reflecting on the key takeaways. Now, practice doing this for each book you read and store these mind maps together, so you can review your research.

CRACKING THE BOOK OUTLINING CODE

"Give me six hours to chop down a tree, and I will spend the first four sharpening the axe." – Abraham Lincoln

So you've interviewed your ideal readers, filled your swipe file and you know what your non-fiction book must deliver... now what?

Well like a grandmaster surveying the chessboard and planning their end-game, you need to be able to step back from your ideas.

You don't want to discover thirty or forty hours into your book that you're up to your eyeballs in research and writing about the wrong things.

Professional non-fiction writers know how to arrange their thoughts... and they often rely on outlines before they put ink on the blank page.

You could write from the seat of your pants, but this uncertain way of writing lends itself better to fiction or literary writing.

A book outline will help you see if you're true to your book's controlling idea, if your arguments stand up and if you're writing what your readers want.

CALCULATING YOUR TARGET WORD COUNT

Your book's ideal word count depends on your sub-genre. Writing books, like this, are typically short while historical biographies often run over 100,000 words.

That said, many successful non-fiction books are approximately 50,000-80,000 words.

For example:

- Malcolm Gladwell's *Blink* is over 70,000 words.
- James Altucher's *Choose Yourself* is 74,500 words.
- Michael Hyatt's *Living Forward* is 64,480 words.
- Seth Godin's *New York Times* best-seller *The Dip* is approximately 24,000 words.

If you're unsure about an appropriate target, buy five of the most popular books in your niche and estimate their word counts.

UNDERSTANDING THE STRUCTURE OF A SUCCESSFUL BOOK

Act one and act three typically comprise 60% of your word count, while act two comprises 40% (excluding your introduction, references and so on).

Stray too far from this rule of thumb, and you risk unbalancing your book.

It's a classic form of storytelling with a distinct beginning, middle and end. The first act connects to the second and the second to the third, forming an arc that satisfies readers.

Act one is the beginning of your book.

Usually, act one begins with a memorable scene, a dramatic incident or a call-to-action. In this act, hook your reader by introducing a problem or by setting up the story driving your book.

Act two is the middle build of your book.

In the meat of your book, elaborate on the problem and heighten the conflict. Show what's at stake and present challenges you or the reader must overcome.

Act three, the final third, brings resolution or closure for your readers.

It includes a climax where you either solve the big problem your book is addressing or offer a resolution. The reader experiences a payoff or gets the solution they paid for.

In the case of this book, the first act reveals what happens when you decide you want to become a non-fiction author (the hook).

The second act covers gaining the skills and work habits of a professional author (the build).

The third act addresses finishing your work and embracing the freedom that comes with being a published author (the payoff).

Obviously, there are exceptions to the three-act structure, such as collections of essays, literary journalism and so on.

That said, the three-act structure is a universal concept. Most aspiring non-fiction authors should embrace it as it will bring a sense of balance to your book.

Now, let's pick an approach for creating your three-act structure.

THE ANALOGUE APPROACH: USING INDEX CARDS

I spent a year reading books about creativity as part of my research for *The Power of Creativity*. I scribbled in the margins of these books, journaled about what I found and bored anyone who asked me, "Where do great ideas come from?"

Then I spent four months organising my ideas. I free wrote about creativity. I extracted ideas, and I turned them into provisional chapter titles. And I recorded these on sixty index cards.

On each card, I created a rough list of ideas in the form of five to ten bullet points. I noted other books and stories to reference. Then, I pinned these index cards to a wall near where I write so that I could live with this outline.

I spent a month working on this outline before transferring it to my computer and expanding on each bullet point.

Did I plan my book like this because I'm an obsessive weirdo? Perhaps.

But I wanted to spend as much mental energy as possible during the planning stage. When the time came to write, I felt more confident about the direction of my book.

Outlining my book with pen and paper, and then later with Evernote, helped me figure out what I wanted to write about in each chapter. It also helped me identify gaps in my research and problems in my work UPFRONT.

Obviously, my outline and table of contents evolved. But, when I was starting from 'Total word count: 0', my outline served as a map. It saved me time and helped me beat procrastination.

Step 1: Categorise Your Book's Key Ideas

You'll need a red and blue pen, a packet of 3x5-inch index cards and a table where you can arrange your ideas. Now, write down a single idea or concept in red pen, one per index card.

Each idea should correspond to the central concept behind a book chapter. For example, in the case of this chapter, I wrote down 'Arranging Your Ideas' at the top of an index card.

Step 2: Expand on Your Key Ideas

Write down five to ten bullet points with your blue pen. Your points should be clear, short and snappy. Try to sum up the key parts forming your single idea. Use sub-bullet points if necessary. If you make a mistake, cross out your ideas or tear up a card and start again.

Step 3: Flesh out Your Entire Book

Keep going until you have broken down all the big ideas for your book on index cards.

Don't get caught up in the exact wording. Your job is to get the essence of each idea out of your head or swipe file and onto the index cards.

The larger your book, the more index cards you'll need. You can outline an article using just three or four index cards, whereas you may need as many as 50-60 cards for a non-fiction book.

Step 4: Arrange Your Ideas (and the Structure of Your Book)

Lay your index cards beside each other on a table. Rearrange your cards, taking care to remove irrelevant ideas and add new ones. Do this until you're happy with the structure of your book and the key topics in each chapter.

Typically, I sort each index card by putting the cards for:

- Act one on the left of the table
- Act two in the centre
- Act three on the far right

Then, I create another section for cards I feel unsure about.

Step 5: Live with Your Book Structure

Spend at least a week considering what's on your index cards and the structure of your book.

I like using a whiteboard for this process. It's less intrusive than taking over a table for days or weeks. Plus, I don't have to worry about the kids or my dog knocking my whiteboard (and my book) over.

Step 6: Start Writing Your Book

You don't need to nail the structure of your book before you start filling the blank page. You can always go back and reframe this structure as you write. But doing this work up front will reduce the amount of time you spend (and the hair you pull out) on a painful rewrite.

If you follow this process of refining, adding and subtracting, you stand a better chance of writing a book true to your controlling idea and what readers want.

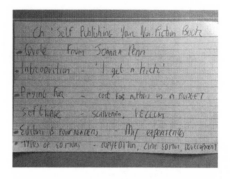

One of my index cards that outlines a chapter in this book

HOW TO KNOW IF THIS APPROACH IS FOR YOU

Pen and paper and other analogue tools come with fewer distractions than a computer. The smell of ink, the dry feel of paper, and a stack of well-worn books are more tangible than any click, buzz or notification from a writing application.

This approach is for you if sometimes wish you could plunge your hand into the screen and get a physical feel for your book.

THE DIGITAL APPROACH: USING SPREADSHEETS

When I was a pale-faced writer with more hair, I told anyone who would listen, "I hate spreadsheets. They're for right-side-of-the-brain thinkers, and they're for accountants who spend too much time looking at profit and loss statements."

Ah, how wrong I was.

You can break down an intimidating non-fiction book using a spreadsheet and write it faster. Zooming out to arrange your ideas is faster than playing with blocks of text in a word processor.

Remember, you're not going to write in the spreadsheet. Instead, your goal is to create a system for categorising and organising ideas for your book.

You can open up on the blank page later.

Step 1: Set up Your Spreadsheet

Create a spreadsheet, and name it after a potential title for your book. Label column A in the spreadsheet as 'Act', column B as 'Chapter', column C as 'Idea' and column D as 'Word count'.

Step 2: Pick an Idea for a Chapter in Your Book

In column B of the spreadsheet, write down the central idea underpinning a chapter you're going to write. Don't worry if you're unclear on what each chapter is about. You can always revise for clarity (and fill in the details of column B) later.

Step 3: Break Down Your Idea for This Chapter

Review your notes, research and reader interview transcript. Then in column C, write down your ideas for the key sections in this chapter. A sentence or two describing each idea should suffice, and you should aim for five to six ideas.

In my case, the key sections include 'Finding out What Readers Want', 'Mastering Your Tools', 'Acting on Feedback' and so on.

Step 4: Set Word Counts for Each Section in Your Book

In column D, write down your target word count for each section. Ideally, each section is the same length, give or take 10%.

You don't want to write an 800-word introduction for a 1,500-word book chapter, just as you don't want a book with a 40,000-word hook and a 2,000-word payoff.

Seek out balance between each chapter and section in your book.

Step 5: Complete Your Spreadsheet

Now, while reviewing your notes, interview transcripts and research, work from right to left in your spreadsheet.

Write down the key:

- Sections in each chapter
- Chapters in your book
- Acts in your book

It should take you about 15-20 minutes to arrange ideas for a single chapter and several hours to arrange each chapter into an act.

Step 6: Review Your Ideas

Now, review your ideas, moving and re-categorising them as required. Again, this will take several hours to get right. Use copy-and-paste to speed things up and re-categorise your ideas by section, chapter and act.

Step 7: Start Writing

Now, you should have a working outline that serves as your North Star. You've broken your large and intimidating writing project into small, digestible pieces. You can tackle these each day.

You see, it's much easier to show up and write a 300-word section for Chapter Four than it is to sit down with the intention of 'working on my book'.

A	B	C	D
Act	Chapter title	Points to cover	Target Word Count
1	So You Want to Write Your First Book?	Decide What Type of Writer You Are Establish what your book is about Robert McKee Ideas and concepts within a book What aspiring writers. vs actually authors do i.e. bar analogy	2200
1	Cracking the book outlining code	Plotter or pantser Provide guidelines for both approaches	2200
1	Finding Out What Your Readers Expect (And Who They Are)	Interview them Research forums etc. Marketing vs. writing Coming up with a controlling idea and positioning statement Provide templates and examples	2200
2	Researching Your Book: The Noble Prize Approach	Types of research The story of Richard Feynman teaching and in Brazil Step 1-4 Importance of reading	2200
2	Taking Charge Your Tools Before They Take Charge of You	Owning your tools Tools I use Analogue vs digital How to dictate a book chapter	2200
2	Taming That Unruly First Draft	Get it out of your head I still can't get started Why you should write every day Knowing when your first draft is done Don't start on page 1	2200
3	Mastering Your Writing Self Like a Zen Master	Setting up your place where you write The tools I use: Scrivener, Google Drive etc. What you can ignore Tools as a form of procrastination Lack of self-belief and turning it into fuel	2200
3	Self-editing Your Book Like a Smart Author Should	Work with an editor How to find an editor Marking up your manuscript Round 1: Editing the Structure of Your Book Chapter Round 2: Editing Your Book Chapter in Relation to Other Book Chapters Round 3: Line-editing Your Book Chapter Proofing and Fact-checking Your Work Provide tips e.g. using the active voice	2200
3	Finishing (And Shipping) Your Work	Set a date What to do when you finish Money, freedom, success. Deciding what to write next	2200

What a book outline in a spreadsheet looks like

HOW TO KNOW IF THIS APPROACH IS FOR YOU

This approach is great for writers who are comfortable with digital tools and don't get distracted. It's faster than using index cards because you can manipulate the structure of your book on-screen.

A spreadsheet outline of your book offers a bird's-eye view that can help you fix problems upfront. For example, you can check word counts for each section and then address any imbalances.

But I Still Hate Spreadsheets!

If you're struggling to get to grips with a spreadsheet, create a mind map of your book and of each of the chapters within your book using a tool like iMindMap.

In the previous chapter, I explain how to use mind maps for your research, and you can follow the same process for your writing.

THE PLEASURE OF ARRANGING YOUR IDEAS

Most professional writers base their books on meticulous research and lots of caffeine.

Once a week, devote yourself to reading your notes, journal entries, research and so on, taking care to categorise what you find.

Consider:

- Which ideas are the strongest, and how can I build on them?
- Which ideas are the weakest, and can I remove them?
- What ideas am I missing?
- How can I reorder my ideas and clarify my writing?
- What are the obvious gaps in my research?

When you review your ideas, you can fix your book's structure without line-editing sentences, paragraphs and sections.

What's more, it's always a delight to find a useful idea in your notes that you'd forgotten.

Pick an approach for outlining your book and work on your structure until it feels solid. You don't need to arrange every little idea before you start writing.

By all means, set yourself a hard deadline if you're worried about overplanning your book.

Once you've established a three-act structure, you'll have a strong foundation for your book, and that's what we're going to build on next.

YOUR WRITING EXERCISES

- Calculate the target word count of your book (and each act) based on other popular books within your sub-genre.
- Front-load the hard work of writing a non-fiction book by organising your ideas using either index cards or a spreadsheet.

TAMING THAT UNRULY FIRST DRAFT

"I have no money, no resources, no hopes. I am the happiest man alive." – Henry Miller

I once wrote the first draft of a book chapter that smelt so bad, I had to open up the office window while reading it.

It's a good thing my first drafts are for me alone, and yours should be too. When you sit down to write a first draft, you may lack confidence or feel uninspired by what you're about to do.

Today, it's you alone wrestling with your ideas and stories, and if you pin one to the page only to decide you don't like the look of it, nobody needs to know.

Most writers, even successful ones, don't write good first drafts. They're more concerned with getting the words out of their heads and onto the blank page.

They know they can fix their drafts during a rewrite.

You may feel like you're writing with a crayon in your mouth, and that's okay.

Most successful authors don't experience moments of white-hot inspiration while writing their first draft.

Instead, there's a determined soul plugging away at their manuscript, one sentence at a time. He or she looks at their word count or the clock and all the while thinking, "It'll do for now. I'm almost there. I can fix this later."

WORK ON YOUR FIRST DRAFT EVERY DAY... UNTIL IT'S DONE

The American non-fiction writer Henry Miller (1891-1980) produced dozens of books, essays and pamphlets during his career. He often wrote about his personal experiences in vivid and shocking detail, and many of his books were banned.

Like many aspiring writers, Miller had little money during the early part of his career. He spent ten years writing in obscurity in Paris relying on the support of fellow writer (and lover) Anaïs Nin.

Miller approached his first drafts as if they were a voyage of discovery, and first drafts often terrified him.

He said:

> I began in absolute chaos and darkness, in a bog or swamp of ideas and emotions and experiences. Even now I do not consider myself a writer, in the ordinary sense of the word. I am a man telling the story of his life, a process which appears more and more inexhaustible as I go on.

Successful authors like Miller sit down in front of the blank page almost every day. They don't wait until the weekend, for inspiration to strike or to feel confident about writing a draft.

They do the work because writing is their job and not a hobby. They write more lousy first drafts than amateurs... and they discover what does and doesn't work.

The author and blogger James Altucher is a more contemporary example. He specialises in non-fiction, and he writes one article a day, every day.

He says:

You can't be a master in one day. You have to improve a little every day.

Now, I'm no Henry Miller, but here's the creative workflow I use to fumble through the darkness and work on an intimidating first draft.

- I go to a quiet room, office, library or coffee shop.
- Depending on where I am, I brew or order a cup of coffee.
- I disconnect my computer from the internet.
- I put my phone in airplane mode.
- I open up Scrivener.
- I arrange the outline for the chapter in question.
- I set a timer for 30 minutes.
- I write, keep my fingers moving and avoid stopping to edit myself (This is harder than it sounds).
- When the buzzer sounds, I stand up and take a two-minute break.
- After this break, I review my outline and notes.
- I repeat my 30 minute writing session two to four times until I hit the day's word count.

When you turn up in front of the blank page to write a first draft, forget your past accomplishments and failures. You may have written a hundred, a thousand or even ten thousand words yesterday. Or maybe you didn't write at all.

Today, you just have to write a lousy first draft... because there are no *good* first drafts. The only job of a first draft is to exist.

You can fix those messy mistakes, take out what doesn't work and put in what's needed during the second, third and fourth drafts.

WHY YOU SHOULDN'T START WRITING YOUR FIRST DRAFT ON PAGE ONE

Many professional writers appear to possess superpowers (Miller, I'm looking at you).

When they sit down to write, they stack up chapter after chapter. They smash through daily word counts that we mere mortals can only dream of.

So does a radioactive spider bite these writers while they were thumbing through the dusty final pages of *Tropic of Cancer*?

Well, if you press a professional writer long enough, they'll tell you that writing the beginning of a first draft is the hardest part.

An introduction to a non-fiction book, or even a chapter, explains or sets up what's about to happen.

But how can you write an introduction if you don't know what comes next?

A conclusion wraps up what was just said. Again, how can you write one if you don't know what you just said!

Whether you're a plotter or a pantser, it's a perplexing conundrum that feels ripped straight from *The Matrix*.

Most professional writers don't care much for conundrums, not when they have a deadline, kids to feed and an overweight cat to manicure.

Instead, they lay out their notes and outlines (if they have them), and they look for an easy way into their first drafts. Then, they often start in the middle of their books and write forwards...or backwards.

Opening up in the middle of your book will help you gain momentum faster. You could:

- Start writing from chapter five or 25, or from anywhere that inspires you.
- Start writing by saying something like, "Then, there I/he/she was..."
- Begin in the middle of a sentence, paragraph or idea.

- Write as close to the end as you can get without stumping yourself.
- Write about what you think of some research or findings for your book.
- Write up an interview you completed for your book.
- Write about a problem you or your readers are having that relates to your book.

Using this approach, write to the beginning, write to the end or jump around if you have to. Work through your first draft paragraph by paragraph, page by page and cup of coffee by cup of coffee.

I STILL CAN'T GET STARTED!

Have you ever looked at the blank page and found it difficult to get started? Well, it was Ernest Hemingway who said:

> There is nothing to writing. All you do is sit down at a typewriter and bleed.

It's no wonder many new writers struggle when they start sitting down in front of the blank page regularly.

So lower the bar.

Pick a single idea from your book and see where it takes you. Give yourself permission to write nonsense for ten, twenty or even sixty minutes. Write for the sheer hell of it without fear or expectation.

When a runner is training for a big race, he or she practices by competing in shorter or more low-key races before the main event. These training races are more about building self-confidence than performing.

When you're starting off, it's enough to turn up in front of the blank page and limber up too. Later on, once you're writing at pace, you can rewrite your earlier drafts or even discard them for something better.

You should also set yourself up for success each day. Prolific

THE ART OF WRITING A NON-FICTION BOOK

writers know how important it is to start writing quickly. So they go easy on themselves.

Ernest Hemingway famously stopped writing in the middle of a sentence so he'd know exactly where to resume the following day.

Here's what happens when you stop writing before you empty the tank:

Your subconscious brain continues working while you're sleeping, working or showering.

Then, when you sit down to write the following day, you'll find it much easier to pick up from where you left off.

WHAT TO EXPECT FROM YOUR FIRST DRAFT

Many writers call their first pass 'the vomit draft'.

In an interview with Tim Ferris, American non-fiction author Neil Strauss said:

> ...your first draft is only for you. No one is ever going to see it, so you don't have to worry about it. You're not going to turn it in. You're not going to show it to friends to evaluate – because it's only for you.

So don't stop to edit yourself, straighten up your sentences or to see if what you wrote sounds reasonable.

If you begin fixing your draft, you'll engage a different part of your brain, the part that belongs to your internal editor. Your editor has a place in the writing process but not when you're trying to reach a target word count.

He or she wants to censor your work and doesn't care that you're trying to hit a word count by the end of your writing session.

So expect misplaced apostrophes. Become friends with dangling modifiers. Invite those hackneyed ideas to dinner.

Don't feel surprised when typos slip out and when your hooks are so clichéd that they make *Days of Our Lives* looks like *Hamlet*.

Your first draft is for getting creative ideas and research onto the page. It takes many revisions to turn a first draft into a book you can publish, and you're going to do all that when you invite your internal editor out to play later on.

HOW LONG IS A GOOD FIRST DRAFT?

First drafts are as long as they need to be. The ideal length also depends on the conventions of your sub-genre.

By now, you should understand your genre's average word count, and you can use this as a target.

So:

- If you write 1,000 words of your first draft a day, you'll produce 6,000 words a week and still be able to take Sunday off.
- If you write 6,000 words a week, you'll have a draft finished somewhere between four and 12 weeks, depending on the length and sub-genre of your book.
- If you write 6,000 words a week for a year, you'll produce over 300,000 words, which is far longer than most popular non-fiction books.

Okay, you won't be able to use a lot of your 300,000 words... but there's gold in there. You'll find it when you sift through your words, ideas and stories during the editing process.

Remember, your goal is to finish writing your first draft so that you have something to rewrite and edit.

While working on the second or third draft, you can gather more people around your writing and fix your messy mistakes. Enlist unsuspecting family members, friends, an editor and even first readers.

Ask what they found confusing in your draft, what worked and what bored them. Then, go about fixing these problems during your next rewrite.

A NOTE ON LOGISTICS

A first draft will cover your desk, floors and even your walls. You've got to crack open a part of yourself and spill what's inside onto the page. You can't do this if you're working in chaos or you don't know where anything is.

When the American poet Raymond Carver was starting off, he wrote on notepads in his car.

The American novelist John Cheever wrote most of his best works alone in a basement in New York wearing just a pair of boxers.

The British author Virginia Woolf worked in a small writing room in her garden, constructed from a wooden toolshed beneath a loft.

These authors, like most true professionals, went to the same place regularly to work on their first drafts.

While writing a book, I often cover my desk (and the ground) with index cards, books, torn-up first drafts and wrappers from half-eaten chocolate bars.

So you're going to need a place to write... and to make a mess each day, without interruption. Creativity demands lots of space, but by all means, tidy up when you're done.

KNOWING WHEN YOU'RE FINISHED WITH A FIRST DRAFT

Raymond Carver spent weeks, months or even years working on his poetry, essays and short stories. And yet, even he recognised the value of writing his first drafts quickly. He said:

> It doesn't take that long to do the first draft of the story, that usually happens in one sitting, but it does take a while to do the various versions of the story. I've done as many as twenty or thirty drafts of a story.

So don't overburden your first draft with expectations. That can come later when you rewrite and edit your book. Once you've finished the first draft of your book, you can take the crayon out of your mouth and relax.

Now, you have a body of writing that you can mould and shape into something your readers will enjoy.

YOUR WRITING EXERCISES

- Set a target word count for your book, and then break it down into targets for each chapter. Now, pick these off one-by-one.
- Do whatever it takes to get the words out of your head and onto the blank page. Record a first draft into the voice app on your phone. Dictate it. Sell your firstborn if you must.

MASTERING YOUR WRITING SELF
LIKE A ZEN MASTER

"From a certain point onward there is no longer any turning back. That is the point that must be reached." – Franz Kafka

You're excited about the progress of your book, but half-way through, you stop and wonder...

Will people really care about what I've got to say? How will this pay my bills anyway? What if I'm wasting my time?

These negative thoughts fester in your mind, and your lack of self-belief paralyses you.

So you stop working on your ideas. You decide against finishing your first or second draft. You put off editing what you've written. You leave your book in a drawer and don't look at it for weeks or months at a time.

Fear not: many authors before you have faced (and overcome) this problem.

EVEN FRANZ KAFKA LACKED SELF-BELIEF

Born in 1883 in Prague, Franz Kafka worked a demanding job as a lawyer for the Worker's Accident Insurance. Each day, he worked from 8 or 9 a.m. until 2 or 3 p.m.

Then, he ate lunch and took a long nap. Sometime around 11 p.m., after dinner and exercise, Kafka wrote until he fell asleep.

Kafka famously said about what it takes to fill the blank page:

> You need not leave your room. Remain sitting at your table and listen. You need not even listen, simply wait, just learn to become quiet, and still, and solitary. The world will freely offer itself to you to be unmasked. It has no choice; it will roll in ecstasy at your feet.

Throughout his life, Kafka suffered from boils, depression and anxiety while not writing. He was an indecisive insomniac who was afraid of living and terrified by the prospects of his death.

He was painfully aware of the toll day-to-day life and ill-health took from his creative work and what he had to do to overcome his problems.

While living in Prague, he published *The Metamorphosis*, (a chilling novella of a man who turns into an insect) to no great acclaim. He also wrote several other books and stories, but he didn't believe in their merits. After all, this was a man who said:

> Writing is utter solitude, the descent into the cold abyss of oneself.

After contracting tuberculosis, Kafka quit his job to recuperate. He continued to struggle with poor health, and fearing that he wouldn't live long, he told his friend Max Brod to destroy his writings once he died.

Despite these personal and physical problems, Kafka wrote consistently. He kept his strict daily routine and cultivated tremendous self-discipline.

Towards the end of his life, he travelled to Vienna for treatment at a sanatorium before dying in Kierling in Austria in 1924.

After his death, Brod read through Kafka's papers and decided to ignore his old friend's request. Brod believed in his friend's writing... even if Kafka didn't.

The following year, Brod published *The Trial*. It's a short, dark novel about a man locked in a hopeless court system.

Afterwards, Brod published *The Castle*. This novel is about a protagonist fighting against the authorities ruling over a village. Over the following years, Kafka's writing became popular in Eastern communist Europe.

Today, we recognise Kafka as one of the literary heavyweights of the 19th century, and yet he never believed in himself.

So you see, it's normal to lack self-belief; the trick is to handle it so that you can learn how to gain confidence as a writer.

STOP WITH THE COMPARISONITIS

It's not polite to talk about jealousy but...

As much as I love writers like Kafka, I cower in the shadows of their natural talents, beneath the towering ambition of the works.

I sometimes compare their accomplishments to my own, and I reach a standstill with my writing.

Even when I think of more contemporary writers, their popularity is enough for me to question what I'm attempting.

No new writer in their natural mind should compare themselves to the likes of famous authors like Malcolm Gladwell, Truman Capote or even Kafka.

And yet, it's difficult.

Their creative works wait for us in bookstores, at airports, on television, all over the internet, on Twitter, Facebook and more.

When I hear a voice whispering, "Look how great Gladwell is, and then there's you, writing about the wrong things," or, "Truman Capote never blogged, why are you wasting your time?" I want to quit.

I have to remind myself what I'm looking at is the summit of their public successes and not their private failures. Their successes represent what they reveal to the world. But nobody sees the abandoned manuscripts, the torn-up pages and unfinished books.

Know that when you compare yourself to successful writers, all you see is what you lack and not how far you've come.

This brings me to...

USE YOUR LACK OF SELF-BELIEF AS FUEL

If you only write about your successes and how well things are going, your readers won't be able to stomach this sanitised version of your ideas.

They want to hear the grubby details.

Several years ago, I became a father for the first time. It was a happy time, but after my son was born, I dreamt about death and how my life would end.

Late at night, when everyone was asleep, I lay in bed clenching and unclenching my fists and trying not to worry, a little like Kafka.

I knew I wasn't depressed, but I worried there was something wrong with me. Then a friend (also a recent father) confessed having the same thoughts.

I learnt as we get older, it's natural to consider mortality and death. To pretend death doesn't exist is to live in ignorance of the bond we all share. So I used these insights to write an essay about becoming a father for the first time and what this meant for me.

So the next time something goes wrong, when you fail and wonder if you've still got it, pause.

Consider what went wrong or what you're struggling with, and ask yourself, *How can I turn this private failure into fuel for my writing?*

Look...

Kafka suffered from anxiety, depression and ill-health throughout his life. And yet, he drew on these experiences for his writing.

In *The Metamorphosis*, his protagonist Gregor Samsa says:

I cannot make you understand. I cannot make anyone understand what is happening inside me. I cannot even explain it to myself.

That's an insight that could have only come from Kafka's inner struggles. So, when writing your book, bleed into it. Because it's all material.

Because it all counts.

PUT ON YOUR LIFE JACKET

When you doubt yourself, it's natural to want to postpone writing because you're tired, bored or 'just not feeling it.' But it's your job to swim through these choppy waters and continue your journey towards becoming an author.

It's not always easy, which is why most successful authors keep to a strict schedule. Like a doctor or an engineer, they rise early, work late or go to the same place every day to work.

Like Kafka, they write because they have to and not just when they feel the hand of inspiration on their shoulders.

Remember, every writer is at a different stage along their journey. For you, it could be something as simple as writing 500 words a day for 31 days. It could be finishing your first chapter. Or it could be self-publishing your first book.

Recognise these small markers as you sail past them.

It's up to you to strap on a life jacket when the stormy waters of self-doubt threaten to pull you under, because committing to your book means developing the mental strength to silence negative inner-monologue... and keep writing.

USING A WRITING LOG

When I'm writing a book, I use a timer on my computer to track my hours and a spreadsheet to record the status of each chapter. I also use Google Calendar to manage my deadlines and a To-Do list for my commitments.

At the end of a writing session, I record how long I spent writing, what I wrote and my word count or writing milestone. At the end of the week, I total up each column.

Sometimes, I try to beat this total the following week. Knowing what I accomplished (or failed at) helps me see if I'm progressing or lying to myself.

I'm a little weird when it comes to tracking my time, but I blame Ernest Hemingway. He wrote standing up and kept a large board next to where he worked. It was there, he tracked his daily word count so as "not to kid myself."

If you want to master yourself, keep a writing log of your progress. Review the past month, three months, the past year and even the past four years.

Don't over think it. It should only take a few minutes each day to record your progress. You could track:

- Your daily word count
- Your target word count for the week or month
- How long you spent writing
- What you wrote
- What you're going to write next
- The current status of each chapter in your book

Do you need help tracking your writing? If so, I've created a freewriting log that will help you manage the progress of your book.

It's part of your book writing bonus that you can get at becomeawritertoday.com/author

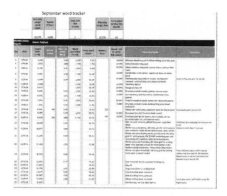

An example of a busy month from my writing log

GAINING CONFIDENCE IN YOURSELF

Kafka's writings only found a rightful audience after he died. Now, I wouldn't like for you to wait that long before you publish your book, start earning money from your writing and find success.

I spent a lot of time waiting to publish my articles and books and for editors and readers to find me.

I waited too long.

So, several years ago, I committed to publishing one blog post a week (perfection, be damned!) and to sending it to readers and subscribers of my email list.

These days, I try to do this every Thursday. I can only do this by keeping to a strict writing schedule, writing even when I don't feel like it and tracking my progress. Some weeks, when Thursday morning comes around, I imagine reasons not to press publish, not to press send.

'You're wasting your time, Bryan. Nobody will read this. Your ideas are half-baked, and you've told all the wrong stories.'

It doesn't help that writing often means getting comfortable with failure.

And yet...

When I press publish, when I press send, it's a minor victory.

So here's the thing:

Self-belief is something writers of all levels struggle with during their careers. All you have to do is learn from your mistakes (because they will happen) and how to gain confidence as a writer.

Today, you can get feedback about your work easily and share your writing and ideas with the world. You don't need a patron like Max Brod or a wealth of resources to do this either.

You can email versions of your book to trusted friends or colleagues. You can blog. You can hire an editor. You can self-publish.

Once you get your ideas out into the world, you'll see you already have everything you need to master yourself and your writing.

All you have to do is to be brave enough to recognise your lack of self-belief for what it is. A marker on your journey towards becoming an accomplished non-fiction author.

YOUR WRITING EXERCISES

- Consider a personal or professional failure related to your book topic and write about it.
- Keep a writing log. There, record your daily progress, and use these insights to improve your craft.

SELF-EDITING YOUR BOOK UNTIL IT'S GOOD ENOUGH TO PUBLISH

"Grammar is a piano I play by ear." – Joan Didion

Learning how to self-edit a book is a little liking having sex for the first time. At first, you may not understand what you're doing or where anything goes, but with practice, it gets better.

Before you even pick up a red pen, finish writing your book's first draft. Otherwise, you risk turning into the frustrated aspiring author who tries to write and edit at the same time.

If you haven't done this before, understand there's more to self-editing than moving around your adjectives, adverbs and nouns.

Distilling a draft into a concise piece of writing takes some discipline and an ounce of self-awareness.

It's difficult to cut a paragraph or a chapter that you love... if it's not working out.

That said, it's also what most successful non-fiction authors do before they send their drafts to beta readers for review or to a professional editor for feedback.

GETTING READY TO EDIT YOUR FIRST DRAFT

After spending weeks or months writing about a topic, the work becomes too hot to touch, let alone edit.

When you finish your first draft, let it sit in your computer for a few days (or longer depending on the length of your book).

Swim. Run. Meditate. Eat steak in an expensive restaurant. Take the dog for an overdue walk. Do something that has nothing in common with writing.

Your ideas will cool and your memory fade. Later, when you open up that messy first draft, you'll look at it and think, "Oh yeah, I remember this."

Before you edit anything, change the line spacing of your work to double-spaced. Change the font to Courier New and the size to 12.

Better yet, download the font Courier Prime. This revised version of the Courier font looks better on larger screens and has all the benefits of its older brother.

(Available at https://www.fontsquirrel.com/fonts/courier-prime)

Many professional journalists and sub-editors format their work this way because it's easy on the eye and takes approximately one minute to read a page. This simplifies spotting errors, and you'll also have plenty of space for writing on your manuscript.

If you're submitting to an editor, you'll need to change the font back to double-spaced Times New Roman 12pt with one inch margins.

Font choice aside, print out your work, sit down at a quiet table and read your first draft in one go.

Confession: I feel guilty about the paper I use while self-editing, and I have great intentions to plant a small forest one day.

MARKING UP YOUR MANUSCRIPT

Don't feel disheartened if your first read-through disappoints.

The American editor Sol Stein likens the process of reviewing a first draft to performing triage on a patient, and that's what you're about to do with a red pen.

Strike through words with your pen, use arrows to move your sentences around, and write in the spaces between each sentence.

Your markups don't have to make sense to anyone but you. If you're in doubt about a change, circle the sentence or word with your pen, and decide on this edit later.

I sometimes read my work aloud and record myself using the voice memo app on my phone.

Then, I listen back to this recording and mark up the manuscript. The act of saying something aloud helps identify problems in a way my eyes can't.

Now that you have a sense of your manuscript, you're going to self-edit your book in at least three different ways.

Round 1: Editing the Structure of a Book Chapter

During this round, concern yourself with how you've organised your book chapter as a whole rather than the finer points of grammar.

For example, during this edit, I re-read the introduction and conclusion to see if they gel with each other.

Ask yourself:

- Does my introduction *invoke curiosity* in the reader?
- Do I invoke at least *one of the five senses* in each page of this chapter?
- Have I *cut the weakest part* of this chapter?
- Have I *included metaphors or similes* that, upon reflection, don't stand up?
- Have I used *compelling subheadings* so that my chapter is more readable?
- Do I need to *reformat my work* or source images?
- Am I *happy with the tone* of this chapter?
- Do I need to *interview* an additional source for this chapter?

- Can I *strengthen* my arguments by including facts, figures, quotes or third-party research?

Round 2: Editing Your Book Chapter in Relation to Other Chapters

Like a general surveying the battlefield before marshalling his troops, take stock of each book chapter in relation to the rest of *your book*.

Ideally, a book chapter falls naturally between the preceding and proceeding chapters. It also has a title and word count consistent with the rest of your book.

It's also sometimes pleasing to sign-post or reference different chapters in your book at this point too, i.e. "I'll talk more about this in Ch.5" and so on.

That said, be careful not to clear your throat so much that you distract your readers.

While editing *The Power of Creativity*, I stepped back and looked at my book as a whole. Then I dumped two unnecessary chapters and wrote a new one.

I was less concerned with pretty little sentences than with arranging my book in a way that agreed with readers. So address the big problems by asking yourself:

- Does the *central argument* of my book stand up?
- Does each chapter hold true to my book's *controlling idea*?
- Is each chapter of a *consistent length*?
- Are the chapters in the *right order*?
- Are the titles of my book chapters consistent with the *tone of my book*?
- Do I need to break my book up into *explicit sections*?
- Have I told an *emotional story* throughout my book that resonates with readers?

- Are the *central ideas or stories* within each chapter specific to these chapters alone or should I sign-post them elsewhere?
- Have I brought an *original insight* into my work?
- Have I checked the *introduction and conclusion* of each chapter so that it intrigues or satisfies readers?
- Do I repeat myself?
- What *metaphors, ideas and turns-of-phrase* do I overuse throughout the book?

Round 3: Line Editing Your Book Chapter

Line editing is like polishing your car. You can spend hours doing it and still not feel happy with how each line looks or your book sounds. That said, it helps to know the basics:

- **Use the active voice:** The chapter was edited by me. Oh dear. I hired an editor to fix my book. That's better.
- **Eliminate unnecessary words:** Look closely for unnecessary adverbs (there's one) and pointless adjectives (there's another).
- **Eliminate clichés** like your life depends on it.
- **Simplify clunky language:** My book, it is filled, with all manner of long sentences that must be edited down. I read these sentences aloud…. and cut them out.
- **Attributing dialogue?** Just say 'said': She gesticulates. He grimaces. We giggled. "That's not how people talk," your editor said.
- **Look for moments of lazy writing:** Do you make a living from your books? Or do you earn a living from your books?
- **Avoid using the same word over and over and over...:** The writing software Scrivener will help you find overused words. A thesaurus is useful too.
- **Kill your mixed metaphors:** Your readers are watching you like you're a hawk.

- **Avoid complicated language:** Your exasperated readers won't have the inclination to ruminate on your warblings.
- **Use suitable formatting:** Put key words in italics and bold, and break things up with lists, like this one.
- **Review your punctuation:** Unless you're tweeting like Donald Trump, cut those exclamation marks!
- **Love the comma:** "Let's eat, grandma." isn't quite the same as "Let's eat grandma."
- **And those dangling modifiers have to go:** You possibly include them because they simply sound good. And your reader's reaction? Really?!
- **In doubt?** Brevity is clarity. Cut 10% of your work.
- **Write compelling sub-headings:** Don't begin your work with a boring Introduction and end it with a stereotypical Conclusion.
- **Check your formatting**: Did you use compelling sub-headings and include images that add value to your book? Did you format your writing using bold, italics, block quotes, lists and so on?

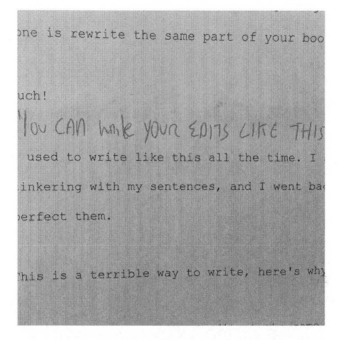

What a line-edit by hand looks like

Hemingway App is a useful free tool that will help you eliminate clunky language and address many of the issues raised above.

GETTING HELP

Should you press enter once or twice after a paragraph? Is it better to refer to an interviewee by his or her first or last name? What's correct: etc. or et cetera?

While self-editing a non-fiction book, it's natural to face questions like these and feel unsure about the right answer

So, let consistency be your North Star. If you wrote "etc." on page one, write "etc." on page 201. If you're still struggling, consider subscribing to a professional style guide like the *Chicago Manual of Style* or the *Harvard Style Guide*.

The authors of style guides like these have already faced and answered these questions many times. If you've got a troubling question, you can just look it up.

What's more, if you're self-publishing your book, you can refer your editor to these industry-standard guides, and he or she can root out any discrepancies for you.

(That said, sometimes it's good to break the grammar police's rules…. once it's a deliberate choice that improves rather than detracts from your book.)

PROOFING AND FACT-CHECKING YOUR WORK

Publishing your book with a typo or a factual mistake is like arriving at a party with your fly open.

Sure, some people will look away. But somebody's going to notice, and when they do, you're going to feel embarrassed.

So it's no wonder typos and bad grammar keep a lot of new authors up at night.

The longer you work on a book, the more likely you are to slip deeper into it and become blind to these typos and mistakes.

Now, you could obsess about typos and bad grammar and never go to that party at all. Mistakes appear in books of all types, even traditionally published ones with a large editorial budget. That's one reason publishers release second, third, fourth and revised editions of popular books.

For example, the first edition of the James Bond novel *Moonraker* by Ian Fleming contained a typo on page 10. The letter "t" was missing from the word "shoot". Today, that version is rather valuable.

Still, nobody wants to turn up to a party (or a bookstore) and embarrass themselves.

Them thar ttypos keep me up at night, so here's my checklist:

- Have you read your work out loud in a quiet place, listening for words that sound out of place?
- Did you check your work for your most common spelling and grammar mistakes?
- Are your figures correct, and do they add up?

- Did you spell your sources' names correctly and give them the appropriate titles?
- Have you cited all your sources?
- Do your links work? If you're editing a book for print, remember to type out the links.
- Did you check your grammar and spelling using Grammarly?

This list is a good start. But all of this will only take you so far, unfortunately. Proofreading is time-consuming, and because you're so close to your non-fiction book, you will inevitably overlook some mistakes.

I wasted a lot of time trying to proof my first book myself, only to have unhappy readers email me about some typos.

Giving chapters of your book to trusted friends and family is one workaround, and it shouldn't cost you much (beyond returning the favour!). However, be sure they're eagle-eyed.

That said, it pays to hire a proofreader, something I cover in a later chapter.

HOW MANY ROUNDS OF SELF-EDITING IS ENOUGH?

Great writing is rewriting.

You should self-edit your book at least three times: by sentence, by chapter and as a whole. That said, you can write, review, edit and rewrite your book many more times before it's good enough to publish.

Take it sentence by sentence, paragraph by paragraph and chapter by chapter. As you self-edit and write (but not at the same time!), your book will teach you how to finish writing it.

While working on your second or third draft, enlist the help of a family member or friend, and ask them to provide frank feedback.

Later on, enlist beta readers, a professional editor and a proof-reader. Ask them to help you turn your self-edited draft into something you're proud to publish.

Working with editors, in particular, is the quickest way to master the self-editing process because they'll teach you things you just can't see.

Some writers rework their book until it goes to the printing press, and today thanks to self-publishing, you can even rewrite your work after publication.

But don't get stuck on a merry-go-round of self-editing your book without an end in sight.

Diminishing returns will set in. If you've taken the time to listen to your editor, you've done your job. So, accept that while your book isn't perfect, it's as good as can be.

And that's all your readers can ask.

YOUR WRITING EXERCISES

- Change the font of your writing to Courier New or Courier Prime, the line spacing to double and the size to 12. Now, print out your manuscript and mark it up.
- After atoning to the environment by planting a small forest, work through your manuscript at least three times. During each pass, edit a different part of your work.

PART III
FINDING LASTING SUCCESS
WITH YOUR BOOK

ACTING ON CRITICAL FEEDBACK
(WITHOUT LOSING YOUR MIND)

"**A**uthors who moan with praise for their editors always seem to reek slightly of the Stockholm syndrome." – Christopher Hitchens

"Welcome to the team," said Deborah, shaking my hand. "It's my job to review all of your news stories and to give you topics to cover each week."

She was a tall, thin, blonde woman in her mid-thirties and the paper's news editor.

"You'll have to bear with me," I said. "I have a lot to learn about writing and journalism."

"I'm sure we'll figure things out, Bryan."

The first thing I figured out was how much everyone on the news team disliked Deborah, and I got right in line. She treated the three other news journalists like school children, even though we were in our mid-twenties.

One Tuesday morning, I was explaining to Emma, another news journalist, about how to find the contact details for a local politician.

Deborah glared across the office, snapped her fingers at us and said, "You two, get back to work."

"Deborah," I said. "We're talking about a news story."

"Well, hurry up. You have a deadline."

Deborah didn't like to see us talking to each other unless she was a part of the conversation. So we spent the rest of the day complaining about Deborah over instant messaging.

Deborah also liked to keep us working late in the office for no particular reason. I disliked her habit of interrupting my lunch break and ringing me at home or on my days off to ask for news updates and story ideas.

I started turning off my phone outside of hours and eating my lunch on another floor.

Events came to a head one Wednesday morning, the day after the weekly newspaper went to press. As soon as Emma, the rest of the journalists and I arrived into the office, Deborah began berating us in front of the rest of the newsroom.

"You're turning over half-finished stories way past your deadline," she said. "If you spent as much time working on your news stories as you do goofing off, we wouldn't have this problem."

"You've no right to talk to us like this, Deborah," said Emma. "Not in front of the entire office."

"Emma's right, Deborah," I said, feeling brave. "You can't treat us this badly... and there was nothing wrong with my story. I sent it on time, perhaps you should check your email."

"I've never met a group of more unprofessional and incompetent journalists," said Deborah.

"You have the nerve to call us unprofessional?" said Emma. "You treat us like school children."

"How dare you!" said Deborah.

"How dare you!" said Emma.

I thought they were going to come to blows, but the newspaper's managing editor stepped in and asked them to come into his office. They spent the rest of day thrashing things out in his office, his door closed and blinds pulled down.

My time came the following day. The editor asked Deborah to wait outside. Then, he pulled out a draft of my news story, which he had marked up with red pen.

"Can you see what's wrong with this story Bryan?" he said.

I scanned through his annotations. I had spelt a politician's name wrong, cited an incorrect figure and, worst of all, I had inadvertently insinuated a public figure was on the take.

My mistakes lined up on the page like rotten eggs.

"Deborah and I were here till 9 p.m. the night before last trying to fix these," he said. "If I let this go to print, we would have been sued, Bryan. You must double-check every name and triple-check every statistic and figure."

As much as I disliked Deborah and her management style, I couldn't blame these mistakes on her. I possessed too much self-belief in the veracity of my work.

So I started questioning every piece I worked on... and I started missing my deadlines because I was so worried about mistakes and getting negative feedback.

I went in search of rounded-out facts and perfect stories when Deborah (and later editors I worked with) wanted a piece on-time. They wanted articles that would stand up in the light of day.

My pendulum of self-belief swung from over-confidence in my work to self-doubt and procrastination. It took me years to find a centre point between the two.

WHY YOU MUST REGARD YOUR EDITOR AS AN ALLY (AND SEPARATE YOURSELF FROM YOUR WORK)

Your editor shouldn't be your friend, but they are on your side. They will help you get your book ready for your readers because that's their job. They're not going to waste their time or money on a writing project that won't sell (or which no one will read).

A book represents a business investment, and they want to see a return. Similarly, if you're self-publishing, your book is *an investment in your business*, and you should have the same mindset as an editor.

Now, you may think:

"What about art? What about my muse? What about writing for myself first?"

Well, I once spent a year writing a collection of short stories only to finish them and realise I had no idea who would want to read these stories. I hadn't written anything people would read, let alone pay for.

I learned the hard way to consider my ideal readers, what they enjoy and what they want before starting any writing project. That's what a good editor will do for you.

When you hire an editor, he or she should help you refine your book, so it speaks to one person rather than the masses. (That said, don't abdicate responsibility for your book's problems.)

Sending a manuscript to an editor is invigorating. But opening a Word document filled with annotations, comments and suggested changes feels like a frustrating step backward.

Many new writers brood about these slights and even feel sorry for themselves (I know because this is what I did). They let a marked-up manuscript sit in their computer for weeks or even months before doing anything with it.

That's a crucial mistake.

Here's why:

When a plumber fits a toilet, they don't view the toilet as an extension of themselves.

When a farmer milks a cow, they don't throw a temper tantrum if someone complains that the milk is sour.

So why should writing a non-fiction book be any different?

When an editor criticises your work, it's not personal. Their criticism is not a judgment on whether you're a good or bad person. Get some distance from your work, and you'll be able to evaluate your editor's advice on its merits alone.

Even if you're working with a publisher, your editor wants you to write a book their readers love and that earns their company a return.

On the other hand, if you're self-publishing, your editor will help you fix the problems in your book, but it's up to you to apply their advice. They've little to lose or gain if you publish a best-selling book or a turd. Either way, you'll have to pay for their services.

So when your editor asks for more research, a rewrite or suggests cutting a section, put your ego aside and listen.

These practical tips will help you handle critical feedback from your editor:

- Read through your editor's feedback and your marked-up manuscript in one go.
- If you're feeling confused, get out from behind your email, ring your editor and ask them questions.
- If you find their feedback tough to take, set your work aside for a day or two before returning to edit your book.
- Set yourself a deadline for working through your editor's feedback.
- Keep a copy of the old version of your work before you start editing. This way, you can undo changes if needed.
- Work on the proposed structural changes first, taking care to update your editor about what you're doing.
- Remember, you don't need to accept all of your editor's suggestions or changes.
- Next, fill in gaps in your research.
- Work through the suggested line edits.
- Send the revised draft back to your editor for another review, if needed.

GETTING FEEDBACK FROM BETA READERS

Musicians often demo early versions of their songs at smaller gigs to select audiences. They use their fans' feedback to improve these songs before recording and releasing them.

For your non-fiction book, find a group of early or beta readers you trust. Ask a more experienced colleague at work, an eagle-eyed family member who is great at catching typos, and readers of your blog or previous books (if you have them).

Many indie authors, for example, ask members of their email list to read their book before they publish it. Ask your beta readers:

- Did you spot any glaring typos or mistakes?
- Did you like the central story?
- Does the book's arguments (or controlling idea) stand up?
- Does the book deliver on its promise (your positioning statement)?
- Did you find any of the book confusing?
- What do you feel the book lacks?
- What should the book include more of?
- Is this book clear and concise?

An ideal beta reader will provide you with frank 'real-world' feedback you can use to improve your book before publishing it.

If your beta readers point out obvious mistakes, correct them, but don't let feedback become a reason for compromising on your entire work. After all, one person's Sistine Chapel is another person's trudge through a boring old church.

Part of becoming a professional author means having confidence in your ideas and your work. No, I'm not suggesting ignoring your beta readers altogether, but do have the courage of your convictions.

It's okay to disagree with your beta readers' feedback. Use a back-and-forth conversation to refine the confusing part of your book or to see if you can strengthen your controlling idea. Alternatively, set two rules for yourself:

- **Rule #1:** If at least one person likes a section in my book, it stays in.
- **Rule #2:** If three or more readers dislike a section in my book, I rewrite it.

After all, you're a professional.

WHAT YOU SHOULD KNOW ABOUT ADVANCED READER COPIES

Traditional publishers often send reviewers and those in the industry Advanced Reader Copies (ARCs) of a book before publication.

A beta reader will provide you with feedback about problems in your book (as you write it). Those receiving an ARC should get something close to the finished product, for example, a print copy of your book.

This approach is a great way of generating excitement about your book and soliciting reviews for the cover or inside of a book. It'll also help you unearth any remaining typos and mistakes.

EVERY AUTHOR NEEDS FEEDBACK

When I first started showing my writing to my mother/father/aunt/best friend, they'd tell me:

"It's great, Bryan. You've got talent."

I was like, "Wow, thanks. Writing for a living is my dream."

But their well-meaning feedback wasn't helpful. I needed someone like Deborah to tell me how it really was.

Now, Deborah and I didn't have a great working relationship. But she (and that newspaper editor) taught me one important lesson: *don't be precious about your work.*

I'm not going to lie to you.

Even today, getting editorial feedback is difficult, but I accept it as valuable medicine.

If you want to take your non-fiction book seriously and become a successful author, handling feedback, both good and bad, is part of the job.

Your internal critic should help you evaluate critical feedback. But don't let him or her prevent you from publishing your book.

Your editor should help you turn a page of lousy prose into something that shines, but know when to push back.

And your beta readers should help you improve your book so it satisfies them, but don't take everything they say as gospel.

Reading critical feedback sometimes feels like swallowing an oversized pill. Even though it's unpleasant, it's still a good idea to take your medicine.

So, get into the habit of putting what you learnt from editors, early readers and yourself into practice. Then, you'll spend less time fixing up first drafts and more time publishing books that readers love.

YOUR WRITING EXERCISES

- Send a second or third draft of a chapter in your book to at least three beta readers, and ask them for honest feedback.
- Spend 30 minutes each week reviewing what you've learnt from your editor and beta readers about the craft.

PICKING A BEST-SELLING TITLE FOR YOUR BOOK

" **A** good title is a work of genius. I have no hesitancy in saying that, for it is genius whether it is the inspiration of a lucky moment or the painful elaboration of a faint idea through an hour of deep thought." – Emanuel Haldeman-Julius

Emanuel Haldeman-Julius (1889-1951) found success by creating and publishing the *Little Blue Books* series of pamphlets, which sold 300 to 500 million copies in the United States and around the world. His company, Haldeman-Julius Publications, sold these books for a dollar, mostly through mail-order.

They sold various expired-copyright classics like the works of William Shakespeare alongside self-improvement books. If a book or pamphlet sold less than 10,000 copies in a year, Haldeman-Julius either withdrew the title from sale or took it into 'The Hospital'.

There, he often picked a more appealing title for the book in question and relaunched it. Here are several examples of title changes from The Hospital that increased sales:

- *The Mystery of the Iron Mask* sold 11,000 copies in a year, while *The Mystery of the Man in the Iron Mask* sold over 30,000.

- *The King Enjoys Himself* sold 8,000 copies a year, but *The Lustful King Enjoys Himself* sold 38,000.
- *Ten O'Clock* sold 2,000 copies a year, while *What Art Should Mean To You* sold 9,000.
- *Art of Controversy* sold no copies, while *How To Argue Logically* sold 30,000.
- *Casanova and His Loves* sold 8,000 a year, but *Casanova, History's Greatest Lover* sold over 22,000.
- *Pen, Pencil and Poison* sold 5,000 a year, while *The Story of a Notorious Criminal* sold 15,800.

You want to sell more copies of your book, right?

Well, alongside selecting a great book cover, writing a captivating book title is one of your most important creative choices.

It's not much use having pretty sentences and great ideas, if your your title doesn't grab the attention of would-be readers.

BUT FIRST OFF...

Before writing your book title, be mindful of Amazon's rules for authors:

- The book title on your cover must match what your Amazon description says.
- You can't make claims about being a best-seller in your title.
- You can't claim deals, discounts or reduced prices in your title.
- No references to other books, authors or trademarks allowed.
- Your subtitle must be fewer than 200 characters.

Now that you know the rules, it's time to cover how to write a captivating book title.

STEP 1: RESEARCH RELATED POPULAR BOOK TITLES

Non-fiction authors traditionally pick self-explanatory book titles. Or they pick titles that rely on a central metaphor.

For example, Dale Carnegie wrote one of the most popular self-help books of all time: *How to Win Friends and Influence People*. Then, there's one of my favourites: Stephen King's non-fiction book *On Writing*.

You know almost immediately what both books are about from the titles alone.

Literary non-fiction writers traditionally pick book titles rich in resonance. They also pick titles that rely on a central metaphor from their books.

For example, consider Truman Capote's 1966 classic: *In Cold Blood*.

It's a non-fiction book about the murders of four members of the Herbert Clutter family in Kansas. This was a high-profile case in the 1960s, but you still need to read a little of Capote's book to discover what he's writing about.

A more recent example is Joan Didion's 2005 memoir: *The Year of Magical Thinking*.

It's an intriguing title, but it gives little away about the book. However, in the introduction, Didion explains the title encapsulates her year of intense grief after the death of her husband John Gregory Dunne.

For your own book, by now you should know the genre, who your ideal readers are and what books they read.

Now, *you can* pick an intriguing non-fiction book title that lends itself towards resonance. However, Capote, King and Didion are (or were) famous authors who could sell books on the strength of their names.

So why compromise?

Today, many successful non-fiction authors combine both approaches. They pick a title that invokes a central metaphor, and they also write a subtitle that sells the benefits of their book.

But before you do all that...

STEP 2: SUMMARISE WHAT'S IN IT FOR YOUR READERS

Consider Tim Ferriss's first book: *The 4-Hour Workweek: Escape 9-5, Live Anywhere, and Join the New Rich.*

In his book, Ferris explains how he uses outsourcing websites to simplify his life, but that's not in the sub-title. Instead, he sells readers on how they can escape the pain of the nine-to-five and follow their dreams.

To distil the benefits of your book, write down a list of five to ten things readers will understand or achieve by the end of your book. Focus on your readers' pain points and how your book will help them overcome these problems.

Use your subtitle to sell the pain.

Self-publishing expert and author Chandler Bolt gave me the following advice:

> It's easier to sell [painkillers] than it is to sell vitamins. When you're in pain, you whip out your credit card, and you will do anything to get out of pain. For vitamins we've got sugary ones, we've got gummy bears. We've got ones in shapes like fruit. It's so much harder to sell because it's not a basic need.

Features are your research, chapters, interviewees, ideas, word count and so on. Benefits, on the other hand, are what your readers *get out of your book.* They represent a problem-solved, kind of like painkillers.

STEP 3: WRITE YOUR BOOK TITLE AND SUBTITLE

Haldeman-Julius had two rules for writing a compelling book title. His first rule was to **make the title describe the book**. He explains:

> The title should contain some dominant word which clearly indicates the subject of the book. If it is biography or criticism, I think the title

should also indicate what the man stood for or what the matter criticised chiefly represents. If human nature can be put into the title, well and good. Every effort should be made to tie up the book with real life, or with the average person's desire for romance, adventure, and fun.

His second rule was to **make the title as distinctive as possible** "so as to compel attention and awaken interest."

PICKING THE RIGHT TITLE

Writing a clever metaphor or a title rich in meaning is tough work. You can simplify things by making a big claim in your title. Try and encapsulate your book's controlling idea in a few words, or make a promise to your readers.

Your title needs to convince people why they should read your book over all the other books clamouring for their attention. Of course, you must back up your claim or promise within your book too.

Dale Carnegie's big claim is clear: he'll teach you how to find more friends and persuade people.

PICKING THE RIGHT SUBTITLE

Your subtitle should be more specific and focus on benefits, rather than features. It should overcome objections potential customers have or be specific about your book's controlling idea.

Here is where hammer home what your book does.

EVALUATING YOUR TITLES

Go about writing ten or 20 variations of your title and subtitle. Ask yourself does each variation:

- Describe what the book is about?

- Explain what's in it for the reader?
- Bring different ideas together in fresh or distinctive ways?
- Consider what readers look for when they type in the names of books into stores like Amazon?

If you write and test multiple titles, you stand a better chance of writing one that grabs readers by the eyeballs.

STEP 4: OPTIMISE YOUR BOOK TITLE FOR SEARCH

Haldeman-Julius would have loved the powerful tools authors can use today to find out what readers search for.

The trick is to identify search terms or keywords and work them into your title, subtitle or book description. Once you do, you should attract more clicks to your sales page and sell more copies of your book.

"According to our statistics, the book that ranks number one for a search term gets 27% of the clicks. The book that ranks number two gets only 13% of the clicks," says author and SEO expert Dave Chesson.

"If you truly want to show up for that keyword, you either need to add it to your subtitle or put it in your description."

The good news is there are lots of free and paid tools that can help you do this.

GOOGLE KEYWORD PLANNER

To use this tool, you must sign up to a Google AdWords account, but it's free.

Google Keyword Planner will generate hundreds of search terms based on your topic. You can filter these by search volume and competition. You can also export your results to a spreadsheet and use this information to inform your title or subtitle.

A DEDICATED SEO TOOL

If you're publishing on the Amazon Kindle Direct Publishing (KDP) platform, you'll have to select seven keywords about your book.

SEO expert, Dave Chesson, says the best approach is to find seven or more popular, relevant keywords and use at least one of these in your title or subtitle.

"When I've nailed those seven, I [ask] which one of those seven is the best representation of my book?" says Dave.

You can find the best keywords using an SEO tool for authors like KDP Rocket.

These tools enable you to find popular search terms or keywords and check the popularity of relevant books.

"I will go ahead and put those seven [keywords] into KDP...but I'll also try to weave them into the subtitle," says Chesson.

STEP 5: TEST YOUR BOOK TITLE

It's easier today to test your book titles *before* publishing your book. If you make the wrong decision about your book title, you can always retest your choices and start again.

LET AMAZON HELP YOU

You can find popular book search terms in Amazon for your genre by typing in a few words into the search bar and letting Amazon auto-populate it for you.

Go to Amazon and type in 'How to' plus '[your book's topic]', and you'll immediately see related book titles that rank highly on Amazon.

Keep a swipe file of popular book titles related to your genre or topic and add to this over time.

Alternatively, study the most popular titles in your niche by using Amazon. It will recommend other titles based on what readers bought on the various sales pages and even via email. This information is a gold mine if you're self-publishing.

ASK YOUR READERS

If you have a mailing list of readers or you're working with beta readers, you could poll them using Google Forms or SurveyMonkey.

USE ADS

Tim Ferriss used Google AdWords to test titles for his first book. His preferred choice was *Broad Bends and White Sands* but after running an ad, he found readers preferred *The 4-Hour Workweek*.

Today, you can test book titles using Facebook ads.

Create two Facebook ads, each one based on a different book title. Then, target these ads at would-be readers of your book or fans of your author page. Let these run for three to five days, and see which one attracts the most clicks or likes.

For this to work, you'll need a modest budget (say $5 a day), a mockup of your book cover(s) and some understanding of how to create and track ads.

RUN A POLL

Once you have two or three book titles you like, you can run a poll. This is a great way of getting instant market feedback. You can post on a relevant Facebook group or use a premium service like PickFu.

I used the latter to A/B test two book titles, and I got more than 100 responses explaining why one title was more compelling than another. This feedback helped me improve the title in question.

CAPTURING THE ATTENTION OF BOOK BUYERS

Crafting a book title is one of your most important creative choices. You need a good title that convinces book buyers to click through to your sales page, download a sample and buy your book.

Now, non-fiction authors today can research and test book titles using tools that Haldeman-Julius and others would have loved.

So, find the middle ground between writing a title that does your book justice and one that readers will search for or remember.

YOUR WRITING EXERCISES

- Keep a list of popular non-fiction book titles you like. If you add to this list over time, then you'll train your brain into understanding what titles sell and don't sell, and you'll have a list you can consult while writing your title.
- Test your book title by running a poll, by asking your beta-readers for their opinions or by creating a Facebook ad.

SELF-PUBLISHING YOUR NON-FICTION BOOK LIKE A PRO

"Writing is about you. Publishing is about the book. Marketing is about the reader." – Joanna Penn

I still get a kick every time I upload a digital book file to Amazon and press publish. It's easy, and it's free... or is it?

Well, you could finalise a draft today. You could prepare your digital book file, knock up a masterpiece of a book cover in Paint (oh, my eyes, it burns!), upload it all to Amazon and have a book for sale within hours.

But should you?

Well, professional non-fiction authors take care to create books that readers love. They work with trained editors, professional designers and more. If you're self-publishing your non-fiction book and you take your craft and readers seriously, you should too.

So how much does it cost to self-publish a book?

According to the *Write Life*, the average amount a writer spends on self-publishing a book falls between $200 and $300. While according to *Book Promotion*, more experienced writers spend several thousand dollars on self-publishing services.

I've spent less than $500 and more than $2000 on self-publishing different books. There are advantages and disadvantages to working on a shoe-string and a larger budget.

I researched the pricing information in this chapter during 2017 and updated it before publication.

Some of the prices may have increased since then, but my advice about *what to budget for* holds true.

Let's dive in.

PAYING FOR WRITING AND SELF-PUBLISHING SOFTWARE

Whether you're self-publishing your book or otherwise, you still need a computer. You also need writing software like Google Docs, Word or Scrivener.

Once you've written your book, you can either hire a designer to prepare your digital book files or do it yourself. It's easy enough if you learn Scrivener's advanced features or use book design software like Vellum (Mac only).

Costs
    Free to $74

For Authors on a Tight Budget
    I'll presume you already own or have access to a computer for writing. At the back of this book, I include a list of free and premium writing software you can use.

A license for software like Scrivener and Vellum costs $45 and $29, respectively. If you can't afford to spend this modest amount on writing software, you're in the wrong game.

HIRING AN EDITOR, COPYEDITOR AND PROOFREADER

Almost every author works with a developmental editor, a proofreader and sometimes a copyeditor or line editor.

A developmental editor will provide critical feedback about the tone and direction of your book in the form of a reader's report. He or she may also provide some light copywriting, depending on your contract.

A copyeditor or line editor will go through each sentence and polish them for you. They will also check that your spelling, word-choice and the overall style of your book is consistent.

A proofreader will eliminate typos and grammar mistakes and may also look for factual inaccuracies.

Some editors also provide developmental and copyedits if you pay extra.

MY EXPERIENCES WORKING WITH EDITORS AND PROOFREADERS

While self-publishing my first book, *A Handbook for the Productive Writer,* I hired a proofreader, but I didn't hire an editor.

Having worked as a journalist and sub-editor, I felt confident about editing a non-fiction book myself. I also turned several chapters into guest blog posts for various websites. Later on, I used critical feedback from these editors to improve my book.

Even though their feedback was helpful, self-editing my book took dozens of hours, and I sprouted grey hairs out the back of my ears.

That wasn't my only mistake.

I hired a cheap proofreader for $200 to check *The Savvy Writer's Guide to Productivity.* This proofreader found some errors (but not all of them) in the book before I self-published it.

Then, after I uploaded the first version of my book, I found some additional errors and typos (the shame!).

After a reader complained to me about some typos, I rained furious hellfire down upon him. When that didn't work, I used the online proofreading service Grammarly to recheck every chapter. Then, I resent this book to a professional proofreader for $300.

A month after self-publishing the first version of my book, I uploaded a new version to Amazon.

I called it Version 2.

Later, I paid to have much of the book re-edited. I also retitled it as *The Savvy Writer's Guide to Productivity*. And I recovered the book so I could position it to the right readers more effectively and increase sales.

For every book since, I've worked with an editor, proofreader and occasionally a line editor.

Typically, an editor sends me a reader report with an annotated version of my manuscript. The proofreader and line editor also make changes in a document and send it back for me to accept or reject.

Feedback like this, while sometimes tough, improves the quality of my books and teaches me more about writing (a nice added bonus).

Now, you can hire an editor, proofreader and copyeditor based on:

- Your total word count
- The hours you want the editor/proofreader to spend on your book
- Your total page count
- Your project as a whole

Before hiring an editor or proofreader, ask them:

- What style they'll use? The Chicago Manual of Style is pretty popular.
- Will they edit your book in British or US English?
- Can they provide a sample edit for you to review (usually free)?
- Do they specialise in any type of writing?
- Can they provide testimonials from satisfied clients?
- How long will an edit take?
- What are their rates?

Costs

I don't have an easy answer for you because it depends on how clean your draft is, your subject matter and what level of editorial support you want. Rates vary widely too, so shop around.

That said... you can hire an editor and also a copyeditor for $40 to $50 per hour, each.

You can also expect to pay an editor and a proofreader $5 to $10 per 1000 words, each.

For Authors on a Tight Budget

If you can't afford an editor or proofreader, start saving! Working with an editor is the single best way to improve your book and your craft.

That said, joining a creative writing group or class is a great way to get free feedback on your writing. All you have to do is provide other people feedback on their work too. So the only real cost is your time.

Similarly, if you write guest blog posts based on your draft, you can get free editorial feedback about your non-fiction. After your guest post goes live, you can always reuse elements of the post as chapters in your book (with some light rewriting).

I caution against self-publishing your book without hiring or getting an eagle-eyed friend to proofread your book.

Those typos will come back to haunt you.

FINDING A CAPTIVATING BOOK COVER

Picking a good book cover is one of your most important creative decisions. It's your book's best chance of standing out against the hundreds of thousands of other books on stores like Amazon.

When I was starting off, I stayed up till two a.m. for nights on end taking online design tutorials. I created a cover that had almost nothing to do with the contents of my book.

Since then, I've run competitions on sites like 99designs and worked directly with book cover designers.

As an author, your time is better spent writing than it is tinkering in Photoshop or Illustrator. So either start saving or reframe the expense as an investment in your craft.

Hiring a Designer

It's relatively easy to find a professional book cover designer, and I've included resources at the back of this book. So find a designer you can afford who has experience creating book covers in your niche.

Then, you'll need to determine if he or she is free to work on your cover and then come to an agreement on price and deliverables. Some budget-friendly designers will let you pick from various book cover templates. More expensive designers will create something new for you.

Before you pay your designer, let them know if you want a front cover for digital publishing, a full cover for print and a 3D mockup of your book for your website.

These extras cost more. Also, insist on the source files (that's the Photoshop or Illustrator files and not just the book cover image), so you can edit the book cover later if necessary.

Decide on Your Budget

You can spend a lot or a little on your book cover. If you spend a modest amount (less than $100), you'll probably have to pick from various pre-designed templates. If you spend more, you can work one-on-one with a designer.

Do Your Research

The covers of thriller books look different from the covers of self-help books. The former relies on dark imagery, while the latter relies on hopeful imagery.

So, spend at least an hour browsing stores like Amazon and saving book covers in your niche that you like (Pinterest and Evernote are both good for this).

Write a Design Brief

If you've commissioned a new cover rather than using a pre-designed template, write a short brief for your designer. Explain what your book is about, the title, key concepts, what book covers you like/dislike and so on.

Are you okay with stock imagery? Do you prefer simple designs, or do you have an image in mind? Are there particular colours and fonts you like?

If your writing draws on key imagery or metaphors, let your designer know as they could work an element into your cover. Include a sample chapter for them to read too.

Providing this information will reduce the amount of time both of you spend going backwards and forwards about a design later.

Give Proactive Feedback

Depending on how much you pay, your designer will go through one or two rounds of changes with you. Tell them what you like and dislike about the cover, and what you want changed.

Remember, your book cover needs to look good at small sizes so it stands out in digital book stores.

But what if you don't know what you like? Ask a friend or your early readers for their opinions about the book cover. They may have a good eye for design or captivating images.

Crowdsourcing Your Book Cover

Sites like 99designs, CrowdSpring and DesignCrowd enable you to run competitions. If you host one, designers will submit covers for you to review. When you pick the best one, the winner gets a prize that you front.

I used 99designs in the past for a book cover, and I was happy with the results.

Two years ago, I wrote an article about my experiences. Some unhappy designers complained in the comments about crowd-sourcing websites. They argued losers get nothing for their submission or hard work.

If you decide on this approach, you'll still need to brief your designer and work with the winner to finalise it.

Costs

It costs $50 to $500 or more to hire a designer, and as with hiring an editor, you get what you pay for. Competitions on crowdsourcing websites start at $240.

Preparing a Print Version of Your Book

What writer doesn't want to hold their book in their hands? If you follow the guidelines on Amazon and CreateSpace, you can do just that. Vellum (Mac only at time of writing) also enables writers to compile print version of their book.

If you can't or don't want to use Vellum, I recommend hiring a designer to prepare your print book. They will take care of headaches like laying out each page correctly. They will also check that your cover is the right depth, break up run-on sentences and so on.

Costs

It costs about $250 to $300 to hire a designer to prepare a 40,000 to 50,000 word book for print. I expect this cost to come down as self-publishing software becomes easier to use.

At time of writing, Vellum Press (for creating print books) costs $249.

For Authors on a Tight Budget

Yes, you could design a cover yourself in Paint or Photoshop or buy a cheap cover for a couple of dollars on a site like Fiverr. You could also rub lemons in your eyes, but that doesn't mean you should.

Unless you've got ace design skills, don't – a cheap cover screams cheap writing. If you can't afford to hire a designer, Canva provides a series of free ebook cover templates that you can adapt. Later on, you can always swap this cover for a more professional design.

There's no cheap shortcut to preparing a book for print, unfortunately. You can always prepare your book file using Vellum, but you'll need the help of a designer to get the cover right for print. If that's an issue, publish a digital copy of your book first and a print copy later on.

THE BOTTOM LINE

Authors today don't have to ask for permission from publishers, editors or even readers! However, you still need the funds to create a great book.

It cost me around $500 to self-publish my first book, $1000 to self-publish my second and over $2000 to self-publish my third.

In each case, I hired more expensive editors, designers and so on to improve the quality of the books in question. I also haven't included extra costs like what I spent on marketing my book using Facebook ads.

You can spend as much or as little as you want self-publishing your non-fiction book.

If you invest a little money, you'll break even on the cost of your book faster. But if you invest more, you'll create a better product and improve your craft with the help of a professional.

Unlike years ago, you're in control of your creative choices (including the budget), and that's a liberating place to be for most non-fiction authors.

YOUR WRITING EXERCISES

- Create a file of book covers from your niche that you like. Add to this file as you go, and show it to your designer.
- Decide up front how much you want to spend on editing, design and so on. Work within your budget, taking care to create a professional product (yes, books are products!) that readers love.

FINISHING (AND SHIPPING) YOUR BOOK

"It all sounded great in the script, and it was doable – just a matter of reps, reps, reps." – Arnold Schwarzenegger

When Arnold Schwarzenegger (b1947) was a teenager, he started lifting weights in the Athletic Union in Graz, Austria.

On the wall next to where they lifted weights, each athlete listed exercises like 'Dead Lift', 'Bench Press', 'Clean and Jerk', 'Shoulder Press' and so on. The athletes chalked a row of hash marks next to each exercise, each one representing a set.

After an athlete completed the reps comprising a set, they marked an X through the first line. To complete a session, the athletes, including Schwarzenegger, had to mark an X through each of the five or six lines.

In his biography *Total Recall*, Schwarzenegger writes:

> This practice had a huge impact on my motivation. I always had the visual feedback of 'Wow, an accomplishment. I did what I set out to do. Now I will go for the next set, and the next set.'

Schwarzenegger applied this mentality of completing reps and sets to find success as a bodybuilder and actor. He even completed his 'reps' to campaign for Governor of California.

There's a famous scene in *Terminator 2* where Schwarzenegger drives down a Los Angeles drainage canal on a Harley. He pulls out a shotgun, fires it, spins and re-cocks the weapon, fires again and so on, until he reaches a chained gate with a padlock. Then, the Terminator shoots the gates and drives through.

Schwarzenegger practiced using a weapon and bike for this scene hundreds of times for weeks beforehand. He worked through his reps and sets so much that he tore the skin off his fingers. He writes:

> I couldn't wear a glove because it would get stuck in the gun mechanism, and I tore the skin off my hand and fingers practicing a hundred times until I mastered the skill.

While governor of California, Schwarzenegger prepared for a big campaign speech by renting a studio. There, he visualised his audience. Schwarzenegger delivered his speech over and over for three days. Each time, he marked his reps on the front page.

If you're worried your book isn't good enough, work through your reps. Schwarzenegger bled into his stunts, and you can bleed into your first lines, books and your craft.

The more sentences you write, the stronger your command of the language will become. The more clichés you terminate, the better you'll become at editing.

The more chapters you write, the better you'll be at articulating stories and ideas. And the more books you finish, the more you'll know about how to write the next one.

And the next.

And the next.

I'M WORRIED THEY'LL JUDGE ME

In December 2016, a friend asked me to help with a street collection for a charity in Dublin. Being introverted, I procrastinated about it for two weeks before agreeing. Then, I donned a luminous bib for the charity, and I wandered out onto the rainy, cold streets.

I held out the bucket as strangers walked up and down the street. They looked at their phones, their shoes, ahead, behind me. They looked anywhere and everywhere but at me and my half-empty bucket.

(I couldn't blame them. I've done the same many times.)

I was jingling the coins inside the bucket and studying a billboard for a new *Star Wars* film when a well-dressed middle-aged woman tapped me on the shoulder.

"I want you to know why I can't donate today," she said, her voice round like an over-sized lemon. "They organised a big collection at church on Sunday, and I gave a lot, *a lot*."

"That's good to know," I wrapped my hands around the bucket. "I best get back to it."

The woman nodded, pulled her handbag onto her shoulder and walked down the street.

That night, I wondered why this well-heeled woman was so concerned about what I thought of her refusal to put a few euro into my lonely bucket.

(I wasn't even thinking about her!)

Many new writers worry their audience will judge them or what people close to them will think of their book or creative works. So they look away from the page, and they hold something back from their book.

I get it. I do it too.

Those messy personal stories – the party where I drank too much, called the host the wrong name and passed out in the bathroom. Or the time they fired me because my maths weren't up to the task. Those don't frighten me. I know how those stories turn out. It's telling you about them. I care too much about what you think.

Many writers worry their readers will judge them.

Last year, I was 100 pages into a non-fiction book by a *New York Times* best-selling author. I was enjoying the author's way with words until he teased a personal story.

He told his readers about a time of inner crisis, only to announce it was too personal to reveal. Then he promptly moved on without revealing anything more. I threw his book across the room.

What was the point in reading on?

This author, as accomplished as he is, was too worried that his readers would judge him. Well, your readers want to know they're not alone. They need you to share some essential truth from your life with them.

In a world of click-bait, fake news and cute cat videos, they crave authenticity. So instead of worrying they'll judge you, be as honest as you can.

I FEEL STUCK

Finishing is harder than starting.

When I was in my mid-twenties, I spent years struggling to finish anything. I wrote dozens of short stories and abandoned them. I researched articles I wanted to write for newspapers, and then I never wrote them.

There wasn't any one moment when I learnt how to finish my work. Instead, I got a job as a journalist writing for a newspaper. There, I had to finish my articles by a deadline because if I didn't, the editor would fire me.

I know this because he called me into his office after I missed a deadline and said so. So I stopped polishing my articles until they were perfect and I finished them.

On more than one occasion, my editor sent articles back to me, saying I'd left out an important paragraph or my introduction needed reworking.

After listening to his criticism, I wanted to quit.

On other occasions, the sub-editors of the paper reworked my articles. This process felt like a brutal dressing-down, but at least I was getting paid to write.

If you're having trouble, act like a professional.

- Set artificial deadlines for each chapter, and stick to them.
- Tell your editor or readers you'll have a draft ready by the end of the day/week/month, and keep your promise.
- Create a book sales page on Amazon, upload your cover and write the sales copy. Then, set a realistic publication date.

The chapters you finish are akin to the threads of a cable, and you'll weave them together day by day until your work is secure.

Then, you'll have more opportunities to gain feedback about your book. In turn, you'll gain the confidence you need to finally finish it.

WHAT IF I FAIL?

So the reviews are in.

So your work sucked.

So your book wasn't any good.

Accept it. Move on.

I don't mean to be harsh.

If you're anything like me or other writers I've met, you'll have far more failures to your name. You'll have more unpublished disasters on your computer than five-star books. And you'll know more about disappointment than success.

I failed to build a career as a news journalist. I failed to hold down a well-paying contract with a magazine I read. I failed to turn a well-paying freelance job into a profitable permanent job.

Worst of all, I failed to write and publish a book before I was 30 (a life-long goal).

Failure – it's tough.

On good days, I felt restless, and on bad days I felt depressed by my lack of progress.

Writing is a personal thing, and not something you can fake or dial in. If you want to finish writing your book and become a successful non-fiction author, you'll fail many times before you get there.

Instead of wallowing in self-defeat, salvage what you can, and use the experience as a lesson to fall forwards. Failure and rejection are pit stops along your journey to becoming a better writer.

Wondering if you've got what it takes, blaming your editor and suffering from a martyr complex won't help you write a better book next time. Feedback is invaluable. It's your chance to learn how to become a better writer for free.

English author Neil Gaiman says:

> Whatever it takes to finish things, finish. You will learn more from a glorious failure than you ever will from something you never finished.

When you publish a book, your career gains momentum. You become a creative professional who can think of an idea, flesh it out, edit, rewrite, polish and rewrite some more, before finally pressing publish.

That takes guts.

WHAT IF I SUCCEED?

One new writer emailed me to say she worried what would happen if her book was a success and she became famous. She said:

> I want to tell stories, and I want people to read them and get joy and satisfaction from them, I just don't want to become a subject under a microscope!

I get it. Publishing a book can feel like you're walking out onto the street wearing no pants.

Will people treat you differently? How will you react when they talk about the stories you told? And will this change you?

Yes, your imagined answers to these questions may feel embarrassing, but your real problem isn't what people think. It's getting their attention in the first place.

The prospects of becoming Malcolm Gladwell—famous for your work are slight. That said, it's natural to worry how those around you will react to your book.

It's normal to wonder what will happen if you become known for being an author.

If you succeed, you'll discover a new side to yourself and your craft, which will only enrich your life. It's impossible to please everyone, so if some people feel uncomfortable with your success, that's their problem.

After all, you will regret not having the courage to see your ideas and your book through later. So hold onto your values, and finish writing your book.

At the very least, you'll be able to afford some new pants or a gym membership.

Schwarzenegger would be proud.

KNOW WHEN YOU'RE AT THE END

Most people spend more time telling their friends they have this great idea for a book than they do turning their vision into reality.

If you've made it this far and finished your book, you're a different kind of writer.

Look:

There will always be a gap between what you want your non-fiction book to achieve and what comes out on the blank page.

The best way to narrow that gap and improve the quality of your book is to put in your reps:

Write more often, finish your book and publish it.

If you've come this far, you're in the minority. It takes a tremendous amount of hard work and mental discipline to release the best possible version of your non-fiction book into the world.

But when you're done, you're done.

Congratulations!

YOUR WRITING EXERCISES

- Work through your reps each day. Practice freewriting. Practice headline writing. Practice editing your book. It all counts.
- Freewrite for 10 to 15 minutes about what your finished book (this book, not another one!) will do for your career/craft/readers. Now, do all you can to turn your vision into a reality.

FREE, FREE AT LAST!

"Life's as kind as you let it be." – Charles Bukowski

So you've finished writing your book, and you're about to release it to the world. It's an exciting and scary place to be.

Should you quit your job, wait for the royalties to flow into your bank account, retreat to the Bahamas and write full-time on a hammock? Or should you strike writing a book off your bucket list and move on with your life?

Well, before you come to any big decisions, wait.

It's always a wise move to ask yourself, "What does success looks like?" Once you publish your book, you're free to decide what happens next.

For some new authors, it's enough to write one book and move on with their lives. Other new authors want to earn a return and even a living from their books and quit their day jobs.

Then, there are authors who care more about reaching as many people as possible with their ideas than they do about their bank accounts.

In this chapter, I'll explain what freedom for most non-fiction authors looks like. I'll also cover what you can expect now that you've finished writing your first non-fiction book.

(Oh, and congratulations by the way!)

WHEN FREEDOM MEANS WRITING FOR THE LOVE OF YOUR CRAFT

I spent almost every Monday in 2007 taking writing classes in Dublin city centre. Twelve of us met every Monday in an airy room overlooking a small park full of old winos near O'Connell Street.

"I'm going to teach you all about great literary non-fiction," said the instructor on the first day of class. He was a balding Texan who took the craft more seriously than his students did. "But first, tell me why you are all here."

"To learn how to write one, true sentence," said a student.

The instructor nodded.

"I have a painful story from my past, and I'm going to write a book about it," said a second student.

The instructor stroked his goatee and smiled.

Perhaps we were all right after all.

"I want to become a rich and famous writer," said a third student.

The instructor's face turned a pale shade of yellow.

"I don't think this class is for you." He stood. "I'm going to give your money back. Please take your things and go."

The student's mouth opened and closed like a flapping seal. Then, he put his notepad in his bag, stood, collected €250 from the teacher and left us to it.

I thought about that moment for years afterwards. I thought about it when I was finishing one terrible literary non-fiction essay after the next, at home alone, again.

I'm just trying to write a great sentence! This is what the craft is all about.

So I gave it a minute.

I gave it five years.

And I got impatient.

Impatient? Yes. But I was in my twenties. I could have done with some advice from Natalie Goldberg, who said:

> Play around. Dive into absurdity and write. Take chances. You will succeed if you are fearless of failure.

Eventually, I learnt not every author wants to earn a full-time living from their book.

While getting paid is nice, lots of authors have well-paying jobs and prefer to write a book around the margins of the day. They want to write without expectation or pressure to succeed.

You could have a story you want to tell and have no desire to go at it full-time. For you, freedom means getting your book out into the world.

That's okay!

What a relief to not worry about shifting copies and creating related products and services, and earning a return on your creative work.

Now, you can concentrate on writing your next book, or you can learn to play *Hey, Soul Sister* on the ukulele.

It's your choice.

I also thought about that moment from the writing class when I looked at my dwindling bank account at the end of the month (I'm conflicted like that).

Why am I spending so much time on something that almost never pays? Shouldn't I spend my time swatting up on investment funds, short selling and currency trades?

Almost no author earns a living from writing literary non-fiction, and I am no exception. Much later, I barely broke even on my first book. I only learnt how to earn an income from the blank page after studying book marketing and copywriting.

But all that writing for free taught me more about the craft than any paycheque ever could.

You see, if your non-fiction book is a labour of love, its existence is a success. You've done more than the thousands of writers who sit in bars and coffee shops, telling their friends.

"I've got a great idea for a book, I just need to actually write it!"

You've listened to the inner muse whispering, *Write, damn it!*

That takes guts.

WHEN FREEDOM MEANS EARNING AN INCOME

My first gig as a professional journalist paid just €100 a day. That's barely enough to cover the cost of childcare, petrol and lunch.

"I can't live on this," I said to my editor. "What's a starving writer supposed to do?"

"Bryan, I've heard that one before," he said. "There are dozens of resumes on my desk from journalism graduates like you."

The sad thing is he was right. I was only starting off, and I couldn't expect a large paycheque. I thought my work would stand for itself and bring in the big bucks.

I spent most of my twenties arguing marketing and writing have almost nothing in common and that my time was best spent writing.

Funny coincidental fact:

I spent most of my early twenties struggling to earn a living as a professional writer.

Was this because my peers were more talented than I was?

At the time, I thought so. Now, I know they were better at telling stories about their work and forming connections with new editors, readers and clients. They marketed themselves and their work, and they got paid for doing it.

A doctor gets paid for attending to their patients, a plumber for installing a shower and even a chiropodist for lopping off those awful bunions.

You can get paid as well.

One book isn't going to earn you a Stephen-King-sized paycheque.

According to a Digital World Book Survey, a typical Kindle author earns about $50 to $999 per year. And, according to a 2016 Author

Earnings report, most indie authors earn approximately $100 per title.

That's not a lot to show for the time and money you spent on your book. To earn a living from your writing, you must develop lots of income streams.

Getting Paid for Writing Books

Take note of the plural heading.

If you're committed to a career as a non-fiction author, starting on the next book is the best marketing and creative decision you can make.

Each time you write a book, you're putting in your reps, building a body of work and improving your craft. When you publish your new book, you'll increase sales of your old books because readers have more opportunities to find your work.

Better yet, you could turn your non-fiction book into part of a series. Indie author Joanna Penn earns a six-figure income from her writing and has published a series of popular *books* for writers.

Then there's professor Yuval Noah Harari whose work *Sapiens* was one of the most popular non-fiction books of 2014. So in 2016, he published a sequel *Homo Deus: A Brief History of Tomorrow*.

Caveat: you still need to take time out from writing to market your books and connect with existing and new readers.

Getting Paid for Your Services

Henneke Duistermaat is a successful copywriter. She self-published a series of books about content marketing and copywriting. She's also drawn upon her experiences to write guest posts for popular sites that her clients read.

"I got all my first clients through guest posting," says Henneke. "I looked for popular blogs that were read by small business owners and business people. I wrote blog posts for them about copywriting."

Getting Paid to Teach

Danny Iny is a teacher and writer who publishes on Amazon short books about his insights. He's a master of turning the information in his books into premium courses for his readers.

Typically, teachers like Danny give their books away for free (or at a steep discount) and sell their courses anywhere from $47 to $3,000.

Getting Paid for Coaching Clients

I met a marketing consultant who sells her book about content strategy on Amazon for several dollars. It has dozens of five-star reviews, but she doesn't rely on her Amazon earnings to earn a living.

Instead, she charges corporations tens of thousands of dollars for teaching the principles in her book to executives. Her non-fiction book is her business card.

Getting Paid for Writing What the Market Wants

Steve Scott is a prolific non-fiction author from the United States. He writes and publishes short non-fiction books for $2.99. Each of these are 10,000 to 20,000 words long, and he publishes one every few months. His titles include:

- *The Miracle Morning for Writers: How to Build a Writing Ritual That Increases Your Impact and Your Income (Before 8AM)*
- *How to Write Great Blog Posts That Engage Readers*
- *How to Start a Successful Blog in One Hour*

Specific. Concise. Profitable.

WHAT DOES FREEDOM LOOK LIKE FOR YOU?

Look, there's a time for being alone in the room and doing the work. There's also a time for telling stories about your book and building connections with other writers, readers and editors.

Successful non-fiction authors who earn a decent living do all these things. They spend time writing, researching and promoting their books. And they also find out what their readers and editors want.

The copywriter wants to attract new, high-paying clients for her business. So she publishes a book about her speciality, prices it for $4.99 and provides details of her services in the book. She cares less about recognition for her literary prowess than she does about attracting leads.

The blogger wants to entertain and inspire thousands of readers around the world. So he publishes a book for $2.99.

He knows that'll barely keep him drinking Mocha Frappucinos, but he doesn't care. He writes for other sites and magazines for free to build his profile. And when he gets a little bigger, he considers coaching some of his readers or even offering them an online course.

The indie author wants to quit her job and write full time. She studies what the market wants and writes her book accordingly.

She knows it's the first part of a series and that it takes a backlist to become a well-paid indie author. She also knows what she's passionate about, and the best way to sell the last book is to write the next one.

The student in a literary writing class regards success as getting his non-fiction story out of his head and onto the blank page.

So he polishes his work until it shines. He submits a few chapters to literary magazines and gets his book published. Then, he either tries again or moves on with his life, after ticking writing a book off his bucket list.

As a new author, you have all you need to answer what freedom means for you. You can turn your vision into a reality.

YOUR WRITING EXERCISES

- What drives you: earning an income, making an impact or

writing for the love of your craft? Use your answer to frame what you write next.

- Until your writing is earning you a decent income, don't quit your job. Instead, regard the 9-to-5 as a crutch that supports your writing.

THE END

We tell ourselves we'll do the work and write a non-fiction book, but often we don't. We put it off until tomorrow. We fuss about our ideas. We worry about not having enough time.

But now, you know better.

In a few months, you could be holding a copy of your finished book in your hands.

Yes, it's hard work. But once you're done, you'll be free to start writing another book. Or you can attract new clients and customers. Or you can even take a break from the craft of book-writing.

Because when you take an idea, turn it into a first draft, edit your work and publish like a professional author, you're free to decide what happens next.

If you want to sell your book, you should go out and tell readers stories about it. Tell them what your book is about. Tell them whether it entertains, inspires, educates or informs.

If you commit to a career as a non-fiction author, start another one... and soon. You can spend a lifetime learning to improve your craft, discovering what readers want and learning how to sell books.

As a committed non-fiction author, you're never really done – you're just out of time.

Now, so am I.

THE TEN COMMANDMENTS FOR SUCCESSFUL NON-FICTION AUTHORS

Behold:

1. Thou shalt commit to writing thy book, for the writer who talks about the beginnings of a book and yet never fills the page shall be cast out.

2. Thou shalt have a plan. In the beginning, there was a controlling idea, an outline and a deadline. And it was good.

3. Thou shalt always be researching, for ideas are the currency of thy realm and thou art richer than thy wildest dreams.

4. Thou shalt honour thy reader for theirs are the problems thy book must solve. Theirs is the boredom thy book must alleviate. Theirs is the soul thy book must inspire.

5. Thou shalt not covet a better writing tool or for tomorrow to come. Abandon ye the error of your procrastinating ways and tremble! Thou must fill the blank page today and thou doth possess all thy need.

6. Thou shalt learn to love thy messy first drafts with all its imperfections, for its only job is to exist.

7. Thou shalt not cloak thy words. Abandon ye thy purple prose, excessive adjectives and adverbs, and passive sentences. Seek out precision and clarity. Let thy editor be thy guide.

8. Thou shalt finish writing thy book for the author who finishes shall raise his or her craft to a higher plain. He or she is free to write something new, something better.

9. Thou shalt not self-publish thy book with shoddy covers and clumsy editing. Woes (and poor book reviews) betide he or she who inflicts upon the world a pale imitation of a book, published only for gold.

10. Thou shalt tell stories about thy book to like-minded souls, for thy readers are waiting.

After you finish writing your non-fiction book and you can hold a published copy in your hands, email me a picture.

We shall spread the good words.

Write on,

– Bryan Collins

REFERENCES

BOOKS

Allen, David. *Getting Things Done*. 2011.

Bukowski, Charles. *The Pleasures of the Damned Selected Poems 1951-1993*. HaperCollins. 2007.

Cheever, John. *The Journals*. 2011.

Chesterton, G.K. *Charles Dickens: A Critical Study*. Kessenger Publishing. 2005.

Currey, Mason. *Daily Rituals: How Great Minds Make Time, Fine Inspiration and Get to Work*. Picador. 2013.

Coyne, Shawn. *The Story Grid*. Black Irish Books. 2015.

Ferris, Tim. *The 4-Hour Work Week: Escape the 9-5, Live Anywhere and Join the New Rich*. Harmony. 2007.

Feynman, Richard P. *Surely You're Joking, Mr. Fenyman!* Vintage. 1992.

Godin, Seth. *Tribes: We Need You to Lead Us.* Hachette Digital. 2008.

Gladwell, Michael. *The Tipping Point: How Little Things Can Make a Big Difference.* Back Bay Books. 2002.

Goldberg, Natalie. *Writing Down the Bones: Freeing the Writer Within.* Shambhala. 2010.

Halbert, Gary C. *The Boron Letters.* Bond Halbert Publishing. 2013.

King, Stephen. *On Writing: A Memoir of the Craft.* Scribner. 2010.

McDougall, Christopher. *Born to Run: Hidden Tribe, Superathletes, and the Greatest Race the World Has Never Seen.* Vintage. 2011.

McKee, Robert. *Story: Substance, Structure, Style and the Principles of Screenwriting.* HarperCollins. 1997.

Nabokov, Vladimir. *Speak, Memory: An Autobiography Revised.* Penguin Classics. 2012.

Pressfield, Stephen. *The War of Art: Break Through the Blocks and Win Your Inner Creative Battles.* Black Irish Entertainment. 2012.

Schwarzenegger, Arnold. *Total Recall: My Unbelievably True Life Story.* Fitness Publications. 2012.

Stein, Sol. *Stein On Writing: A Master Editor of Some of the Most Successful Writers of Our Century Shares His Craft Techniques and Strategies.* McMillan USA. 2014.

Woolf, Virginia. *A Writer's Diary (1918-1941).* e-arrtnow. 2014.

Zoe Segal, Gillian. *Getting There*. Harry N. Abrams, 2015.

ARTICLES

Als, Hilton. *"Joan Didion, The Art of Nonfiction No. 1."* Paris Review. Spring 2006. Accessed at https://www.theparisreview.org/interviews/5601/joan-didion-theart-of-nonfiction-no-1-joan-didion.

American Psychological Association. "Multitasking: Switching Costs." American Psychological Association. 2006. Accessed at http://www.apa.org/research/action/multitask.aspx on January 29, 2017.

Author Earnings. *"May 2016 Author Earnings Report: The Definitive Million-Title Study of US Author Earnings."* Author Earnings. 2017. Accessed at http://authorearnings.com/report/may-2016-report/ on January 28, 2017.

Cunningham, Anne E., and Keith E. Stanovich. *"What Reading Does for the Mind." Journal of Direct Instruction.* University of California, Berkley. 1998. Accessed at http://mccleskeyms.typepad.com/files/what-reading-does-for-the-mind.pdf on March 27, 2017.

Desta, Yohana. *"10 Famous Writers Who Don't Use Modern Tech to Create." Mashable.com.* February 15, 2014. Accessed at http://mashable.com/2014/02/15/modernwriters-technology/#DijnxwtYZkqd on January 28, 2017.

Gladwell, Michael. *"Hi, I'm Malcolm Gladwell, author of The Tipping Point, Blink, Outliers and--most recently--David and Goliath: Underdogs, Misfits and the Art of Battling Giants. Ask me anything!" Reddit. June 2, 2014. Accessed at*

https://www.reddit.com/r/IAmA/comments/2740ct/hi_im_malcolm
_gladwell_author_of_the_tipping/ on September 26, 2017.

Greene, Robert. *"I am Robert Greene, author of The 48 Laws of Power, The
Art of Seduction, and others -- AMA."* *Reddit.* April 18, 2013. Accessed at
https://www.reddit.com/r/IAmA/comments/1cmb0d/i_am_robert_-
greene_author_of_the_48_laws_of_power/ on January 28, 2017.

Office for National Statistics, United Kingdom. *"United Kingdom;
Office for National Statistics (UK); 2011 to 2014; 42,000*; UK households .
Total Number of authors, Writers and Translators in the United Kingdom
(UK) from 2011 to 2014 (in 1,000)."* Statista. 2017.

McGrath, Matt. *"Wood Density Key to Violin Sound."* BBC. July 2, 2008.
Accessed at http://news.bbc.co.uk/2/hi/science/nature/7484975.stm
on January 28, 2017.

Mueller, Pam and Daniel M. Oppenheimer. *"The Pen Is Mightier Than
the Keyboard: Advantages of Longhand over Laptop Note Taking."* *Psychological Science* 25, no. 6 (April 23, 2014): 1159-68. Accessed at
https://sites.udel.edu/victorp/files/2010/11/Psychological-Science-
2014-Mueller-0956797614524581-1u0h0yu.pdf on February
14, 2017.

Nelson, Kelyse. *"How Much Does It Cost to Self-Publish a Book?"* *Bookpro-
motion.com.* 2015. Accessed at www.bookpromotion.com/how-much-
does-it-cost-to-self-publish-a-book/ on April 26, 2017.

Sitar, Dana. The Write Life. 2015. *"How Much Does It Cost to Self-
Publish a Book? 4 Authors Share Their Numbers".* Accessed at
thewritelife.com/cost-to-self-publish-a-book/#.j0dxzg:Xy7M on
April 26, 2017.

Vonnegut, Kurt. *"8 Rules for Writing."* *New York Writers' Intensive.*
Accessed on

http://newyorkwritersintensive.com/morningpages/kurt-vonneguts-8-rules-for-writing/ on January 28, 2017.

US Bureau of Labor Statistics United States. *"Bureau of Labor Statistics; 2011 to 2015; Excluding Self-Employed Workers."* Statista. 2017.

Weinberg, Dana Beth. *"Lessons and Expectations as the Digital Book World and Writer's Digest Author Survey Evolves."* DBW. 2014. Accessed at http://www.digitalbookworld.com/2014/lessons-and-expectationsas-the-digital-book-world-and-writers-digest-author-surveyevolves/ on January 28, 2017.

Weinschenk, Susan. *"The True Cost of Multi-Tasking."* Psychology Today. September 18, 2012. Accessed at https://www.psychologytoday.com/blog/brain-wise/201209/the-true-cost-multi-tasking on August 5, 2017.

TOP TOOLS AND RESOURCES FOR TODAY'S AUTHORS

What follows in this section is a list of tools I use and rely on as an indie author.

The list is relatively long, and (depending on what your book is about) you won't need to use all of these tools.

If you're facing a technical problem, these tools can help.

Remember, writing your non-fiction book is more important than mastering any tool. So pick a useful tool and get back to writing and marketing your book.

If you're reading this on print or you want more information, you can find my always-up-to-date list blogging and writing tools at http://becomeawritertoday.com/writing-apps/.

FOR WRITING YOUR BOOK

Nuance Dragon Naturally Speaking

I use Dragon software to dictate early drafts of blog posts, book chapters and articles. This piece of software enables me to write faster, and it also reduces the amount of time I spend struggling with repetitive strain injury (RSI). In this article, I explain how to get started with dictation http://becomeawritertoday.com/speech-to-text

Evernote

If I have an idea for a book that I don't want to forget, I keep it in here. I also save articles I like into Evernote as part of my personal swipe file. Sometimes, I take photos of mind maps on my whiteboard with my phone and put them in Evernote too. It's my digital brain.

IA Writer

This is a useful minimalist writing app for Mac and iOS. The font Nitti Light is worth the price of admission alone. I use IA Writer for writing short articles on the go.

iMindMap

I've used these affordable tools to create mind maps in the past. They're easy to learn too. Alternatively, you can create a mind map using pen and paper. To see how I use mindmaps for writing, visit https://becomeawritertoday.com/mind-mapping/

A Moleskine notebook

No, there's no need to use a Moleskine notebook for writing or capturing ideas, but I'm drawn to the build quality of these notebooks and the feel of the paper. I've a box full of these near where I write.

Scrivener

I can't recommend Scrivener enough. I use it to write blog posts and books. I've used Scrivener to write feature articles for newspapers, reports, a thesis and books. Other useful writing apps include Ulysses, Pages and IA Writer. Get my free Scrivener blogging template at http://becomeawritertoday.com/using-scrivener-blogging-ultimate-guide/

Vellum

This application enables indie authors to edit and create professional looking books for every store and device with ease. I write books like this in Scrivener, export to Vellum, lay the book out and then create the relevant file for Amazon, Kobo, iTunes and so on. Sorry Windows fans, it's Mac-only for now.

FOR EDITING AND PROOFREADING

Autocrit

This is a critiquing tool for fiction writers. It costs $29 per month.

Grammarly

This is my proofreading and grammar checker application of choice. It costs $29.95 per month, but there are discounts available for quarterly and annual subscriptions. See https://becomeawritertoday.com/grammar-checker-review-grammarly/

After the Deadline

This is a somewhat less powerful but still useful alternative to Grammarly. It's free.

Kibin

Unlike many proofreading and editing services, Kibin will edit for grammar, spelling, punctuation, sentence structure and more. I've sent book chapters and articles to this service. See http://Kibin.com.

ProWritingAid

This software integrates with popular writing applications like Word and Scrivener. It costs $40 per year.

Hemingway Editor

If you're not a confident writer, don't worry. Hemingway App will review your text and, in the spirit of Ernest Hemingway, it will tell you what to remove or edit so your writing is bold and clear.

Reedsy

If you want to find a book editor, proof-reader or cover designer, Reedsy takes the hassle out of it. When you sign up, you get access to a community of self-publishing professionals that are ready to work with you and on your book. See http://Reedsy.com.

FOR COMMISSIONING A BOOK COVER

Reedsy enables authors to find editors, designs and more.

The Book Designer runs a monthly competition featuring some of the indie industry's best book cover designers. Find a cover you like and then contact them. Visit https://www.thebookdesigner.com/

I've used **99designs** to find a designer to create a book cover for one of my books. If you want a professional design (like a logo, business card or packaging) for your online business, 99designs is a good place to start too. See https://becomeawritertoday.com/99designs-competition/

The **Book Cover Designer** offers a large selection of pre-made covers that you can customise. Visit: thebookcoverdesigner.com.

Joanna Penn provides a list of book cover design resources on at thecreativepenn.com.

OTHER TOOLS I RECOMMEND FOR AUTHORS

A whiteboard

I keep a large whiteboard next to where I write. It's a great way of capturing and organising ideas. I also use it for mind maps and for creating outlines for articles, chapters and even books. I find a whiteboard less confining than traditional digital tools.

Audible

As a writer, your inputs (what you read, listen to and watch) are just as important as your outputs (what you write, paint or draw). I spend at least an hour a day listening to audiobooks that I purchased from Audible on my smartphone.

If you sign up, they'll give you your first audiobook for free. To learn more about creating your audiobook, please see https://becomeawritertoday.com/how-to-make-an-audiobook/

BookFunnel

If you want to send copies of your book to beta readers or distribute Advanced Reader Copies (ARC), use BookFunnel. Once you upload your files, send readers a link. It automatically provides them the correct version of your book alongside instructions about how to open it.

Brain.fm

Brain.fm provides AI-generated music for focus, relaxation and deep work. When I use this, I find I can enter a state of creative flow faster. Plug in a pair of headphones, and you're good to go.

Buffer

I use Buffer to share articles, photos and social media updates by myself and others on Instagram, Facebook, LinkedIn, Twitter and Pinterest. Buffer simplifies sharing social media updates across multiple networks and enables you to schedule your updates in advance. You can enable others to manage your social media profiles… leaving you more time to work on your creative projects.

Day One

For years, I wrote journal entries in a password-protected file in my computer. When I last checked, the file was over 150,000 words long, it took several seconds to open and was slow to navigate.

Now, I use Day One. It supports Markdown (a method for converting plain text to HTML) and pictures. It also simplifies finding older entries. There are versions for Mac and iOS.

Freedom

If you keep getting distracted while writing, use the app Freedom. It will disable your internet access for a pre-determined period, allowing you to focus on writing and not on cat videos!

G Suite

It's time to put the hard-drives and USB keys away. Essentially, G Suite enables me to send and receive emails from the becomeawritertoday.com domain (bryan[at]BecomeAWriterToday.com) using the Gmail interface.

I also get lots of additional cloud storage and can easily collaborate with other writers, editors and designers.

Google Forms/Survey Monkey

Both of these tools are great for capturing the opinions of beta and ARC readers. It only takes a few minutes to set up a survey, and you can send it to members of your email list (if you have one).

Kindle Spy

Kindle Spy is a great tool that will help you see what books are selling on Amazon and how much they earn. Then you can use this information to increase sales of your book.

KDP Rocket

KDPRocket is the other tool in my arsenal for doing market research and checking out what sells on Amazon.

LeadPages

I use LeadPages to create landing and squeeze pages for my books. I also use it to create sign-up forms for my mailing list. See https://becomeawritertoday.com/leadpages-review/

Logitech MX Master 2S/M510 Mouse

I use these wireless laser mice alongside gel-wrist supports. They help me avoid RSI.

Web-hosting

For your author website or blog, I suggest hosting with Siteground. If you need help, check out my detailed guide on how to start a blog: https://becomeawritertoday.com/start-a-blog/

Screenflow for Mac

This is a great tool for recording video and screencasts. It's also relatively simple to edit your recordings and export them to a format suitable for Facebook, YouTube or your website. Also consider Camtasia.

Sumo

Sumo is an all-in-one tool that enables you to gather email addresses, set up a share bar on the side of blog posts and also track how people interact with your work online.

If you're sharing your work online, I highly recommended it. See https://becomeawritertoday.com/sumome-review/

Upwork

No matter how talented or hard-working you are, it's impossible to do everything alone. Upwork is a great service for finding designers, editors and more who can help you with time-consuming tasks so you can spend more time writing books.

I've used Upwork to hire video-editors and also developers who fixed problems on my website.

PickFu

This poll service is useful for A/B testing book covers and titles.

VXi Headset

This affordable headset is purpose-built for dictation and when I switched to it, my accuracy dramatically increased.

REMEMBER YOUR BONUS

I created a **FREE video masterclass** that will help cut months off how long it takes you to write your book by using my best tactics and strategies.

DID YOU CLAIM YOUR FREE BONUS?

VISIT
becomeawritertoday.com/author

If you want to get this free video masterclass today, please visit and sign up here: http://becomeawritertoday.com/author

THE POWER OF CREATIVITY

Learning How to Build Lasting Habits, Face Your Fears and Change
Your Life
(Book 1)

An Uncommon Guide to Mastering Your Inner Genius and Finding
New Ideas That Matter
(Book 2)

How to Conquer Procrastination, Finish Your Work and Find Success
(Book 3)

http://thepowerofcreativitybook.com

ABOUT THE AUTHOR

In this life, Bryan Collins is an author.

In another life, he worked as a journalist and radio producer. Before that, he plucked chickens. He is passionate about helping people accomplish more with their writing projects, and when he's not writing, he's running.

At becomeawritertoday.com, Bryan offers new writers practical advice about writing, creativity, productivity and more. His work has appeared on *Fast Company*, *Lifehacker* and *Copyblogger*.

Bryan holds a degree in communications and journalism, a diploma in social care, a master's degree in disability studies and a diploma in digital media.

You can reach him on Twitter @BryanJCollins, via email at bryan@becomeawritertoday.com or join his Become a Writer Today Facebook page.

Bryan is also the author of the novella *Poor Brother, Rich Brother* and a three-part series *The Power of Creativity*.

He lives an hour outside of Dublin.

becomeawritertoday.com
bryan@becomeawritertoday.com